SLAVIA   BULGARIA

RANIA

GREECE

TURKEY

Aegean Sea

NEAN   SEA

CYRENAICA   Derna
Martuba

kra   Tobruk Bardia
El Sollum
Buqbug
Sidi Barrani   Mersa
Matruh   Alexandria

EL ALAMEIN   CAIRO

R. Nile

OM EL ALAMEIN - OCTOBER 1942 - TILL DECEMBER 1943

MONTGOMERY

[*Photograph by Frederick Maillard*

MONTGOMERY, 1946
Chief of the Imperial General Staff

MONTGOMERY

A BIOGRAPHY

BY

ALAN MOOREHEAD

HAMISH HAMILTON LTD
LONDON

First Published November 1946
Second Impression January 1947
Third Impression November 1947

PRINTED IN GREAT BRITAIN BY
MORRISON AND GIBB LTD., LONDON AND EDINBURGH

To My FATHER

"To preserve a becoming brevity—that, surely, is the first duty of the biographer. The second, no less surely, is to maintain his own freedom of spirit. It is not his business to be complimentary; it is his business to lay bare the facts of the case as he understands them."

From LYTTON STRACHEY's Preface
Eminent Victorians

NOTE

THIS, I think, is the first attempt to tell the full story of Montgomery's life, and my sources therefore are as various as the story itself.

Apart from an abundance of military documents, letters, memoranda and newspaper articles, there was very little printed material to be used as a guide. However, I have read with profit two books by the Field-Marshal's father: *A Generation of Montgomerys*, produced privately for the family, and a memoir on the life of Sir Robert Montgomery.

A third book, *Bishop Montgomery*, written by the Field-Marshal's mother and published by the Society for the Propagation of the Gospel in Foreign Parts in 1933, was most helpful. And then there were Lord Montgomery's own pamphlets and speeches and his two books: *Alamein to the Sangro* and *Normandy to the Baltic*, both privately printed for the Army.

Still another source was that mass of undigested spoken folk-lore which encompasses any living man in the public eye; the anecdotes, the changing legends and the conflicting and some-times apocryphal tales that pass from mouth to mouth getting richer as they go. This required sifting.

In the end, I suppose, I have relied most heavily on my own observation of the Field-Marshal and the generous help of the men and women who knew him well at the different stages of his career. For the story of the early years I am particularly indebted to Colonel C. R. Macdonald, Mrs. Andrew Holden, Colonel D. A. L. Day and Brigadier C. T. Tomes.

General Sir Frederick Pile, Major-General Sir Charles Gwynn, Sir Edward Crowe and Sir Alan Herbert gave me many valuable details of Montgomery's later life. For the most recent part of the story I have relied heavily upon Major-General Sir Francis de Guingand, the late Colonel J. O. Ewart, Brigadier E. T. Williams, Sir James Grigg, Field-Marshal Lord Alanbrooke, Lieutenant-General Sir Archibald Nye and Lieutenant-General Sir Bertie Fisher. Mr. Bernard Shaw and Mr. Augustus John have kindly consented to the publication of the correspondence appearing in Chapter Eleven. I am in-debted to Mr. Augustus John and the University of Glasgow for permission to reproduce the John portrait.

Finally, there were very many others like Mr. Alexander Clifford, the Reverend L. A. Wilkinson of the Abbey Church,

Shrewsbury, and Dr. William Moodie who helped me for no other reason than their disinterested generosity.

None of these people should be associated necessarily with the opinions or any specific information in this book; it is a pie baked to my own recipe. As the research progressed and each new piece in the jig-saw found a place, a theme developed in my mind; and while I believe this theme to be a true explanation of Montgomery's career, I hesitate to suggest that any of my kind informants automatically subscribe to it as well. They may strongly oppose it.

At all events here is the story as I see it and as my wife has revised and edited it. At least it is a story with a happy ending.

ALAN MOOREHEAD

June 1946

NOTE FOR THE THIRD IMPRESSION

I HAVE made a number of alterations and amendments in this revised edition. For the most part they were suggested to me by the following, whose names are recorded with my grateful thanks : Lieut.-General Sir James S. Steele, Lord Wavell, Major-General Sir Clement A. Milward, Lieut.-General Sir Richard O'Connor, Canon Hughes, Field-Marshal Sir Archibald Montgomery-Massingberd, Brigadier Henry Wood, Captain Liddell-Hart and Major-General H. W. Higginson.

A. M.

London 1947

CONTENTS

CONTENTS

LIST OF ILLUSTRATIONS

MAPS

Drawn by
ARCHIE HARRADINE

MONTGOMERY

CHAPTER ONE

1066 AT FALAISE

I

WHEN Montgomery went down to the War Office in London
in June 1946 to become Chief of the Imperial General Staff,
he was just on fifty-nine years of age, and still one of the most
controversial figures in England.

For many hundreds of thousands of soldiers and millions
of their relatives the war-time glory persisted. He was still
"Monty", the dynamic little man in the black beret, still the
hero of a proven legend of invincibility. They believed that he
had succeeded as no other British soldier since Wellington, and
that he had brought something else to his work besides—a
plain devotion, an inspiration, and a talent which sealed him
up in history along with the very greatest leaders.

But to others Montgomery was no such hero. He was a
Judge Jeffreys in the Army, a harsh, narrow and ruthless man,
much overpuffed with personal publicity. True, they argued,
he had had a remarkable run of victories in the war; but he
had had extraordinary luck as well. Always there had been
behind him more capable men who managed the real brain
work while he harvested the glory on the battlefield. Greatness
had been thrust upon him. And had he not been over-cautious
in his campaigns? Too slow, too quarrelsome, too contemptuous
of advice?

In America the arguments broke out afresh in the spate of
post-war books: and Montgomery, in fact, became the sounding
board for emotional Anglo-American rivalries. One interesting
thing emerged in all this: he found his friends among either
those who had known him intimately or those who admired
him from afar. His enemies, with one or two exceptions, stood
in the middle distance, men who had neither gone hero-
worshipping with the crowd nor had yet been high enough to
sit with the leaders in the actual conduct of the war.

But whether you believed or disbelieved in Montgomery,
whether you hated or loved him or were merely indifferent, on
one point at least nearly everybody agreed: there was no one
quite like him. He did not even look like the accepted picture

of a British general. Where for the most part his predecessors since Wellington had been big and handsome men, Montgomery was small and wiry. He had neither the ruddy complexion nor the deep voice nor the heartiness which usually goes with men who have succeeded on the battlefield and come home at last among their friends to a life of privilege and power. At fifty-nine the Field-Marshal was a soft-spoken little man, rather more dapper than resplendent in his uniform, and his movements were quiet and precise. His thinning grey hair had left him bald across the temples, and his complexion was sallow, his face sharp and taut, his nose pinched and slightly aquiline. There was something almost of a mediaeval ascetic in his spare appearance, something of the ecclesiastic or the hermit; at all events if you had come upon him unawares in his civilian clothes you would scarcely have taken him for a regular soldier.

And despite his evident love of the crowds, his gregariousness stopped short of his private life. He shared with General Gordon of Khartoum a contempt for "dinners", for the normal club-life of other soldiers. He went to bed early, and while the port and cigars went round in his absence a hundred stories were hatched about Monty's abstemiousness, his eccentricities, his simplicities and, as it seemed to others, his absurdities. There can scarcely have been a British general so much discussed, so often the butt of pleasantries which ranged sometimes beyond gossip into malice. And yet perversely he seemed more and more to obtain a respect not for his office but for himself. He was a character in his own right.

It was not so much the tight and rigid mouth, the set of the chin, which arrested your attention: it was the light blue-grey eyes. They had a peculiar steely remoteness, a coldness altogether washed of emotion, and they gave you the impression that he was searching rather than seeing, always watching intently rather than merely looking from place to place. Half a dozen of the best British artists attempted to capture that expression and were baffled; and it was never quite revealed in the millions of photographs that flooded the country.

If Montgomery was still popular among the mass of the people in England, and even enlarging his following in the Army, it was almost in despite of his behaviour. He had consistently done the one thing that was not permissible: he had broken the traditional rules. Instead of being silent he had approached the soldiers and the public directly. He had quarrelled with men to whom he ought to have deferred. He had unceremoniously and publicly dismissed others who should have been regarded as sacrosanct within the brotherhood of the Regular Army. He had exulted in his own leadership. All this to traditional minds was unforgivable. And even in the country at large there was still an innate mistrust of showmanship, an acute dislike of any man who, having succeeded, revealed that he was perfectly aware of the fact. A few who knew Montgomery in his earlier days recalled that he used to say: "One has to be a bit of a cad to succeed in the Army. I am a bit of a cad."

These things would certainly have been enough to have blocked Montgomery in his career but for one inescapable fact: at a time of extreme national peril, and after a period not notable for British generalship, he had come through with one victory after another, without a single serious reverse up to the ending of the war. That fact had fixed his reputation with the public.

To the experts he had achieved a number of other things. He had established a new system of higher command. He had perhaps done more than anyone else to settle the long dispute which had bedevilled the relationship between the R.A.F. and the Army during the opening years of the war. And he had evoked morale in Britain with an almost revivalist gusto.

There was a third group of adherents—the very large number of soldiers and people at home to whom Montgomery had acted with kindness and encouragement. These people, with whom he corresponded regularly, were acquaintances rather than friends, but they remained a staunch band of loyal support that cut through all the levels of society.

In 1946 these three groups—the public, the experts and the personal acquaintances—were more than enough to launch the Field-Marshal solidly on his job as the country's first soldier in the Atomic Age. But inevitably criticism and argument were going to rage round his name throughout his three years of office and long afterwards. He attracted trouble as other men attracted indifference. It even seemed a natural part of the Field-Marshal's career that he had never worked in the War Office before he took over the position of Chief of the Imperial General Staff—and indeed he had spent a considerable part of his career sniping at some of the incumbents of that institution. One curious thing was that so little was known of his private life.

The story of Montgomery is like one of those explosive rockets which the Germans fired upon London at the end of the 1939–1945 war. For the first few thousand feet the

missile struggles slowly and awkwardly upward, leaving an
acrid trail of smoke behind. Then suddenly it alters course
for no apparent reason and shoots off at tremendous velocity
into the stratosphere.

In 1942 few people outside the Army had ever heard of
him. The war was half over. More than half his life was spent.
Suddenly, at the late age of fifty-four, this obscure figure seizes
command of hundreds of thousands of men, apparently with
the utmost ease and confidence. He walks among kings and
commanders with complete, even aggressive assurance, and
manages battles on a cosmic scale as though he had been
accustomed to this exalted atmosphere all his life. The minor
soldier who had spent half a century inside the narrow walls
of a regular army life becomes overnight an inspirational
leader, a household word among millions, a public figure
approaching the war-time popularity of Churchill in Britain
and Roosevelt in America. To the outward eye there are no
mistakes, no back-slidings. He advances from one victory to
another, cramming the events of five lifetimes into these few
tumultuous years until even his eccentricities become part of
the legend of his success.

What happened to Montgomery in 1942 at Alamein, the
critical moment of his life, the point where he shot off into the
stratosphere? Was it merely good luck and a certain amount of
native cunning? Is there something unknown in the years
before and a good deal unrevealed in the years thereafter?
Was he a good man who was simply kept down until that
perilous moment because of his idiosyncrasies and his vanity?
Was there some mystical experience in the desert?

The questions are irresistible. One feels the need to plunge
in search of the answers, to burrow backwards from the point
of his birth and upwards through that early secluded life,
to establish some kind of pattern and explanation for this
seemingly disjointed and two-sided career. And in their very
nature the questions seem to suggest that we might emerge at
the end of our search with a character who bears only slight
resemblance to the popular figure of Montgomery as he was
known to the public during and immediately after the war.

2

First, to glance briefly backward.
The family background bristles with attractive analogies
and coincidences which might mean anything or nothing at

all. It was from Falaise in Normandy, for example, that Roger de Montgomery, the first well-known member of the clan, set out for the invasion of England in 1066. He was second-in-command to William the Conqueror. A thousand years later Field-Marshal Montgomery landed from England and fought his greatest battle at Falaise. And here near the very site of the conflict you will find an old hotel that descends from ancient Norman times: the Hotel Ouest et Montgomery. In happier days the place was famed for the excellence of its omelettes.

Even more remarkable is the matter of Field-Marshal Rommel. It was an intensely personal struggle between Montgomery and the German commander. Having pursued him across Africa, Montgomery fought him again in Normandy, and at last that long intimate rivalry between the two men came to an end when Rommel was struck down with a wound in the head. The village in which he was hit is called Sainte Foy de Montgomery—the Sacred Faith of Montgomery.

Normandy indeed seems to have been the cradle and the testing-place of the family. Mons Comericus on the River Dives is said to be the origin of the name (though undoubtedly there are several other theories). At all events, early in the eleventh century you find the family well established in the district with their castle and 150 feudal dependencies, and later historians describe the Montgomerys as "one of the most illustrious of Norman families".

Roger was a cousin of William the Conqueror. He commanded on the right flank at Hastings, and we have a brief picture of him in the old Norman chronicles of the battle:[1]

> William sat on his war-horse and called on Rogier, whom they called de Montgomeri. 'I rely much upon you,' said he, 'lead your men thitherward and attack them from that side.'

And again:

> Roger de Montgomeri (presumably the same man) came galloping up with his lance set, and heeding not the long-handled axe which the Englishman wielded aloft struck him down and left him stretched upon the ground. Then Roger cried out, 'Frenchmen strike! The day is ours!'

Evidently Roger fought well, for presently we find him in the gift of large estates on the Welsh border and created Earl of Shrewsbury. He probably had command over the Welsh county now known as Montgomery.

Roger had in him that familiar blend of soldier and church-

[1] Sir Edward Creasy: *Fifteen Decisive Battles of the World.*

man. At Shrewsbury in 1083 he founded the Abbey in fulfilment of a vow, and a monastery grew up around it. Three days before his death the old soldier was received into the Benedictine Order. Twentieth-century tourists visiting the Abbey came upon a stone slab bearing the representation of a knight in armour with his sword and shield. The stone is very old and very worn and it has this inscription:

> *Sir Roger de Montgomery*
> *Second in Command of the Army of His Kinsman*
> *William the Conqueror*
> *At the Battle of Hastings, the First of the Family of Montgomery in*
> *England. He was advanced to High Honour as the Over-Lord of Many*
> *counties, and created*
> *Earl of Shrewsbury*
> *He Founded the Church and Abbey, wherein he, as a*
> *brother of the Benedictine Order*
> *Died, the First of August MXCV*

From this strong plant the Montgomery clan grew up. The records are obscure and they had a way of being burnt at intervals. A Robert Montgomery turns up in Scotland in the twelfth century, and early in the seventeenth century there begins the migration over to Northern Ireland. In 1628 a branch of the family settled at Killaghtee in south-west Donegal, near Dunkineely. There is a John Montgomery, then a David, and finally one is on sure ground at last with the birth of a Samuel Montgomery in 1723. Samuel was a prosperous Londonderry merchant dealing in wines and spirits and other goods. By 1773 he had amassed sufficient wealth to buy a thousand acres of land on the north bank of Lough Foyle and erect thereon a country home called New Park, which has been the centre of the family life ever since. To the dignity of the new estate Samuel added the Montgomery crest with its motto "Gardez Bien". An arm holding a broken spear rises above the shield and this commemorates the Montgomery who rode in a tourney upon King Henry II of France and drove his lance into the King's eye.

Another Samuel, a churchman, succeeds the first, and then in 1811 Robert Montgomery, the grandfather of Field-Marshal Montgomery, is born. From here onwards we might justly look for the first definite roots of the squalling and difficult grandchild who was to be born towards the close of the century.

Robert Montgomery, the grandfather, was a stern and gifted man. At the age of seventeen he set out from New Park with three hundred pounds in his pocket to make his fortune in India. From the first he prospered in the Indian Civil Service.

He belonged to that generation of Englishmen, who, having gone abroad, identify themselves with the country of their adoption. He married in India and brought up a family. As a commissioner at Cawnpore he had some success in dealing with a murderous sect known as the Thugs. Then, in May 1857, the mutiny flared up. Robert was in Lahore in the Punjab at the time and he obtained word over the telegraph that the mutineers were entering Delhi. It could only be a matter of time before the revolt spread to Lahore and Robert struck first. As Lieutenant-Governor of the province he seized control of the town, and disarmed the native garrison. It proved (from the British point of view) to be a decisive stroke in saving the situation. The Punjab remained under control, and two years later Robert was rewarded with a knighthood and the thanks of both Houses of Parliament in London. He continued until a late age in control of the sixteen million people in his province and died in 1887, leaving as his chief monuments a marble bust, still standing in the India Office in London, and the model irrigation settlement town of Montgomery in India.

Some ten years before the mutiny a second son was born to Robert Montgomery at Cawnpore. This was Henry Montgomery, the father of Bernard. A curious gentleness and saintliness seemed to pervade the whole of Henry Montgomery's long life. His father, a strong churchman, trained him from an early age for the Church, but there was something here beyond the ordinary observance of religion, an other-worldliness, a kindness and forbearance which made people speak of him with affection long after his death. There is a strong facial resemblance between Field-Marshal Montgomery and his father, but in the father the eyes are softer, the features more rounded and there is an air of decorum and Victorian dignity of manner which never descended to the son. None would have accused Henry Montgomery of being dynamic or ruthless. Yet he enjoyed an extraordinary influence in his lifetime. Henry Montgomery believed passionately in his Church and he lived out his life to the last letter of its strictures. Yet something—perhaps revealed in the humorous lines about his mouth—saved him from rigidity and a churchly coldness, and he is remembered more as a kindly gentleman than as an Anglican prelate.

Henry wrote well. Describing his first memory—that of falling off an elephant in Cawnpore—he says, "My father feared I was killed. He took me up covered with dust, hardly a feature visible. A little hole appeared in the dust followed by a roar and all anxiety was banished."

"I think I may say", he wrote later, "I was brought up on

almost undiluted hell-fire. On the whole such diet has done me immense good."

Still later, in the course of passing on this doctrine of hell-fire to his children, he adjured them: "You come of a family of 'gentlemen'. You know that word does not signify mere outward refinement. It tells of a refined and noble mind to which anything dishonourable or mean or impure is abhorrent and unworthy."

From the first there could be no doubt about Henry's piety or of his obedience to his somewhat overwhelming Victorian father. It was also evident that Henry was no brilliant scholar. He yearned for sports with a more than schoolboy eagerness. Sir Robert was able to indulge him; the family was prosperous. New Park in Ireland had flourished and the village of Moville or Bunnyfuddle had grown around it in the feudal tradition. Henry was sent to Harrow, where he soon became captain of both football and cricket. At eighteen, when he was ready for Cambridge, he was a tall, sensitive, strikingly good-looking youth, obviously embarked on a successful career. At the University he took his degree in the Moral Sciences Tripos, but he was chiefly remembered among his contemporaries there for jumping up the steps leading out of Great Court up to the Hall at Trinity—a remarkable leap ten feet in length and four feet high.

In 1871 Henry, at the age of twenty-four, was ordained in Chichester Cathedral and his ecclesiastical career had begun. About this time a Dr. Farrar was obtaining a remarkable success in England as a popular preacher and a writer of improving books. Dr. Farrar was a stern churchman, a pronounced teetotaller and a great teacher of boys (he had been both a schoolmaster at Harrow and headmaster of Marlborough). But writing and preaching were the passions of his life, and in these he exhibited a certain flamboyance, even a theatricality, which was looked on by the more crusty elders of the Church with some misgiving. He excited the parishioners. He stirred up emotions in a way that was reminiscent of Mr. Charles Dickens at his public readings. And soon the Doctor's *St. Winifred's* and *Eric, or Little by Little* were to sweep around the English-speaking world. He was a best-seller. There was no restraining his success either in the pulpit or at the desk, and he applied himself to both with an abounding energy. His *Life of Christ* became a standard work. Eventually he died, it is said, of writer's cramp.

There is little in Dean Farrar's works which the modern reader will find sensational. To take a typical sentence:

"Pish!" said Eric. "It was the unhappy lad's first oath." Nevertheless the stigma of modernism and over-popularity was there and some people looked askance when the Doctor came up to St. Margaret's, Westminster, one of the most important pulpits in the Anglican Church. Henry Montgomery came to Westminster with him as his curate.

The good-looking athletic boy was at once plunged into a pleasant whirl of comings and goings, of impressive services, of weddings and ceremonies and church teas and dinners. Dr. Farrar was at the top of his form. Whenever he preached in the Abbey the building overflowed and a notice had to be posted on the door: "Abbey Full".

The Doctor's house was an hospitable place and his curates were welcome there. While the Doctor wrote mightily in his study at his best-selling books and his sermons, there were his five comely daughters to entertain the callers. Four of these girls married their father's curates. It was the third daughter, Maud, who, while still a schoolgirl of fourteen, became engaged to Henry Montgomery.

On July 28th, 1881, after two years' courtship and when Maud Farrar was still but sixteen and Henry thirty-four, they were married in Westminster Abbey. Henry by now had left the exciting bustle in Westminster for the living at St. Mark's in Kennington, where life was less a matter of high church business and fashionable congregations than of ministering to the deserving poor. The young couple plunged into the work with exemplary energy. They canvassed the district in search of parishioners. They worked strenuously upon charity organizations. They set the church finances to rights. Maud Montgomery had had, in reality, no adolescence. In an age when women were essentially feminine, essentially under the dominance of men, she went straight from her school to her marriage. This vicarage atmosphere at Kennington was simply an extension of the secluded world she had always known in her father's home. A strict and pious Victorianism and a life compounded equally of household duties and Church observances gave her little opportunity of gaining experience of the world. But she was young. She was devoted to her much older husband. And she had an exceptionally strong will.

The London of the eighteen-eighties was an interesting place for a newly married couple to set out upon their life together. Victorian England was rising to the full height of her abundance and prosperity. The Established Church, and every other established institution, like the Throne and the Bank of England, held immense sway. Sunday among the devout was a day of absolute observance when no game was played, no theatre was open and no light book was read. The rest of the week fairly hummed with prosperous life. Hansoms and growlers and horse trams bowled along the gaslit streets. Gilbert and Sullivan had commenced their tremendous vogue along with the music-hall and the pub, where oysters, the poor man's dish, were a penny a dozen. The penny-farthing bicycle was going out and a craze for the new "safety" machines was sweeping England. Whistler had won his case against Ruskin without doing much to shake the popular belief that every painting should be a faithful and photographic representation and, if possible, tell a story. Oscar Wilde had arrived on the scene and the forces of outraged morality were soon to break on top of him. It was the age of accepted practices, of solid bourgeois tradition, of righteous commerce and confident self-esteem; the high watermark of placid living between the hurricane of the Napoleonic wars in the nineteenth century and the German campaigns of the twentieth.

Henry and Maud Montgomery in their vicarage overlooking the Oval at Kennington were well and securely launched upon this carefully organized and regulated world. With youth and intelligence and family backing they had only to follow in the predestined grooves of the Church to make a dignified and useful life for themselves and their children. The world stretched out comfortably ahead. Behind them lay generations of worthy but unremarkable ancestors. If the Montgomerys had produced no great crusaders since Roger, no writers or statesmen or soldiers of any great distinction, they had at least done their share in populating England with a solid and respectable community; they were gentlemen.

Henry Montgomery was probably much too modest to have expected any momentous future for himself. In any event his exacting sense of duty to his religion and his immediate work would have chilled any worldly ambition that might have descended to him from his successful father. He devoted himself to his parish. Children were not long in coming; first Queenie, then Harold, then Donald, and still the young mother was barely past twenty. And now in the summer of 1887, in the midst of this world of placid clerical gentlemen, of parish meetings and the steady routine of the Victorian household, Mrs. Montgomery was expecting another baby. Almost anything could be expected of the unborn child— perhaps a compound of the father's piety and the mother's strong will, of Sir Robert Montgomery's adventuresome spirit and Dean Farrar's flair for personal magnetism. If you liked to be fanciful you might even cast the child's horoscope back through the centuries and discover for him some of the war-like and crusading zeal of his first ancestor who crossed the Channel at the head of the invading army in 1066.

Everything or nothing could be hoped or feared for this new young sprig of the Kennington vicarage. The only thing that was certain was that he—or she—would be born into a respectable and comfortable household under the blessing of the Church of England.

Already 1887 had been a momentous year for the growing family. Sir Robert Montgomery had died and Henry had inherited the properties at New Park. And now there was talk of Henry being offered the bishopric of Tasmania.

At length, on November 17th, in one of the vicarage bedrooms abutting on to Kennington Oval, a fourth child was born to the marriage. They called him Bernard Law Montgomery.

CHAPTER TWO

THE BOY IN THE BERET

I

In 1889 Henry Montgomery was consecrated Bishop of Van Diemen's Land—or Tasmania—in Westminster, and the whole family set off by sea for the other side of the world.

It must have been an extraordinary upheaval for them. Another child, Una, had already followed the birth of Bernard, so that now there were five small children, and Maud Montgomery herself was still little more than a girl. Tasmania in those days was regarded as the outer wilderness, and with all his missionary zeal and his sense of duty Henry Montgomery must have had deep misgivings at abandoning his Irish home, his friends and the formalized life he loved so well in London. His wife, however, seems to have tackled the business with extraordinary determination. She was an exceptional girl, strong-willed, handsome and quite unusually methodical. From earliest girlhood she had been quick and intelligent at her lessons, and she shared her father's gift for precise and fluent writing. The rapid birth of her five children had still left her with abounding vitality. Not for one instant was she daunted by her youth, her lack of all experience in the life that lay ahead; while Henry prayed in his church for guidance, his wife was bundling up the trunks and boxes and keeping a firm hand on the excited children.

To understand Montgomery one has to keep in mind these early relationships, the resolute mother, the gentle father who was twice the mother's age, and the intensely busy "family" atmosphere which was now about to close round the boy in Tasmania.

They embarked on the steamship *Tainui*, and, making the long journey round the Cape of Good Hope, arrived in the harbour of Hobart in October 1889. Hobart of the 'nineties was an astonishingly beautiful place, a neat country town with many brownstone houses and wooden shingle roofs that ran down to the very edge of the clear water. "Victorias", with pairs of white ponies, trotted about the streets. Immediately behind the settlement Mount Wellington soared up, a gay wooded slope just coming at this season of the year into its spring freshness against the sky and the bright sun. Many green apple orchards straggled down to the harbour, and in the lovely harbour itself sailing-boats and coastal luggers were at anchor. In every direction they turned, the Montgomerys saw new stretches of eucalyptus trees, homesteads and orchards and pleasant coves where the forest came down to meet the sea. This was no wilderness of blackfellows and kangaroos, but a sleepy and comfortable country town, as beautiful as any they could remember.

Elated by the scene but feeling strange and diffident, the family came ashore and settled into their new home, Bishop's Court, on the lower slopes of the mountain. It was one of those gaunt stone houses which reflected the austerity of religion in the nineteenth-century colonies. There was even said to be a ghost—an old grey lady—who haunted the chill corridors. One can imagine the strain and awkwardness of this first arrival. The Montgomerys knew no one. They felt very English and rather lonely. This much they could have endured well enough, but something far more serious intervened. Queenie, the eldest child, fell critically ill. No amount of desperate nursing could throw off the effects of the long sea voyage. Three weeks after the family came ashore the little girl died.

If anything were needed to sharpen Maud Montgomery's determination to protect and preserve her family in this strange colonial world, then this most untimely death was the inspiration. She flung herself into the organization of the house. First it had to be enlarged and brightened. A new façade of warm red brick was added, with wide bay windows thrown out on the sunny side. Red gravel paths were constructed through the gardens. Next a schoolroom was built, and tutors and governesses were brought out from England. Although few of them stayed more than a year or two, Maud Montgomery persisted all through the 'nineties in running her own school, to which a few carefully selected children from the town—the sons of judges and dignitaries—were also invited.

Everything appears to have been done with the utmost method and precision. The children, for example, were rigidly guarded against acquiring an Australian accent. When Bernard mispronounced a word he was made to stand before the family and repeat it endlessly until he got it right. The same penetrating care was taken of the family's health. Australian children's teeth decayed quickly. This possibly was due to the lime in the water or some other agency, but Maud Montgomery decided that it was caused by the eating of sweetmeats. She thereupon entirely banned the children from having them.

They had strict instructions to refuse sweets even when they were offered at other children's parties.

Little by little the rules grew up until every corner of the day was organized and disciplined. The children rose at dawn, tidied their rooms, cleaned their shoes and chopped wood for the fires. Lessons began at 7.30, followed by an inspection of the bedrooms (the children standing on parade at the doorways), and then chapel. After chapel, breakfast and then lessons again all morning. At midday the family lunch, with the Bishop at the head of the table. Games in the afternoon for a fixed period. Supper, the children prepared for themselves, and ate in the schoolroom. And finally the day closed at the appointed hour with family prayers.

Saturday was a day of relaxation when the children might perhaps ask a few friends to a party. Sunday was a time when all games and worldly things must be put aside and the entire day devoted to religious readings and services. This was the fixed unalterable rule of the house and Maud Montgomery would allow no breaches of it. A Christian life was a serious and Spartan thing, and if she was firm then it was simply for the children's own good. Minor illnesses were no excuse for being absent from the daily round of duty. The children had to be tough. They learned that if they woke in the night with some possibly frivolous malaise they could not call on her; they must wait for the morning. If they wasted their pocket money they were beaten.

To a world which has had its customs loosened by two major wars this set routine seems harsh and repressive. It may even have been severe by Victorian standards, but it was certainly not exceptional for a churchman's household. The Rule was all. Sin had to be closely watched. It lay across a thin dividing line from virtue, and the safest thing was to observe a very definite code of behaviour from which it would be an effort to escape.

Here and there no doubt Maud Montgomery, in her zeal to do the best she could for her family, made mistakes. Possibly she was too firm in some ways. Possibly the children might have responded to a looser rein and a less guarded affection. But it must be remembered that she had no older relations in Tasmania to guide her in these things. In the absence of friendly advice she simply obeyed the Victorian law to the letter.

Henry was ready enough to hand over the household to his vigorous and capable young wife. He had much travelling to do in his diocese. Often he would be away for weeks tramping in the unexplored bush; he was a passionate walker. And everywhere he was loved. He took ship to the distant islands around Tasmania. He was determined to see everyone, and his missionary faith drove him on long beyond the point where a normal man would have returned to the comfort of his metropolitan home. He asked very little of life. He neither smoked nor drank. Each week his wife handed him ten shillings for his ordinary out-of-pocket expenses, and for the rest, his meals, his clothes and his ways of living, he was almost as much attendant on his wife as his children were. To them he behaved with an excessive gentleness and friendliness. He rarely scolded. He never interfered with his wife's routine; she was the head of the domestic arrangements and the final authority in the children's lives.

2

All this time young Bernard had been growing up. If he was a remarkable baby no one has taken note of the fact. He thrived. He was small-boned, but tough and wiry. He was barely two years of age when he was brought to Tasmania, and his first memories are of the busy life around Bishop's Court in the midst of the other children. From the first the Montgomerys were very clannish children; they played and worked together in an intimate communal life. Although other small boys were brought into the Bishop's school, the Montgomerys were sufficient unto themselves. Every afternoon (except Sunday) they played together in the garden. They rode ponies, they swam, they went off on picnics in the bush where they drank "billy" tea and explored the surrounding hills. It was a vigorous and healthy life. Inside the house they had a series of hectic games. Despite their mother's stern control there was constant noise and laughter in the house.

And now, almost imperceptibly, before he was yet ten years old, Bernard began to develop a nature and strong character-istics of his own. It was not an easy nature. He (unlike the other boys) had inherited his father's blue-grey eyes and fair brown hair, but there for the moment the resemblance stopped. The child was restless almost to the point of nervousness. He was forever plunging into some new project. He was more than ordinarily impatient if he was thwarted, and he began to exhibit a passionate eagerness to be the leader in the games. He seemed less capable than any of the other children of keeping within the rules laid down for him by his mother. Presently he grew mischievous. One row succeeded another, and each was followed by the inevitable recoil of wounded pride. What was becoming increasingly apparent was that the child had inherited in a very marked degree his mother's strong will. The clash between them was inevitable.

Outwardly there was nothing very dramatic about all this; Bernard's misdemeanours were of the usual schoolboy variety. He spent pocket money on the forbidden sweets, or, worse still, against his mother's strict injunction accepted them at other people's houses—and then went roaming in the fields to clear his breath before he got home. Once, it is true, in a blind rage he pursued a little girl through the house with a carving knife (in after-life the victim said she felt like Rommel). But for the most part his sins were those of simple disobedience—of being late or noisy—of defiance and deliberate forgetfulness. It was not so much the quality of his transgressions: it was the importance which he, even as a small child, attached to them. He seemed incapable of taking life as easily and calmly as his brothers and sisters. Every incident was a challenge. Every row was a personal battle. Neither he nor his mother would give in. He might have accepted the routine but he hated the way it was applied. And in challenging his mother he found himself battering vainly against a will that was just as strong as his own. He was aware that he was being naughty, but he was unable to stop himself; something drove him on to put each issue to the test. And he began far too early in life to know fear. Sometimes, when he knew he had been naughty and that it would not be long before punishment overtook him, he would go coursing through the garden, and then, throwing himself down in the long grass he would whisper; "What have I done? What have I done?"

The problem was equally difficult for the mother. She judged it her duty to be firm rather than indulge him. At times, as it happens with most parents, the boy would drive her to the limit of exasperation. Then, standing at the head of the stairs she would call him, "Bernard, come here". He would walk up staunchly, and having taken his beating, would come down again, still in control of himself but with a trembling lip.

Possibly Bernard would have defied any control that was set upon him, even at so tender an age as this; he was irritable of all restraint. But he was also sometimes lonely and unhappy, and unconsciously felt himself in need of more affection than he found. Somewhere in that dark incommunicable world of early childhood a character was being formed. But to reach it and touch it and guide it—this was no easy thing for an unsubtle age which believed it had already discovered the correct methods for the behaviour and the bringing-up of children. How often do we ourselves look back into our first memories and find there nothing but a confused series of isolated fears and bewildered prejudices? Odd remembered things—a smashed toy, an angry scene in the nursery, the look on the face of some chance visitor in our lives—suddenly strike sharply across the intervening years with the unreal clarity of a dream. They apparently have no pattern or significance. And yet the remembrance is accompanied by a nameless fear, and one hastily thrusts it back into the limbo of unconscious mind from which it has escaped. Even when we deliberately seek to break down the silence of early childhood and the reluctance of memory, even when the pain is fully explained, we feel that a scar remains and that our characters have already been formed from the mass of these tiny unconsidered trifles which were all the world to us when we were young.

So very little of all this shows upon the surface—either then or now. Looking back many years afterwards Maud Montgomery wrote: "I need hardly say that Bernard was often naughty like other little boys". Donald, his elder brother, went somewhat further: "He was the bad boy of the family, mischievous by nature and individualist by character".

The truth probably was that they were all extremely high spirited Irish children, and their mother found it necessary to invoke a series of drastic measures to keep them in order. They certainly stood in awe of her, and with Bernard, possibly the most sensitive of them all, the effect went deeper. He began to conceive that life was simply an unending struggle, a constant pitting of oneself against superior force. One was hemmed in. One was opposed. One had to break out . . . somehow, anyhow. He set his will to it and waited for his chances. As the years went by he became entrenched in this attitude. Outwardly his life went by merrily and easily enough along with the other children. As it often happens in large families, this inner struggle of one member passed by unregarded. It was simply noticed that the thin and active little boy was sometimes silent. Often he wandered off on his own.

Mrs. Montgomery at this time was a striking-looking woman, usually described by the neighbours as "aristocratic". On Sunday it was one of the sights of the cathedral to see her sweeping in with a rustle of black taffeta skirts, her children trailing in behind her. Frequently she startled the people on the holiday beaches by galloping along at breakneck speed, riding side-saddle in her dark blue habit. They wondered how it came about that this fiery young woman had become the wife of the venerable Bishop, with his gentle unassuming manners. The Bishop usually walked.

"I remember the first day I saw the family", says the account of a contemporary. "They were walking down a street in Hobart. To us they seemed to have stepped from the pages of a picture-book. The Bishop, with his silky beard and kindly face, was always to us a picture bishop. Mrs. Montgomery was the most beautiful woman I have ever seen, that truly perfect Irish type. Black hair, cream and roses skin, and deep violet eyes heavily lashed. She was more like the eldest sister than the mother of her children.

"Una, the daughter, was very pretty, with a wistful little face, a frail child wearing a Greenaway frock of black velvet half-way down her legs, little white socks and dainty shoes. Then the sturdy Harold, and Donald, so beautiful that he took your breath away, with peat-stream eyes and gold curls lying in flat ringlets against his head. Finally the irrepressible Bernard. Perfectly straight hair and cool grey eyes, exactly as he is now, beret and all, only the beret was a scarlet one. All four wore scarlet berets, and the boys' knickers of black facecloth, with little buttons on the outside seam, and short covert coats, seemed to us the height of elegance.

"We climbed trees and swung down the outside branches like monkeys. We played hide-and-seek all over the roof. We climbed out of upstairs windows and in at others by linking hands. Many times I quailed at the tasks set by Bernard.

" 'Who's afraid?' he shouted once to a line of children before him. 'I'm not', said a newcomer, stepping forward. 'Liar!' shouted Bernard. He tied our hands together, made us climb up a ladder, step on to the roof, walk round it and come down again. I remember fighting against this until the string ate into my skin, but in the end I went under his escort. To my astonishment I found myself back on the grass unhurt. Coolly he whipped out his pocket-knife and freed my wrists. There was trouble after this. Parents on both sides were displeased.

"The last time I saw him was at a Bishop's Court Christmas party. He was standing half-way upstairs with that slight scowl that we see even now in his photographs. He looked the picture of elegance with his white silk shirt, black velvet pants and long, slim, black-stockinged legs."

The scowl evidently was meant seriously. Bernard had just been ordered to bed by his mother for misbehaviour.

It was upon his father that all the boy's pent-up affection flowed from even his earliest days in Tasmania. Here was the essence of patriarchal kindness and justice. Bernard worshipped him. Secretly he began to imitate him.

One night the Bishop called his sons together and read

MONTGOMERY, AGED 8

them a paper upon their future lives. It was a moving little speech. He begged them to put God first in their lives whatever profession they chose to pursue. Overcome by the gravity of the occasion Bernard broke down and confessed that he had sold his bicycle in order to buy some stamps for his collection. "The bicycle", his mother related later, "was a present, and he had no right to sell it. I bought the bicycle back, but Bernard had to go without pocket money until every penny was paid up."

Some years later there was a terrible occasion when Bernard was discovered smoking. Deeply grieved, his father took him into the chapel and the two of them knelt there in silence for a quarter of an hour. When they came out the Bishop told the boy that all would be well now that he had confessed his sin to God. Bernard then left him to face the less spiritual correction of his mother. This question of smoking was to continue right into Bernard's young manhood. He would never give his promise that he would not smoke. When finally he was told that he was old enough to decide for himself and he could do what he liked, he practically abandoned tobacco, and from that moment, to use his own words, he "never felt the need of it". In the same way he steadfastly refused to sign the pledge against drinking. "No. I will never sign it and nothing will ever make me," he declared flatly. If any strictures were to be placed upon him they were to be of his own making.

However, these scenes never grew to the importance of creating a visible neurosis, and life flowed by unconsciously enough in Tasmania. Tutors from England came and went. The children had wild and free holidays in the Tasmanian countryside. Sometimes they stayed with friends on the Australian mainland. It began to seem that they were fixed in Tasmania for ever.

After a gap of several years more children began to arrive; first Desmond, then another girl, Winsome, and finally two more boys, Brian and Colin. In addition there were often young relatives and friends staying at Bishop's Court. Each day the family gathered for the midday meal—even the youngest babies were brought to the table. No wine was drunk in that house, nor did the men sit late over their dinners. But it was a busy and cheerful place and the colonial life had grown into the family's heart.

There were set-backs. Having inexplicably escaped all the diseases of the other children—measles, whooping-cough, chicken-pox and mumps—Bernard contracted typhoid and almost died.

Then there was the evil day when the banks failed. The
coach and the gardeners disappeared. For a time the family
travelled second-class in the trains, and the Bishop's wife took
some pride in the fact that she was "the worst-dressed lady in
Hobart". The Bishop was forced to sell some of the family land
at Moville.

In 1897 Henry was summoned home to England for the
Lambeth Conference, and he took the family with him. They
lived with Dean Farrar, and the boys were temporarily placed
at King's School, Canterbury. But soon they were back in
Tasmania again, and the round of entertainment and work
went on at Bishop's Court.

Just at the turn of the century the children were immensely
excited to see a contingent of troops setting off from Hobart
for the Boer War in South Africa. Soldiering meant nothing in
Bernard's life (he was barely twelve), nor was it much mentioned in that religious and peaceful household. But now the
uniforms and the guns fired his imagination, and for some
months afterwards he would play nothing but military games.
It was a phase that flared up and passed, apparently leaving
no trace behind.

Then in 1901, when Bernard was thirteen years old, his
father was suddenly asked to resign his bishopric and come
home to take charge of the Society for the Propagation of the
Gospel, in London. Henry Montgomery was entirely reluctant.
The family had grown to love Australia. They wanted and
expected to spend the remainder of their lives there—Bernard
in fact was already entered for St. Peter's school in Adelaide.
But the Bishop in the end decided that he must go, and at
the end of the year the family arrived back in London.

They took a large house in Bolton Road at Chiswick, close
to the point on the river where Oxford and Cambridge Univer-
sities rowed in their annual boat race, and they named it
Bishopsbourne. Harold, the eldest boy, at once enlisted in the
Army as a trooper, set sail for Africa—and never returned.
Eventually he became a colonial civil servant and retired to
Kenya. Donald and Bernard were sent off as day boys to St.
Paul's School in Hammersmith.

3

They were hardly prepared for the life of an English public
school. They were "colonials". Neither of them had been to a
public school before except for a few months. They were
strong swimmers and runners. They had grown sunburnt

and tough in the Australian bush. But they knew nothing of
organized games like cricket and football and they had had
no preparation for the elaborate social structure of a public
school. Beyond a passing liking for Longfellow's poem
"Hiawatha", *Tom Brown's Schooldays*, *St. Winifred's* and the
books of Henty, Bernard had shown even less than the normal
schoolboy's interest in reading, music, painting or any of the
arts. Nor was he anything more than an average scholar.
Sports and the out-of-doors were the passion of his life, and
from the moment he took the bus down to the front-door of the
school on his first morning, he plunged into every sort of game
with gusto. Within three years he was the captain of the first
eleven (as a batsman) and of the first fifteen. He was in the
swimming team. He was the head of one of the boys clubs.
He had a two-sided motive in every activity he took up—he
wanted to excel as a player and he wanted to control his
companions as the captain of the side. As an ordinary member
of a team he was argumentative and sometimes obstructive. As
captain he was perfectly happy.

In a quite conscious and deliberate way he keenly enjoyed
the popularity and the schoolboy hero-worship for the successful player. He played at his best with an audience. Better still,
he loved to order other people about just as much as he de-
tested being ordered about himself. Always the proposition
was: all right, I will play provided I have control. It was more
than a superiority complex. It was a fixed and rooted determination that the other boys should obey him, not so much
because he enjoyed command but because he sincerely believed
he could manage affairs better than the others.

He was extremely happy at the school. It widened his scope
for command. For the time being the period of struggle was
over. To a great extent he had escaped the routine and the sub-
servience of life in his own home. At school he was a success.
He was in control. Outside the playing-fields of the school he
hated life in London. At home he was often silent for hours at
a stretch. His mother scolded him: "You must talk. You must
be agreeable and sociable." But he had nothing to say. At
Bishopsbourne he was still under orders.

A contemporary at St. Paul's describes Montgomery then
as a small boy "with mousy hair and undistinguished appearance". His brother Donald, years later, remarked somewhat
trenchantly that Bernard, since his schooldays, had "developed
a streak of showmanship he never had before".

"Years ago", Donald Montgomery went on, "he had no
social graces and no social contacts but remarkable powers of

inspiring devotion. He had an inflexible determination and he was tremendously confident. I believe there are many people who do not regard him as a lovable character."

Looking through contemporary papers one comes on many references to Bernard as the star young man in schoolboy sport. Thus in *Wisden* for 1906: "When the full team (St. Paul's) were able to play they gave a good account of themselves and showed their ability to play an uphill game . . . Cooper and Montgomery putting on over 100 for last wicket when severe defeat seemed impending".

This was young Bernard's world and he was deadly serious about it. Work at school did not impinge too strongly on him: he passed and that was all. The whole business of lessons appears to have been rather nonchalant, although he did work rather harder in his final year and passed his examinations without difficulty. On his very first day at St. Paul's an interesting and not altogether explained event had taken place. Scholars who eventually intended to go into the Army were given an opportunity of entering a special group known as the Army Class. When the proposition was put to Bernard he unhesitatingly replied, "Army Class". In later life he could not remember why he made the choice. There is the obvious explanation that he had been stirred by the Boer War and the departure of his elder brother in a resplendent uniform. But the idea of soldiering as a career had never really entered his head. There was no family background for it, and certainly no encouragement from his parents; indeed the very reverse. His mother, he knew full well, would certainly not approve. Already she was planning something very different, the Church for instance. Somewhat defiantly he went off home on this first night to tell his parents. He was met with hurt astonishment.

"But why the Army?" they asked him. "Why did you choose that?"

"I want to be a soldier", he answered stubbornly. That was his decision. He was going to stick to it. Arguments were useless. The more his mother demanded explanations the more he was resolved. Grieved and uneasy, the Bishop left the room. If this was the boy's desire then perhaps it was the will of God. Exultantly Bernard went back to school the next day and started work in Army Class "C", which was the lowest category then offering. When he emerged three years later at the age of eighteen his graduation to Sandhurst was more or less automatic. He left St. Paul's as the best-known boy in the school and a prefect of Army Class "A".

The next two years at Sandhurst were a curious foreshadow-ing and yet a denial of the whole of Montgomery's subsequent career. Already he had passed unconsciously through two distinct phases of emotional development. As a remarkably self-willed child he had rebelled against the family routine in Tasmania; rebelled and come off second best. There was very little repose in his nature. Feeling thwarted and confined he did not have it in himself to forget the rebuffs and set-backs which attended his every sally against authority. He felt with all the pain and urgency of small children that he *had* to succeed, he *had* to have his own way. And when one frustra-tion was added to another he had the child's usual recourse to an inward bitterness, an outward silence, an outraged feeling that he was being wronged because he was not under-stood. If he had had a weak nature things obviously would have been easier for him. As it was he could see no escape, only an unending struggle ahead. He was sometimes frightened. Yet something forced him to put himself in the way of fear again and again.

Had he been an artistic child he might have found some release in music or books or some hobby. Had he been able to form quick emotional attachments, all his early years might have been warmed with affection, and he might have known the vivid pleasure of those glancing light-hearted friendships which come to a normal child. But no mental attachment had yet charmed his mind and no marked friend (unless perhaps it was his younger sister Una) had appeared to soften and leaven his passage through these early years of life. He was perforce one of a large family of children, and a part of a rigid system not of his own making, and he stood strangely remote from them and it, engrossed in this private struggle, this utter determination to exalt his own ego at any cost. As an only child he would have engaged his father's attention much more strongly and satisfactorily. But the Bishop was a busy man with a large family; he had to be shared and adored from afar. Religion may have been a palliative to this uneasy spirit but the boy was much too young to explore and under-stand it. There remained simply the outlet of boisterous games where one could legitimately exert one's determination to lead and control and be an individual. But Bernard suffered a fate common in large families; he had two older brothers who were stronger than he was, and the younger children were too young to play with.

Inevitably, then, he arrived at the age of fourteen a restless, extraordinarily single-minded boy of very few attachments, of no talent for the minor decoration of life, of no mental brilliance, of little patience and—somewhere in the middle of all this—a vague, nameless hunger for a sense of adjustment, for a feeling of well-being and an acknowledgment that he was succeeding in life. He was much too strong minded to lapse into a state of introspective neurosis. Anyway, his life was made too busy for this. But the lack of affection and fulfilment was very strongly in the background of his mind. By the time he came to St. Paul's he was as sharpened and as ready for combat as a pointed flint. He was asking no quarter and giving none. If he had no charm to win friends and seduce people to his will then he would fight for their obedience. Already, as one sees from contemporary photographs, this conflict was strongly marked in his intent young face. At fourteen there are no humorous or easy-going lines in his cheeks; the mouth is tight, the eyes direct, almost snapping, and the set of the thin young face has no schoolboy carelessness in it. He is as tense as a mousetrap.

At St. Paul's, the second stage, you get almost a complete reversal. He competes; he succeeds. Suddenly he breaks out into the clear intoxicating fields where he leads and the others follow. His mother no longer controls his days. This is the very luxury of life. This time he sets the pace. He makes the routine. He plans the game—and the cheers come very pleasantly across the football field. Fortunately it is still a narrow world wherein you have but to excel in sports to claim the attention —and the obedience—of the others. And young Bernard is very good at sports. St. Paul's is a very happy time indeed. He has found his place in the world. If people will only continue to understand this—to understand that if he is given control then he will be quite happy and everything will be done with the utmost efficiency. It is all quite simple: they— the others—need a captain and he is the man for the job.

But now we have him entering manhood at Sandhurst, and this third stage is much more complicated. Things are not nearly so simple. Sport still plays a strong part, but it is not all. There are many other considerations—such as one's personal manner, one's ability to learn, one's relationships with the officers. There are such factors as money, the family background and the social pleasures of life. The family code he threw off on leaving Tasmania for the freedom of sport at St. Paul's is now replaced by the larger code of adult social behaviour. At nineteen Cadet Montgomery enters into the third main struggle of his life.

4

The course at Sandhurst consisted of three terms of six
months each: the junior, intermediate and senior stages. It
was very much an academy for young gentlemen. They were
essentially gentlemen first and cadets afterwards. The atmosphere tended more towards good-breeding and decorum than
to any fanatical interest in the art of war. But it provided
within its rigid limits a solid grounding in army life, and there
was scope for the promotion of the intelligent and hard-working
boy. After the first six weeks the most promising of the juniors
were made lance-corporals for the remainder of the term. They
could then reasonably hope for advancement to the rank of
sergeant as the course went on. Such promotion was eagerly
sought—for one thing, a non-commissioned officer could not
be punished for misdemeanours. And the sergeant's sash was
very decorative.

Montgomery plunged into Sandhurst with the same
enthusiasm with which he had entered St. Paul's. He was
promptly selected as a lance-corporal. Once again he began to
take the lead in games; hockey and one or two other sports
were added to his repertoire. He could play anything well.
But now something most unlooked for and unwelcome intervened. He fell foul of his instructors. In particular the officer
who was immediately in control of his destiny looked on him
with sharp disfavour.

Whether it was the confidence and assurance of the boy,
or his intransigence and inability to compromise, or perhaps
his lack of personal charm, the fact remained that he was
unpopular with his masters, and probably there were some of
his equals as well who looked upon him as over-aggressive and
even arrogant. Montgomery did not work hard at his studies.
He became part of the noisy group of young cadets who amused
themselves by beating up the people they happened to dislike.
Very soon he was back again in the childhood atmosphere
where he found himself maladjusted to the routine and therefore determined to fight it. This time he had reserves to call
on. He was a notable player of games and could always command a following there. And by now he was getting into the
technique of opposition. The beatings-up continued. Escapades
that began as "rags" ended with pitched fights in which pokers
and sticks were used. Cadets were injured and still the hearty
gang, Montgomery in their midst, continued blustering their

way nonchalantly through the course. Finally one incident brought things to a crisis. An attack was made on a certain cadet, and he was surprised at the moment of undressing. Under Montgomery's directions the youth was pinned from the front with a bayonet while Montgomery set fire to his shirt-tails behind. The victim was badly burnt and sent to hospital. The conspirators were appalled. Although the injured cadet never revealed the names of his attackers the incident sobered them down considerably, Montgomery most of all.

He began to see that he had been wasting his time. If he was to proceed with his expected promotion to the rank of colour sergeant he had better get down to work. But already it was too late; he had been marked down as unsatisfactory. When the promotion lists went up he was passed over. It was a slight that no one at Sandhurst could altogether ignore. Montgomery, full of angry pride, found that he had been reduced to the rank of cadet, and when this occurred he tore the corporal's stripe off his arm and defiantly framed it over his mantelpiece.

Then he began to work. There was a good deal in his temperament and his circumstances to help him to this simple decision. He was far from wealthy. The Bishop spared him two golden pounds a month to put in his sovereign case—not nearly enough to enable him to join the other cadets in their occasional jaunts to London. Nor enough for the cadet drinking parties. Barely enough for tobacco. Certainly not enough to entertain girls to dinners and dances. But none of this was of much importance. He drank very little, and smoked still less. And the matter of entertaining young women was wholly outside his interest. All this was not merely the result of a severely religious upbringing. He was neither prudish nor assertive about his abstemiousness; others could do what they liked. He had no wish to convert them. There was simply a strain of innate asceticism in the boy. It was no effort at all for him to reject the normal minor vices and pleasures of life; he was simply not interested. While all around him his companions were toiling awkwardly through their first calf-love affairs he was not even embarrassed by the presence or the idea of women. He knew them, he had grown up with them, and they were not interesting. The thought of kissing a girl was not so much ridiculous as a waste of time. He began to perceive the existence of a world in which he had no part, and he neither hungered for it nor consciously resisted it. There was a barrier separating him from other people and that was that. He was greedy for only one thing in life, and that was success and the authority that goes with it.

Little by little he grew interested in the idea of soldiering; as the work advanced it fed on itself. He developed a passion for exact detail. For the rest he had his games, the family holidays, and in this narrow world he began to focus his life with a peculiar concentration. One of his contemporaries remarked long afterwards: "Imagine a horse with blinkers staring straight ahead with searchlights instead of eyes. There you have Montgomery." He passed out of Sandhurst marked "excellent", and thirtieth on the list of 150 candidates.

None of this made much impression on his superiors. To them he appeared as a troublesome and erratic figure, far too self-opinionated and grievously lacking in the polished manner one liked to see in a Sandhurst graduate. One of the officers had a final word. "You are quite useless", he said. "You will get nowhere in the Army." What a violent contrast Cadet Montgomery was to that able and intelligent and tremendously popular youth named Alexander who followed him into Sandhurst a year or two later.

5

At home in Chiswick Mrs. Montgomery still presided rigidly over her family. Each Sunday the children gathered round her in the drawing-room for a religious reading. Each day the family Bible came out and the whole household— servants, gardeners, coachmen—bowed in prayer before their meals. Month by month the growing children followed that steady direction which never faltered. The mother was still the guiding hand. Of late, though, the routine was somewhat relaxed, and the younger group of children were indulged as the elders had never been. Henry Montgomery was growing into his sixties with all the flowing dignity of his Church and his simple kindly faith. He was now an influential churchman, and presently he was to be elected Prelate of the Order of St. Michael and St. George. He was a very striking figure in his robes; he had become the friend of Royalty.

Each summer the entire family packed up and went off to the home at New Park in Northern Ireland for six weeks' holiday. It was a formidable cortege. Quite apart from the nurses and the cook and the other retainers, each child was allowed to invite one friend, and from the first these annual expeditions had a gaiety and joyousness which makes them stand quite apart in the family history. Liberated from the streets of London the children ran wild. They tramped off sometimes for twenty miles over the mountains and along the coast. They called on the cottagers and ate teas of Irish pancakes and soda bread and butter. In the evenings hectic games raged through the old house. Shouting and screaming, the children raced round the dark passageways. There were noisy practical jokes, the girls against the boys. Sometimes they played charades, and often when they were tired Mrs. Montgomery would read to them from books of ghost stories and improving novels. She had a very beautiful reading voice. A squash court was built, and the local people remember especially the piercing yells when Bernard was playing.

All this was a heritage from a similar set of rompings and festivities which the children were allowed every Saturday in Tasmania, and now, just for a moment each year, they escaped from the drab life of London into the same exuberance and freedom.

Bernard planned endless expeditions. With his sister Una and a cousin aboard, it was his practice to take an open sailing boat straight out of Lough Foyle and into the Atlantic. When the boatmen refused their boats for these unnecessarily dangerous trips Bernard took the boats just the same. Often they were caught in squalls and Bernard would shout to his sister to loosen her skirt and her shoes and be prepared to jump for it. Once the boat was entirely out of control. As the swell rushed them past the submerged rocks and they were on the point of capsizing, a coastguard caught sight of them. Rushing along the cliff-tops he hurled curses and directions down upon the children, and somehow they managed to beach the boat and scramble ashore to face a six-mile walk in their wet clothes. Of such escapades they said nothing when they got home. It was part of the freedom of their holiday. Next day Bernard would set out again to catch conger eels in the Atlantic.

Sunday was the only brake on their excitements. In the morning all members of the household would troop down to the garden to select their Sabbath buttonholes—a tradition handed down from Grandfather Robert Montgomery. Morning and evening church services followed. The Sunday dinner invariably included six puddings. In the afternoons the Bishop read to the children in his study and answered their questions.

As the years went by the atmosphere of innocence and hilarity persisted in Moville. Even when the children and

MONTGOMERY. AGED 15

LADY MONTGOMERY
The Field-Marshal's mother

their friends were growing into young men and women no attachments developed between them. By some form of mutual and unspoken consent "flirting" was "not done", and the aura of boisterous romping continued as though the family was reluctant to abandon its childhood and there was some magic in the place to make time stand still.

In Moville village close by there were reputed to be some forty public-houses; no drop of liquor ever crossed the threshold of New Park. The family generated its own gaiety. They were young. They were free. They were enjoying the last spacious years of a century of unexampled security and prosperity. And as though they had some foreboding of the tragedy that was about to fall on Europe, as though they knew that the step into an adult life could be delayed only a moment longer, they squeezed out of these long days by the sea the last atom of happiness. Years later Bernard and his brothers and sisters were going to look back on New Park as a lost and lighted island in their lives. The place indeed had magic.

CHAPTER THREE

PROBYN'S HORSE

I

LIFE in the Regular Army in Edwardian times was a period piece of a very special *genre*. Sadly, the bloom and the bouquet has blown away. Old soldiers, looking back across the upheaval of two cataclysmic wars, are apt to fumble in their recollections and all that is left are a few remembered names, a mass of English colour, a pageant, a brassy compound somewhere in India, a sense of spaciousness and time. It seems now that the whole period is lighted with a curious feeling of warmth, a sense of theatre, as though one were looking at it across a row of footlights.

There was no war to speak of. Indeed nearly a hundred years had gone by since Waterloo, and none of the subsequent nineteenth-century engagements—the Mutiny, the Crimea, the Sudan and the Boer War—had engulfed the nation or fully engaged the Army. The Army was free to develop in its own peculiar way. Nothing like the American Civil War had occurred to disturb its traditions or its ceremonial. No citizen army had been grafted on to the regular service. No unorthodox amateur had come up through the ranks. The institution was based not so much on the terrible experience of the battlefield as upon the accepted practices of peace or rather of keeping the peace. In the nature of things the emphasis was rather less on fighting and rather more on soldiering.

And yet the spirit was there. The discipline was excellent. The life was healthy and hardy. The drill most professional, the uniforms very decorative. And there was all the Empire to play with, especially India. The one thing really lacking, perhaps, was enthusiasm. For some time it had been the practice for families to send younger and less inspiring sons into the Army. Moreover, one really needed at least a small private income to maintain an officer's status with a proper dignity, and so the Army was a rich man's, a gentleman's, profession. This naturally narrowed down considerably the number of first-class men available for high command. It also meant a dearth of new ideas. One entered the Army because it was an amusing life, a gentleman's life. And there was a pleasing dash of colour to it as well. The red tunic and the sword. The polo pony. The bustle and excitement of going abroad. The long periods of leave. Where trade was distasteful, farming too dull and a life of politics apt to overtax the mind, the Army was obviously the congenial and correct career. In the Service one could progress with dignity and leisure.

It would be monstrous to suggest that there were no brave and intelligent officers in King Edward's Army; nevertheless it was certainly not the repository of the best and sharpest brains in the Kingdom, and the time was going to come when it was to pay for this with its own blood and its own wasted courage.

Meanwhile the respected traditions went on. The pleasant circle of regimental balls and race meetings. The ceremonial parades, the dinners in the mess, the sports, the not-too-onerous routine of drills and manœuvres. One had one's servants. It was a life free from commerce and the care of money, and if one married then the Army offered facilities for that as well. It was all very pleasant provided one's wife got on with the colonel's wife. And these agreeable dealings were spiced from time to time—if you were lucky—by border skirmishes and expeditions against the native.

One is hard put to it to think of anyone so peculiarly unfitted for this life as Second-Lieutenant Bernard Montgomery when he emerged from Sandhurst at the age of twenty-one. He could not dance and he was not interested in betting. He was far from being a robust and handsome figure in the fashion of the time and he was without the ordinary young man's vanity in a smart uniform. He was never good at ceremonial parades. He had yet to taste his first whisky and soda and he did not smoke. He never went out with girls. He was not wealthy. He nursed a carping discontent with established authority and was apt to argue with his superiors especially at moments when he should have been dumb. He was no horseman. He was religious. He had no family military influence. And what was much worse than all this—very much worse—was that lately he had developed an unblushing enthusiasm for the profession of making war. He was aggressively full of ideas which he wanted to put into practice—so full of them that he committed the solecism of talking shop in the mess. Even when he was fined by paying for a round of drinks he was not cured. It looked as though the Sandhurst officer's appreciation of him was a sound, even conservative, judgment.

The one thing that told in his favour was that he excelled in sports.

Montgomery has since expressed what he, on his side, thought of the Army. "The average young officer went to India to drink gin, play polo and have a good time. You were not supposed to show keenness in soldiering. A great number of these officers—and the older men at the top—were useless, quite useless. They were divided into two groups: those who had brains and those who had not. The majority with no brains got, subsequently (after the chaotic experience of the war had intervened) to the rank of major or lieutenant-colonel, seldom more. The minority with brains were divided into two classes: those who wanted to understand war and those who did not. Those who did not bluffed their way up to the rank of brigadier and sometimes major-general before they were found out. The others with brains and enthusiasm shot up to the top at once when war broke out. In 1939 there were not half a dozen good generals in the British Army."

It was just the sort of downright statement which irritated and antagonized the Army, especially the older regular officers. Montgomery was already beginning to deliver such opinions when, as a very junior lieutenant, he was posted to the Royal Warwickshire Regiment in 1908.

2

Almost at once he was ordered overseas to join the first battalion of his regiment on the north-west frontier of India at Peshawar. No one especially remarked his arrival; it was the custom to ignore young subalterns for the first few months after their arrival. Montgomery quietly set himself up in his billet. He had his kit, his tropical clothes, his red tunic and his swords. He had his pay of five shillings and threepence a day, or about nine pounds a month. His mess bill alone would amount to eleven or twelve pounds a month, but his mother had warned him that he would have to get along as best he could on his pay; over and above this the family could spare him just a hundred pounds a year. This did not worry him unduly except that, just at this moment, he wanted a horse. It was now Christmas 1908 and the Peshawar Vale Hunt Point to Point was due to be run in January. Montgomery was determined to enter.

Just why, as an indifferent horseman, he should want to do this is not entirely clear. Possibly he wanted to show that he was capable of something. More probably he simply looked on the event as one more field of sport to conquer. In any case the other wealthier young officers had their own horses and Montgomery decided he must have one as well.

Eventually a sporting captain in the regiment found him a beast which had been used as a baggage animal or something of the sort in an Army unit known in India as Probyn's Horse. The attractive thing about it was the remarkably low price of one hundred rupees.

Montgomery called it Probyn, trained earnestly for the event and started a rank outsider. He was so light he had to carry a good deal of added weight. His performance at the start was scarcely promising; he fell off. . . . Unwilling to give up, he pursued his charge, re-mounted and urged it forward with such abandon that the astonished animal bore him to the head of the field. In a wild fury of unorthodox horsemanship Montgomery lost all contact with his stirrups. He dashed madly past the finishing post and catapulted from the saddle again as the judges were declaring him the winner. This incident won him considerable esteem in the regiment. Very soon we find him on the way upward again on much the same lines as at St. Paul's and Sandhurst.

From the beginning he loved the work of the Army. Privately he might rail against the system and the men in authority, but now at last he begins to step with certainty and direction. It is still an extraordinarily limited life, unmoved by books or music, uninterested alike in politics and the teeming Indian millions around him, and equally undistracted by pleasures or family responsibilities. There is not even a ripple in his health and bodily well-being. But now he begins to perceive that there is something beyond the round of sports and the purely physical approach to life, and all his latent unused abilities for learning focus upon the technique of the Army.

He performs every job given him with intense earnestness. He learns Hindustani and the local dialect with such thoroughness that thirty years later he is still able to issue commands to Indian troops in their own language. He organizes a troop of army scouts for work along the north-west frontier. He organizes the battalion sports. He lives almost entirely with the little section of men under his command, exploring with apparent fascination all the minutiæ of musketry, shooting and drilling. Long after a more intellectual officer woold be bored to extinction Lieutenant Montgomery is found on the parade ground instructing the recruit in the final nicety of grounding his rifle butt or presenting arms. Rarely has the Army so fascinated one of her children. There was nothing down to the last indent in triplicate for a tent peg that escaped his simple and enthusiastic boy scoutery. He was thorough. He was keen. He was hardworking. And he was honest. The authorities could hardly help noticing him.

As for his life in the mess he progressed unexpectedly well. It was, after all, not much more than an extension of the crowded family board in his own home and the communal atmosphere in which he had grown up at St. Paul's and Sandhurst. If he had no especial friends he had a certain impersonal gregariousness, and he was young enough to adjust himself. He drank a glass of port after dinner. He smoked occasionally. Once again his prowess at hockey and cricket gave him an entrée. And if occasionally he was isolated from the others by his religious fervour, his genuine simplicity of habit and his undercurrent ambition, he had at least become an accepted member of the regiment.

The Warwicks was not a fashionable regiment. The great families of England sent their sons to regiments like the Guards, the Hussars or the Rifle Brigade. Nor did the Warwicks offer much opportunity for quick promotion. The turn-over in older officers was slow and the young lieutenant had to wait years for a captaincy. Moreover, it so happened that the north-west frontier was quiet at this time; a spell of fighting against the tribesmen had just come to an end and there was no opportunity for gaining distinction in the field. Steadily and enthusiastically Second-Lieutenant Montgomery plugged away with his little section in a world of dust and mule carts, of boiling heat and leave in the hill stations, of regimental sports and Homeric arguments in the mess. Little by little the family background faded away. The important thing was to pass the Transport Course and qualify at musketry. By now he had grown to his full physical stature, and although he looked a good deal more robust than he did later in life he was no heavy-weight. He was five feet eight inches in height, under eleven stone in weight, his face was thin and pointed and there was already an air of tautness, a curiously quick and bird-like quality in the way he held himself. In the end the word for him, one supposes, was wiry. It was not an intellectual or especially sensitive or good-looking face, but it was interesting if only for the fact that it expressed a certain wariness, and it gave the impression that there was something held back. For a man who had devoted a great part of his life to British sports he was spectacularly lacking in heartiness. In the early regimental photographs he sits among the jutting jaws and the massively folded arms like an alert fox-terrier in the midst of a collection of bulldogs. Two years on the north-west frontier had given him resilience, a certain poise, an acceptance of life rather than the old struggle against it.

3

In October 1910 the battalion came down from the open space and the dry heat of Peshawar to the close and humid atmosphere of metropolitan Bombay. With that curious island-English characteristic of being in a place and not part of it the soldiers tramped into this milling hothouse of stinks and scents and coloured poverty, mixing no more than oil and water. The Army, a compact intrusion of igneous rock in the shifting native soil, went about its own business rigidly. Once they were called out to quell an Indian riot. And, dispassionately and impersonally, they quelled it. To the young subalterns politics were something quite aside and undefined. They were simply there as soldiers to keep the peace, the status quo. The efficient means of doing this, of sizing up the tactical situation, of posting troops and distributing ammunition and rations, frankly fascinated Montgomery. About this time he began tentatively to read books beyond the prescribed curriculum. He tackled Clausewitz and could make neither head nor tail of it. Unperturbed he went on grasping for information that would lead him somehow up that slow and ponderous ladder of promotion. He had been made a first-lieutenant in April 1910 but the way ahead seemed endless. At last a little kink opened up in the opposing armour of authority—he was given the job of Assistant Adjutant. It was a start. Then something better happened. The Regimental Quartermaster went home for a year's leave. There was some debate about the appointment of anyone so young as Montgomery; the post was one for an older man with more senior rank. Montgomery was watched and interviewed. In the end he got the job. This was a considerable rise, a definite step above his contemporaries. The matter was debated with pained surprise among some of the officers. It was impossible not to notice his peculiarities, his absence from the more earthy and boisterous parties in the mess, his friendship with older and more senior men in the Service, his devotion at Church parades, and his rather boring over-concentration on his military duties. He was not unpopular. But he had moved into a position where he was watched. As for his seniors, now they reported on him most favourably. He was a little headstrong and argumentative perhaps, a little too apt to take decisions into his own hands, but he did the job thoroughly. He was keen. It was an agreeable thing for a hot and busy captain to hand over the more dreary of his duties to the young lieutenant and know they would be well done. Each one of these crumbs of authority Montgomery gathered up eagerly and cherished. He applied for promotion to captain and began to study in earnest. By mid 1911 he was passing his qualifying subjects with regularity and apparent ease.

Meanwhile the sports went on. He was officer in charge of games. He became secretary of the sailing committee of the yacht club and sailed his own boat, the *Antelope*. *The Times* of India for November 21st, 1910, speaks of his winning a handicap race by unorthodox methods vaguely reminiscent of his boyhood jaunts in the Atlantic in search of conger eels. Furthermore—and this was distinctly erratic for an officer in India in 1910—he purchased a second-hand motor-cycle. In that era of horses and regimental decorum his senior officers were pained to see him, covered in grime and with an air of desperate seriousness, careering through the native quarters of Bombay.

There was also the incident of the *Gneisenau*, which came into Bombay with the German Crown Prince on board. Montgomery formed part of the guard of honour, and then, as games officer, hurried off to field his football team in a friendly match against the Germans. Etiquette counted for a good deal in 1911. Higher instructions were that the Germans should be treated with hospitality and decorum. Since the Warwicks' football team was a notable combination Montgomery was instructed to field only a second-class side. It was apparent, however, as the British and German staffs sat watching the game, that something had gone painfully wrong. The Warwicks won forty goals to nil. Montgomery was summoned to report to his colonel. He confessed that against orders he had fielded all his best players, and he added "I was not taking any risks with Germans".

In November 1911 his three years of service was up, and he sailed in the *Plassy* for six months' leave in England.

Nothing very much had happened at Chiswick. The family life still revolved steadily around Mrs. Montgomery. The Bishop was gently rising to the height of his influence in the Church. One other child, Desmond, had died as a schoolboy at St. Paul's, but the rest of the children were growing up as uneventfully and methodically as children did in a well-conducted middle-class London household.

But for Bernard the break with his childhood was now almost complete. He was returning as an established adult, entirely convinced of the rightness of the career he had chosen for himself and sure of his independence, or nearly sure. Yet, during his leave when he brought his friends to stay at Bishopsbourne, they were astonished to see how much he was engulfed in the family and Mrs. Montgomery's rule of the house. They found they were obliged to push their luggage from the railway station in a wheelbarrow, and once inside the house, they too, were drawn into the circle of family prayers, punctual hours for meals and early risings.

Again and more strongly than ever Montgomery came under the spell of his father, and the Bishop on his side began to regard the boy with special interest. There were great resemblances between the two: their simple piety, their abstemiousness and a certain patriarchal quality which was to develop later in Bernard when he began to visit his soldiers with the same eagerness as the father moved among his parishioners. The Bishop now began to see in his third son unusual qualities beyond his other children; he began to single him out as the coming head of the family.

To the rest of the family, however, Bernard had no such mission, nor to them was there anything remarkable about him at all. He was "the difficult one"—and, thank goodness, he was settling down in the Army.

4

In the midsummer of 1912 Montgomery was back again with his regiment at Bombay and six months later his battalion came home to England to take up its headquarters at Shorncliffe. Again the steady unremarkable climb, the infinity of little regular steps upwards. He passes out top of the musketry school at Hythe, he plays hockey for the Army, he heads the list of batting averages with 57·5 and a highest score of 88 not out.

The years of the Victorian age and its Indian summer, the Edwardian age, are running out quickly now although there is nothing much to remark the fact among the lights and the crowds of London, and still less in the barracks of provincial England. In Montgomery's narrow world especially, everything conspired to suggest that there was no need for alarm, no call for apprehension about the future. The habit of peace was entrenched. In 1914 Montgomery was not yet 27. All his life he had been surrounded by apparently unshakable institutions; the supremacy of the British Empire, the Church, the Army, the Family, everything moved inexorably forward in its predestined groove. Life, to be sure, could be interrupted in its normal course by sickness, by accident, by debauchery or sudden poverty, but for the rest it was a sane and well-ordered world. No young officer in the Army saw any need to set the Thames on fire. Politics were a thing apart, a slightly unsavoury business best left alone. Because they had no information and no particular interest Montgomery and his friends held no decided views as a rule on the Irish question, Trades Unions, Colonial Government or Britain's foreign policy. They read no controversial books. A dozen heated quarrels about Impressionism in art, or Marxism in the modern state, or the balance of power in Europe might rage over their heads without their ever being aware that such matters existed. The average middle-class boy of the governing class had his ideas of the world in general handed out to him pat and ready made; and usually the Army or the Bank or some other institution swept him along with the tide, evoked and engaged his interest in the existing order of things, before he could branch out and think for himself. If you were in the Army you stuck to that and kept your nose out of other people's business. If you were an officer you were almost automatically Conservative, Church of England and a horseman—or at least interested in cricket. It was "not done" to write, to paint, to engage in business or become exercised over political theory.

Montgomery's struggle had been purely personal. He had rebelled in varying degrees against his family, his schools and the Army, not to establish any abstract idea, nor to alter the order of things, but as an individualist who simply disliked any authority except his own. Latterly he had begun to engraft on to this somewhat anarchistic strain an enthusiasm for soldiering. With this enthusiasm came the obvious desire for experimentation and reform; but it was experiment and reform within the existing rules. He would have been shocked at the notion of abolishing the authority of parents. He would have regarded anyone who called the Army a ruthless imperialistic machine as a dangerous mutineer.

His struggle with the family was now over. He had successfully made his way in the Army. It was a passive and balanced moment in his life, a lacuna in the upward climb. The long scale of promotions stretched inevitably ahead. He was agitated by no love affairs or private worries of any consequence. He had his place in the world and the world itself was very solid.

As the drowsy days of 1914 went by he was even more detached than most people from the passing scene. There was nothing especially sinister in the fact that the Tsar was talking of mobilization or that "incidents" began to develop between France and Germany or that the "threat to Belgium's neutrality" was spoken of in Parliament. This did not mean that Montgomery and his young friends were entirely cut off from reality. War in early 1914 was not such a terrible prospect. It meant expense certainly, and did much damage to trade. But it could not last. There was no real reason why Britain should be dragged in.

In a way, some people argued, it might be a jolly good thing if war did come; teach the blighters a lesson. But war against whom? There was no Munich conference to clarify the issue in advance. For many a young subaltern it was simply war against "the foreigners" on the other side of the Channel. And when the foreigners gradually resolved themselves into Germans, then that was good enough.

> "We don't want to fight, but by Jingo if we do,
> We've got the ships, we've got the men,
> And we've got the money too."

The old song was still applied. There is a certain fascination in the sublime self-confidence of 1914, in the appalling ignorance of the future that was rushing on. Montgomery was propelled along by the current as it slowly began to quicken. He was sent down to Sheppey Isle at the mouth of the estuary of the Thames with a battalion of regulars. Just a precautionary measure. Nothing serious; obvious thing to put the defences of the island in shape just in case there was a raid across the Channel.

The long summer days of July passed agreeably beside the sea. Montgomery had acquired an old Ford car and he was gathering a reputation among his friends as a somewhat reckless driver. In the outside world the rumbles of war went on.

As July turned into August Montgomery drove in his car down to Folkestone for a game of tennis. In the midst of this the abrupt, the shattering summons: general mobilization. All personnel to return to duty immediately.

Montgomery was appalled. Why such short notice? No time to go home. No time, no time, no time. The long leisured meandering stream of life had suddenly, without any real warning at all, plunged headlong over a precipice. Many a year would go by before anyone had any time again. Very few of that generation would be able to climb back into the prosperous valleys of the Edwardian days. But an afterglow and a delusion persisted. "At least," Montgomery said to himself as he packed his tennis clothes, "the thing will be over in three weeks."

CHAPTER FOUR

D.S.O. IN FRANCE

I

THE Army rushed upon the war in France. During the first few weeks of August tens of thousands of men with only the vaguest conception of the shock of modern war and the most delirious idea of its consequences were suddenly plucked from England and bundled across the Channel into the fighting. As a display of the gallantry of the human spirit it was inspiring. As an exhibition of the science of making war it showed how little we were prepared, how much we had to learn.

There was at first a machine-like horror about the whole operation. Tragically determined young officers, without proper maps or sufficient equipment, giving and taking confused orders, flung themselves forward on to that highly organised German assault. The luckier ones came reeling dazedly out of the battle without any clear notion of how or why it had all happened. For a while there was no discernible order in this tossing human sea. Here and there and at a dozen places the chain of command broke down and the front line became a ragged and unpredictable edge, steady at this point because of some imponderable outburst of human bravery, fluid at that point because there was none to give a clear command.

Pitched battle at the place of contact is usually a state of barely controlled chaos, but properly organised men can cling to their reason there and make defined and coherent movements, provided they are not hopelessly outnumbered; and then there is some sort of sanity in the general madness of noise and pain and destruction. But here, in France in August 1914, men had to fight pretty well on bravery alone. And their anger—or whatever it is that gives them the feeling that they are superior to their opponents.

In the headquarters of the generals and in the reports to Cabinet no doubt the situation appeared coherent and opti-mistic enough. Sir John French, the British field commander, was even talking to Asquith, the Prime Minister, of breaking through to Berlin. But there was no such coherency or optimism at the Front. An appalling muddle was raging. This much at least was seen by Winston Churchill, the First Lord of the

Admiralty who, throughout September, was oscillating violently back and forth across the Channel, at one moment a Cabinet Minister in London, at the next a commander in the field in Belgium.

On an undated day in October Asquith noted blandly in his diary: "Having, as he (Churchill) says, tasted blood these last few days, he is beginning, like a tiger, to rave for more, and begs that, sooner or later—the sooner the better—he may be relieved of his present office and put in some kind of military command. I told him that he could not be spared from the Admiralty but he scoffs at that . . . his mouth waters at the sight of Kitchener's new armies. Are these 'glittering commands' to be entrusted to 'dugout trash' bred on the obsolete tactics of twenty-five years ago, 'mediocrities' who have led a sheltered life mouldering in military routine, etc. etc.? For about a quarter of an hour he poured forth a ceaseless cataract of invective and appeal and I much regretted there was no shorthand writer within hearing, as some of his unpremeditated phrases were quite priceless." [1]

Along with the rest Lieutenant Montgomery was swept into the cataclysm. He was bustled from Sheppey (where the territorials took over) to Shorncliffe, then up to York (as a minor cog in the 4th Division). Then down to Harrow where the 10th Brigade under Brigadier-General Haldane finally formed up and embarked at Southampton for France on August 22nd. The date is interesting. They had missed the first awful clash with the Germans at Mons and were now plunging into the midst of a retreat.

Early on August 23rd they landed in Boulogne and the 10th Brigade (with Montgomery) raced full tilt to get into the fighting that was rapidly coming towards them. On the 24th they reached Le Cateau and at 2 o'clock in the following morning, barely forty-eight hours after leaving England, they made contact with the enemy outside the town and ran blindly upon him.

As far as Montgomery could see there was no plan. Section leaders were simply told; "Attack that hill." Up they rushed waving their bayonets. At that time the quota of machine-guns to each battalion was two. The casualties were frightful. Montgomery, charging ahead with C Company, got on to the hill and presently, along with everyone else, was flung off it again, having apparently achieved nothing whatever. Captain Day, the Company Commander, fell wounded and Montgomery decided to go back with two men and bring him in. They

[1] *Memories and Reflections*, by the Earl of Oxford and Asquith, K.G.

found the captain lying with a broken leg on the hillside and somehow struggled back as far as a church where they dumped him with the other wounded. By now their repulse, far from being a local affair, was turning into a general retreat—or rather a continuation of the retreat which had been going on since Mons. Cohesion in the line had vanished. No one could be sure of what was happening on either flank or even in the rear. By the irresistible pressure of events it had been decided in the High Command of the British Expeditionary Force to withdraw behind the Marne; but how to get those orders through to the right people and how to carry out the manoeuvre with any sort of balance and efficiency was beyond anyone's control.

The orders did in fact get through to Montgomery's battalion after they had been lying out on the exposed slopes all day; they were to retire at dusk. Unhappily the battalion was split up and those (including Montgomery) who lay on the forward slopes did not receive the orders at all. At nightfall they sent back for instructions only to find that their companions had vanished; they were alone in the void without information of the enemy or indeed of anything or anybody. The sensible thing was to beat a retreat and the major in command rounded them up for this purpose. Day and the other wounded were loaded on to country carts and the expedition set out. It must have been an alarming march. All round them were the noises of the enemy—in fact they were now between the main German line and the advanced cavalry screen of the Crown Prince's Death's Head Hussars. The convoy of British wounded making towards Peronne was quickly rounded up by the Germans, but the other survivors struggled on. Once they were charged by their own cavalry. For three days and nights the retreat went on—hiding by day and marching by night; and at length they rejoined. Even now they were not in much better condition. An indescribable confusion raged through the rearward areas. There were stragglers everywhere. Thousands of men had lost all contact with their formations and were roaming aimlessly about. It was impossible to sort them out so close to the enemy, and eventually the majority were bundled on to trains and taken farther back for regrouping.

The German tidal wave still threatened to break on Paris, but now something remarkable occurred. The whole line steadied. A kind of second wind took possession of the British Expeditionary Force. Out of their professional training (all these men were regulars), out of their courage, and out of the knowledge gained by that first brutal experience, the Army began to fit its tattered pieces together again. It was seen that Le Cateau had, in fact, achieved a great deal. It had acted as a major brake on the speed of the German advance. At Le Cateau the British had been outnumbered two to one and they had given ground. But by fighting there they had provided a desperately needed breathing space, and now, with their reformed ranks, they were ready to hold. The confusion ebbed away. The defence of Paris began.

Montgomery fought with the Warwicks on the Marne and subsequently along the Aisne where the line was temporarily stabilized. Then towards the end of September began the race for the sea and the Channel ports. The battalion went into the first battle of Ypres, and October 13th was probably the worst day of Montgomery's life.

In the morning he led his platoon in a bayonet charge on the village of Meteren. They carried the objective, but the enemy fire still continued from farther back where German sharpshooters were sniping out of the houses. Montgomery was standing up in the pouring rain reorganizing his platoon on the newly won ground when a rifle bullet entered his chest on the right-hand side from the back and passed entirely through his body. As he fell in the mud a man ran to him with a bandage, but he, too, was hit. Mortally wounded in the head he fell across Montgomery's body and the two of them lay there, one on top of the other, while the Germans continued to shoot bullets into them. Montgomery was struck a second time in the knee. He now was entirely unable to move, but he was still conscious and he shouted to the rest of his men to remain under cover. It was barely three in the afternoon and clearly no one could venture into that open space before nightfall. For the next three hours Montgomery lay motionless under the dead man in a welter of blood and mud while the rain poured down and the bullets passed by and life slowly drained out of him. At nightfall two men came out and got him. Hardly conscious, he was slung in a greatcoat, passed through a hedge and got to the forward dressing-station.

He was now in a shocking condition, badly wounded in one lung and scarcely alive. Indeed in that nightmarish place in the midst of the firing, with so many others wounded and dying, he seemed to be dead. Another officer who was brought in just ahead of him had already expired and orderlies were set to work digging graves for both of them. With some slight unconscious movement Montgomery attracted the doctor's attention. He was re-examined and it was decided that since

MONTGOMERY AS SPORTS OFFICER, BOMBAY

BISHOP MONTGOMERY
The Field-Marshal's father

he had a bare chance of living he was worth putting into an ambulance. Montgomery woke up in a hospital in England to find that he had been made a captain and awarded the D.S.O.

2

Moreover he was surviving. The years of Tasmanian fresh air, of endless sport and his natural hardiness began to build him up. True, one lung was permanently affected. He would have to control his diet. Tobacco smoke would tend to make him cough and his voice was weak. But for the rest he was whole again and fit at least for staff duties in the field. On the whole he rather enjoyed hospital; it was the first period of enforced idleness and rest he had ever known—and perhaps the only period he ever was to know. Early in January 1915, after a remarkable recovery, he was discharged from the wards. In February he was back on duty as a brigade-major at the age of twenty-seven.

In this first contact with battle something much deeper than a merely physical crisis had happened in Montgomery's life, although he had neither the time nor the inclination to explore it. Eight short weeks of chaotic and agitated active service had culminated in the sudden shock and pain of his wounds and he had come very near to death. He had done the thing that is always vital to a man's ego—he had presented himself in the way of danger and found that he was able to stay and endure it. Then the long weeks in hospital under the successive balms of his D.S.O., his promotion and the sympathy of the nurses. And now the sweet fields of higher command.

Outwardly there were one or two obvious changes. He was thinner. His face was warier and tauter than ever, his voice was incisive. His very clear blue-grey eyes had always given the impression that they were constantly watching, constantly on the alert. Now they had added to them a certain hardness, It appeared to many people to be the sharp and piercing glance of the martinet.

A black-and-whiteness in his character was for the first time coming out. To his fundamentally simple mind there were few half tones. He hated strongly and unforgivingly. Equally he loved steadily and deeply. And both functions were performed without fuss or outward passion or sentimentality.

For those he loved he was capable of endless little attentions; a flow of letters, unexpected gifts, a naive and whole-hearted confidence. All his childhood is studded with sudden little gleams of personal kindness. In Tasmania a little girl who was being teased by his elder brothers found Bernard rushing gallantly to her aid and helping to smoothe out her dress which had become dirtied in the scuffle. In Ireland a peasant bemoaning the breaking of a cream-jug is suddenly presented by Bernard with two jugs from the village shop. And with the same egocentric concentration he pursued his chosen enemies.

This basic dichotomy in his nature, never permitted full expression before, begins from now on to grow more and more marked. Even in the smallest things he went through a process of thought so profoundly uncomplicated that in later years it passed at times for a kind of mysticism. Every new thing was reduced to its utter simplicity. Was it good or bad? Was it right or wrong? Having taken a decision he stuck to it blindly, persistently and, at times, bigotedly. And all his subsequent dealings with the subject were on the same simple level. All the doubtings and misgivings and half interests and desires which lie at the periphery of a normal young man's mind, did not exist here. There was no outer periphery to Montgomery's mind. His mental world, like the world of the geographer of the Middle Ages, was flat. If you went past the edge you fell off. Ruthlessly, calmly and clearly he lopped away all the impedimenta that he judged were without importance to his life. Other things might exist but he was not interested. No point in investigating them. Stick to what you wanted. When it was necessary to advance into unexplored country plan a campaign in advance. Never get beyond the reach of your bases. Clear up the new country entirely before you set out again.

This incisive logic—a logic that sometimes excluded evidence—was already giving him immense advantages over other young men of the same age. He concentrated. He rarely squandered time in the pursuit of hobbies or half-hearted pleasures. Everything in Montgomery's life was done with a purpose and persisted in to the bitter and sometimes barren end. He rarely made conscious emotional judgments. As for the small prejudices he was born with (for example he disliked cats and he did not eat fish), he never investigated them. They existed and that was that.

At twenty-eight he was developing the fixity of mind and purpose of a man ten years his senior and he was far beyond his age in everything except experience. It was this that gave him a bearing that sometimes lacked charm and suppleness and patience—unless by chance you happened to be on the right side of his mental fence; and then he was capable of a precise consideration and indulgence that made him a remarkable friend.

From 1915 onwards there is an irresistible comparison with General Gordon of Khartoum in everything but one major particular. The same compact and wiry frame, the same rigid almost fanatical set of the head, the Bible reading and the stark emotional fervour, the contempt for convention and authority, the self-assurance and the ruthless determination, the quick outbursts of charm and generosity, the restlessness and the misogyny, the physical bravery and the impatience and quarrelsomeness, the indifference to money and the love of praise, the compelling instinct towards leadership, the painstaking study and the asceticism, and finally, sublimating all this, an inward glory in the risks and the colour and the skill of war. It is a remarkable resemblance. It fails only in this: quite unlike Gordon (or at least unlike Lytton Strachey's portrait of him), Montgomery had complete control of himself. He had no need whatever for brandy and soda or any other kind of escape. It seems almost impossible that a man, without being a stupid bore, could be so impervious to weakness, so entirely without a chink anywhere in his armour. Yet there it was; he was self-sufficient. He had formed no deep attachments outside himself, nothing that he could not cut away and forget. He was perfectly content without the society of women. He had largely out-grown his family. He was apparently inspired by a series of abstract loyalties—to his regiment, his country, to himself and to his God. Of the humble loneliness of other men he seemed outwardly to have no part.

All these qualities had been obviously building up in him since his earliest days in Tasmania, and the element of struggle had become part of his life. But now, unconsciously, the effect of his adventures in France was to gather the qualities tightly together and fix them into the permanent cast of his character. Up to now he had lived in a physical world. Now by virtue of the experience of his wound and the stimulus of his promotion he switches over to a more mental condition. The games subside. The desk comes in. Others will do the running about while he directs. As he himself might have put it, "I ceased to be a player and became a coach".

From hospital he proceeded to a new division and trained with them in England all through 1915. The Citizen Army, the unskilled farmer and the city clerk, were moving into the ranks at the rate of tens of thousands every month. Professionals like Montgomery were urgently needed as instructors and as officers in the key staff posts to grip the young army together. All Montgomery's sense of tidiness and efficiency had been outraged by what he had seen in France and he flung himself avidly into the job of training recruits. In 1916 he was back on the Somme in France. Early in 1917 he was General Staff Officer Grade Two of the 33rd Division. Later in the year he became GSO2 of the Ninth Corps and remained with the Corps in the big offensive at Chemin des Dames. In July 1918 he was promoted to GSO1 of the 47th London Division with the rank of lieutenant-colonel (brevet major).

All this time Montgomery was suspended between the men at the front and the higher command of the war. In his billets on the divisional level just behind the lines he never saw Haig or the senior commanders. The orders simply came down in writing and the junior planners were left to work out the details of the local tactics. When he went forward Montgomery no longer had personal command or any opportunity for inspirational leadership. Yet he was gulping in experience at a tremendous rate, and now with all his oddities he was regarded as an exceptionally able soldier. Eight times he was mentioned in dispatches. He had no time to argue. No authority to criticize. But the long urgent tide of work ran on and he seemed destined eventually for high command. Then the war stopped, and with it all promotion. As a major with the rank of GSO2 Montgomery went into Germany with the British forces of occupation, their headquarters at Cologne. As the British advanced into the zone the Germans fell back; little or nothing happened to guide the Allies in their future dealing with Germany. The British never penetrated beyond the borders of their zone. Somewhere in the interior of the Reich the German Army, still more or less intact, still resentful, went its own way.

3

In all the inevitable repugnance to war and soldiering that swept the world in 1919 Montgomery had no part. The jazz era rose to its height, the world of bobbed hair and short skirts, of cocktails and cars, of cynicism and exhausted disillusionment, of the restless and hysterical clutching at little pleasures, and of dancing, dancing, dancing. Montgomery remained tucked in his little military world, hopelessly out of tune with

the times, labouring at a career which was regarded as out-
moded and bottomlessly dull. He was that ridiculously
anomalous figure, a soldier without a war in a world hating
war. While pacificism and disarmament and a Wilsonesque
perfectionism and idealism captured nearly every intellectual
brain, he went on plodding solemnly at his indents and drills.
Furthermore, he was enthusiastic about it.

The reasons for this were neither political nor emotional,
nor really prophetic. He was not moved by a blind and unrelenting desire for revenge. He did not clearly foresee that the
Germans would rise again. His knowledge of politics was weak,
to say the most of it. The idea of mass slaughter appealed to
him no more than to anyone else; and his basic Christianity
subscribed to all the ideals of a League of Nations and the
concept of peace and goodwill to all men.

But something else intervened: he could not bring himself
to believe in peace. War, to his mind, was as inevitable as
that sparks fly upward. There would always be need of an army.
Idealism was well enough but you had to be strong to back it
up. The British throne was the personification of justice in this
world and it needed a police force to keep the foreigners in
order. The amateur and idealistic politicians could only talk
effectively with the support of a professional army. And now
that he had time to think he was increasingly coming round
to the view that the conduct of the late war had certainly not
been professional. There had been no science in that vast
slogging match. There had been a vast and useless wastage of
soldiers and weapons, a poverty of planning, a deplorable lack
of training; except for chance brilliant moments the whole
thing had been disgracefully mismanaged. It had not been
neat, or skilful. The Army must be reformed so that next time
everyone would know what to do.

From Cologne in 1920 he was selected to go to the Staff
College at Camberley in England, and he laughed outright
at the course prescribed there.

To him and a group of the young veterans who had been in
France the curriculum was "all nonsense", entirely out of
date, and unrealistic. Montgomery in particular was regarded
by the authorities as quarrelsome and argumentative, "a bit
of a bolshevik". He appeared to think he knew better than his
instructors or anyone else. The course was of one year. Montgomery and his friends went through it jeering, deriding,
arguing—and passed. Almost immediately afterwards he was
posted as Brigade-Major to the 17th Infantry Brigade at Cork,
in Ireland, and this meant war again, an especially dangerous

and vicious kind of war. The Sinn Fein rebellion against British rule had flared up and it was a murder campaign through the damp back streets of the towns, in some respects worse for those who were there than the recently ended war. It was the old story of a British Government with the most worthy of intentions promising freedom to a people and then delaying the execution of the promise.

The Sinn Feiners had already had one abortive rising at Easter 1916, and the revolutionary spirit had been simmering in Ireland all through the war. Now that the war was done and still the Cabinet was shilly-shallying over its promise of Home Rule, moderates in Ireland began to flock to the Sinn Fein Movement; shooting and sabotage began. There was nothing for it but to send troops over from England. Montgomery, with his Protestant northern Irish background, did not have his loyalties divided; he went most willingly and technically into the fight and continued in it until all the leading rebels were killed or caught; and Lloyd George having got his truce, withdrew the British troops.

In many ways the Irish rebellion was an ominous forerunner of the crisis that was to occur in Palestine two decades later. The British troops and their dependants were grouped into a "security area" around the barracks overlooking the city of Cork, and Montgomery lived in a small house in a terrace near by. It was impossible to carry out normal military tactics since the Sinn Feiners wore civilian clothes, and having carried out an ambush simply vanished among the ordinary crowds of the city. They made night attacks on isolated British outposts, kidnapped policemen, destroyed bridges, dug trenches across roads and threw bombs into military buildings. Week by week the hatred on both sides grew more bitter. There was a typical incident one day when the band of the Second Hampshires was marching to barracks. A bomb, worked by remote control, exploded in their midst killing and wounding a number of the men and some of the band boys. Not long afterwards the Hampshires trapped about 20 Sinn Feiners in a thatched building at Clonmult. The rebels refused to surrender and fought back. Eventually the roof was set on fire and as the survivors ran out the Hampshires shot them down.

It was in this overcharged and merciless atmosphere that Montgomery worked; his job was the organising of house-to-house searches and other security operations against the rebellion. He seems to have been successful in a dispassionate and thorough-going sort of way, judging from the reports of his superiors at the time. He was developing a talent for organization. The Cork Brigade under General Higginson had been a large affair of nine battalions, and as brigade-major, Montgomery had had a large area of control. His promotion in rank was not affected—indeed it took him sixteen years in the slowly grinding military machine to get back to the rank he had held in the war.

This was the time—the early nineteen-twenties—of ruthless retrenchment in the Service budgets. Disarmament governed all. Regular officers were being "axed" right and left and many felt themselves lucky if they got out with a pension. The hectic backwash into peace had even gone to the point where army officers returning from France were heckled in London streets, called warmongers; and in a world of growing hunger and unemployment, they were accused of hanging on to safe and idle jobs at the public expense. It was the final swing of the pendulum from the days when hysterical women went about offering white feathers to civilians.

Gloom and lethargy pervaded the Army. Sorrowfully brigadier-generals unpicked the red tabs and the pips from their uniforms. There were no longer enough senior jobs to go round. Battalions going out for service in India frequently numbered generals and colonels among their majors and captains; and Montgomery suffered along with the rest.

From Ireland he was shifted to the same duties with the 3rd Division stationed at Plymouth. By now he was becoming known inside the Regular Army as an unusually assertive and busy officer, a little odd, a little too ready to take things into his own hands, but still hard-working and efficient. At Plymouth he had the luck to fall in with a commanding officer whom he liked and admired and, what was better still, a man who would also give him a certain amount of rope to play with. Brigadier-General S. E. Hollond seemed to Montgomery to be full of the right ideas. He had definite theories about the art of war. He also believed that the basis of it all was to whip some enthusiasm into the junior officers. They should be made to see that soldiering was not a long wearisome routine from which one escaped gratefully to the mess at the end of the day. Drill had to be varied, manœuvres made exciting, a sense of competition spread abroad. While the General planned and encouraged, his Brigade-Major, Montgomery, jumped into the actual control as his executive officer. It was Montgomery who issued the orders, Montgomery who was always on the telephone at headquarters, Montgomery who hurried about in a whirl of new training schemes and projects. The Brigade-

Major was stepping a little above his position but he was
certainly useful.

Little by little under the stimulus of Hollond's ideas
Montgomery advanced from one experiment to another. These
were the days of collecting and tabulating his war experiences,
of digesting what he had learned; and inside his mind it was
the first tentative beginning of a new theory of the training of
troops for the next inevitable war. 1922 slipped by very pleasantly. When he made a mistake or overstepped his authority
he was tough skinned enough to pass off the ensuing rumpus.
All the missionary purpose of his father, the desire to instruct
and reform and convert, was coming out in him. Most strongly
he felt he knew the answers. Now he wanted to teach. He was
entering the period of his life which was to end in his becoming
one of the most notable pamphleteers ever produced by the
British Army. Still there were no distractions from his military
love. His long honeymoon with the Army was coming into its
full flower.

4

In 1923, when he was approaching his thirty-sixth birthday,
Major Montgomery was posted to the 49th West Riding
Division, stationed in Yorkshire, and here he began conducting
private military classes of his own. Junior officers were invited
to a weekly course on tactics. Montgomery was the sole
lecturer, and, he talked all day long. In the evenings he
visited the rooms of the more enthusiastic students and coached
them in the higher branches of his theory of war. Most of what
he taught is accepted practice now and it makes unremarkable
reading for the layman. In 1923 it was a distinct and almost
revolutionary break with tradition.

The 1914–1918 war had been fought largely between huge
masses of men, more or less equally armed, who were committed against one another in set-piece open battle. First there
was the heavy artillery barrage, then the massed assault for the
limited objective—perhaps only a few hundred yards. Each
battle was fought to a standstill, to the point of exhaustion
when tens of thousands of men lay dead and wounded on the
field, and no more reserves were available. Then the whole
process was repeated at some other point along the line. In
each case the objective was usually some obvious enemy
strong-point like a hill or cross-roads.

It was the steam-roller method. Surprise did not count for
much and stealth still less. Most commanders attempted to

batter and numb the enemy by the preliminary bombardment and then demolish him with overwhelming numbers of infantrymen. Always the key to the battle was "Who has the greatest numbers, the most fire power?" The individual soldier counted for little. He was one among millions, and if he knew how to pull a trigger and run with his bayonet that was enough.

To Montgomery this was all wrong. The individual soldier, far from being an unconscious cypher among a million others, was the most important person in the battle. The utmost care and attention must be lavished upon him. He must be trained for many months beforehand. Instead of being kept in ignorance, his role in the fighting and the whole battle itself must be fully and clearly explained to him beforehand. He must never be used in the mass, blindly striking against another mass. Morale was everything, and the only way to achieve high morale was to make the soldier feel he was part of a team carrying out an intelligent plan that was bound to succeed. General officers, and especially the commander-in-chief, should mix freely with the men and talk to them frankly. They must stay up forward at the front leaving the working out of details of planning to their subordinate officers.

Under Montgomery's theory the old slogging match was out. Stealth and cunning were far more important than the massing of overwhelming numbers. One must never strike directly at important objectives, but go round them. The cutting edge of the Army must consist of strong highly trained and highly mobile columns, capable of making narrow but deep penetrations and then fanning out in the rear of the enemy line.

Every battle must be preceded by exhaustive reconnaissance to discover the enemy's weakest points. Elaborate deception plans must be drawn up to confuse the enemy on the timing and direction of the main thrust. Everything must be sacrificed to the object of getting in a quick deadly blow at the weak spot while the enemy was not looking. Nothing must be done until the whole operation was supplied and keyed to the last detail and every man perfectly aware of his part. Before the battle began every possible risk must be examined and provided for. To Montgomery a battle was as precise and technical an act as building a house, and no one should go into action until he was absolutely certain he was going to prevail.

In the past war it was the defence and not the attack which usually succeeded. In the new war Montgomery believed that the attack should always succeed.

And now sitting up at night with the young subalterns in

3

Yorkshire he urged them to forget the old parade-ground drills, the forming fours and the endless marching. The thing to do, he believed, was to behave like a cat-burglar and a gangster.

Among those who listened to him and took fire from his enthusiasm at this time was a young subaltern named Francis Wilfred de Guingand. De Guingand was wholly unlike his mentor. Along with the other younger men he used to smile at Montgomery's oddities and such dour pronouncements as this: "Marriage is not a good thing for officers. You cannot be both a soldier and a husband." Yet a liking grew up between the two men and many years later it was to develop into one of the most remarkable combinations of the war against Hitler.

From York, Montgomery went back to his regiment to command a company. For eleven years he had been away on the Staff and some of his brother officers were not wholly overjoyed to see him back. For one thing he had a trying habit of suggesting that they were hopelessly out of touch with the real business of soldiering.

Then in January 1926 he got a job which was entirely to his liking. He was sent back to Camberley as an instructor. General Ironside was the Commandant, and Brooke and Paget, two future leaders of the Army, were on the Staff. In addition, half a dozen of Montgomery's future subordinate commanders—men like Leese and Harding—were students at the school, and for three years he settled down to the enjoyable business of telling them exactly how he believed battles should be fought.

CHAPTER FIVE

SWITZERLAND TO BURNHAM-ON-SEA

I

In 1925 Montgomery decided quite bluntly and simply that it was time he got married.

All his life he had avoided women; never had he formed so much as the slightest attachment to a girl. He was even regarded as a woman-hater, and he held strong views about their "emancipation from the home". Quite apart from his puritanism, women were to him an impediment to the simple and monastic progress of one's career.

Now suddenly in his thirty-eighth year he decided that marriage was a necessary and desirable thing, and he devoted himself to the project with the same intense concentration with which he usually approached a military operation. An excursion with several friends was organized to Dinard in Brittany—France presumably was the sort of terrain where this business could best be studied. As usual Montgomery made all the arrangements for the party. He got the tickets, struck a bargain with a hotel on arrival. He then instructed the manager of the hotel to procure him a dancing teacher. While the lessons were in progress (they did not proceed very well), arrangements were made to obtain introductions to the eligible young ladies then holidaying in the neighbourhood. A few mixed tennis parties ensued.

These preliminary manœuvres produced no one quite suitable, but at least they constituted a definite opening to this new campaign, and Montgomery proceeded amiably to Switzerland for the winter sports a short time later, choosing an unpretentious place, the Wildstrubel Hotel at Lenk in the Bernese Oberland.

He was scarcely a romantic figure. There was no nonsense about his ski-ing clothes. He wore gaiters, baggy grey sports trousers, a large and shapeless V-necked sweater that hung far below his waist, and all this was surmounted by a black beret which he had bought somewhere in the village (the first appearance of a beret on his head since childhood). Stuck in it was a local ski club badge (third class).

Rising early in the morning he attacked the mountains fiercely on his skis. He was interested less in the finesse of the sport than in long-distance explorations across the snowfields. Rapidly he became organizer of the sports at the hotel. He made up parties of the guests for cross-country runs and led them at a tremendous pace up the steeper slopes. With equal gusto he performed on the skating rink. But alas, when evening fell he had little to commend him in the social life of the hotel. He did not dance or play cards, and there was not much small-talk to be had out of the ascetic bachelor-major of the Warwicks. He knew sport and he knew the Army, and that seemed to be about all.

It was in these circumstances that Montgomery met and fell in love with one of those unusual women who are befriended and liked by almost everyone they meet. Betty Carver, the daughter of an Indian civil servant, was a widow with two small boys. There was hardly a point on which she could have sympathized or agreed with Montgomery. Her husband had been killed at Gallipoli in the war, and this had made her into an ardent pacifist.

Though she had been surrounded by a military family she loathed war to such a degree that she even disliked her children to play with toy soldiers.

Most of her life was given up to her two sons. She painted both in oils and water-colour, an enthusiastic amateur. She sculptured and was interested in pastels and wood carving. She lived contentedly among a little colony of artists and writers at Chiswick village on the Thames, not far from Montgomery's old home.

Betty Carver made no pretension to being a beautiful or a fashionable woman; but she had a wit and an infectious gaiety that made her loved among her friends. She was one of those natural and completely unaffected people who live life easily and without ambition. In all her kindness and gentleness the one violent emotion seemed to be this fixed hatred of anything to do with war. In the normal course of events she might easily have married another artist or continued pleasantly painting and bringing up her children beside the Thames.

As it was, Montgomery, in his large V-necked sweater, stepped firmly into this placid life. It was through Betty Carver's children that he came to know her. Montgomery was already a natural leader of boys. At Lenk he devoted himself for hours to these two children, teaching them skating and the first steps in ski-ing. They responded enthusiastically to this new man in their lives, this eager and devoted figure who was never tired of devising new games and sports. Betty Carver could hardly fail to be impressed.

When she returned to Chiswick, Montgomery called upon her in his car. For him too this courtship was a considerable adventure. Artists and writers were something wholly outside his experience: a rather tricky proposition with their loose talk and their strange and untidy interests. When he pulled up his car outside Betty Carver's riverside house he would not go inside, he waited on the pavement until she left her odd friends and came out to him.

It must have been an unusual courtship. Betty Carver's friends describe her at this time as "a charming eccentric with a tremendous vitality and zest for life".

"She had", says one, "very light-grey twinkling eyes, no make-up, a large nose and rather untidy dark hair. She was not very tall, and she wore, as we all did in those days, shapeless washing silk dresses with very low waists and strings of beads round her neck. She was excellent with the children—but then everybody loved her. She was always laughing and always full of mental vitality."

By the spring of 1927 something altogether new was happening in Montgomery's life; he was being impelled by a force which he had not evoked or designed himself, and moreover it was a force over which he had no control. He was falling deeply in love. The event had a double psychological importance. Throughout his life things had never "just happened" to Montgomery. He himself had planned each step in advance, he himself had forced every issue. When outside influences sought to take hold of him he resisted and often violently. That was one side of his mentality. But then again, and coincident with this, he had erected a network of prejudices and dislikes in the course of this long struggle from childhood; and one of the strongest of these prejudices was his aversion to women, or at least the idea of a woman controlling his life.

For nearly forty years, therefore, it had been an unbalanced life, even a somewhat unnatural life. All the energy, the interest and the affection which normally would have flowed into a marriage and the rearing of a family had been blocked and diverted towards the Army. Now suddenly, and almost at one stroke, nature reasserts itself. Betty Carver restores the balance. The prejudice makes a violent swing to the opposite direction; the antipathies of years dissolve delightfully.

No doubt during the courtship Montgomery still had the illusion that he was the master of events, since he did all the pursuing in a most masculine way. But the unexpected, unevoked interior passion was there, willy-nilly carrying him onwards.

On Betty Carver's side the same affection had swept away all her aversion to the military life. They were married most happily in the summer of 1927, and set up house in married quarters close to Montgomery's lecture-rooms at Camberley.

2

There began now for Montgomery such an era of affection and happiness and companionship as he had never known or imagined. For nearly forty years he had envisaged life as a kind of lone-wolf struggle against society, a fight to break down other people's wills to his own. Suddenly all this was changed. Here in a world of opposition and conflict was another person who was constantly and unquestioningly and loyally on his side whatever he chose to do. Here was someone to encourage and approve everything he wanted out of life. Here was a home and an unimagined friendship. In an excess of released affection and gratitude he devoted—almost dedicated—himself to his wife. He surrounded her with little attentions and kindnesses. When she was ill he was always there with hot-water bottles and medicines. Nothing was allowed to distress or disturb her. The tradesmen's bills all came to Montgomery. He seized control of the whole household, ordering the groceries and the fuel, installing the furniture, organizing the routine, arranging the boys' schooling.

Wisely and sunnily Betty Montgomery laughed and let him have his head. As an eager young husband he made many mistakes. There was the day when the entire garden was cluttered up with coal and logs which he had ordered under the belief that the house would consume fuel by the ton in the winter. But he learned, and he loved learning. Running a house was simply a matter of pure organization, which could be reduced in the end to pure logic.

On August 18th, 1928, the final climacteric happiness arrived: a son was born and they called him David. Montgomery immediately set about organizing the care, the clothing and upbringing of the boy. Finding this a most intricate labour, he complained quite seriously one day that he did not think he would have another child "since it entailed too much staff work".

Outwardly at Camberley the Staff and the students did not find much change in him. He pursued his work with a more remorseless interest than ever. The more exuberant students found him dry, hard and much too severe. They complained that he was "inclined to be bossy", and that he "rammed facts down their throats". There was a sharp quarrel with a full colonel who was senior to Montgomery on the Staff.

Indeed Montgomery's mannerisms were hardly endearing at times. Even his kindly gestures tended to be emphatic. Major-General Sir Charles Gwynn, who was in charge of the Staff College, remembers opening his front door one day and finding Montgomery on the threshold clutching a radio set.

"You have no wireless set", Montgomery announced, coming inside. "Here is one and"—glancing narrowly around the room—"*that* is the place to put it."

The General protested mildly that he did not want a wireless, and if he did have one he would not put it in that particular spot. Montgomery enthusiastically pointed out how wrong the General was about the whole thing. In the end the set was accepted, placed to Montgomery's liking, and he left.

Among a thousand stories of Montgomery which were current at the end of the war (most of them exaggerated or wholly wrong), there are none which give a more accurate flavour of his acquaintance than this passing incident at Camberley with its ingredients of simple kindness, of slight crankiness and the air of convinced rightness with which he went about.

One gathers that many people were slightly frightened of him: one could laugh light-heartedly with Mrs. Montgomery, but when her husband came into the room there was a pause, a slight air of restraint. Once when the Montgomerys were guests at a house party in Italy a fancy-dress dinner rparty was arranged. Montgomery (as it was expected) refused to put on a costume, but his wife appeared weeving his evening clothes, a moustache painted on her upper lip. With one accord the guests glanced apprehensively at Montgomery to see how he would take it. Betty Montgomery alone appeared to be at ease. Lifting a glass she cried, "The ladies—God bless 'em", and the party relaxed.

3

The marriage had astonished Montgomery's friends. Few believed that that dry unrelenting figure was set upon any other course than permanent bachelorhood. If they had chosen a bride for him it would have been some strong country girl wearing sensible rough tweeds, a good horsewoman, and a leader in the local charities.

But this dark vivacious woman with her infectious giggle, her paint-box and her books was something entirely unexpected. What was even more remarkable to the onlookers was the ease with which she handled her husband. The spectacle of Montgomery dancing attendance upon anyone was something which no student at Camberley at that time could lightly believe in. Yet there it was.

Actually Betty Montgomery had made great concessions to her marriage. She did not force her life or her friends upon her husband, and because she was in love she accepted happily and naturally the military atmosphere which he drew around her. She did not abandon entirely her old life but took selected parts of it into her new household. Her Chiswick friends found her able to laugh at Montgomery's rigidities. They remarked that she could apparently "do what she liked with him". And they also found that she admired and respected him; in a curious way she made a bridge between her old friends and her new husband, between the soldier and the artist.

The Chiswick circle discovered that Montgomery was only dogmatic and emphatic about military affairs. When they talked of politics and painting and books he was modest and unassuming. He would listen and question with respect and unending patience. They even found him charming. And he on his side probably transmitted some of his simplicity and direction to their ideas. People whom Betty brought into the house, like A. P. Herbert and his wife, became close friends. Then, too, she had no difficulty in making a conquest of the military people around her and of Montgomery's own family. Out of a maze of opposites she was making the perfect wife.

A great deal of this time Betty Montgomery was not very well. She had married at forty. When, after the marriage, Montgomery took her back to Lenk for a second season she was expecting her child and unable to take part in winter sports. The birth of the baby left her weak and she was never afterwards very robust. This weakness was enough to redouble Montgomery's devotion and kindness. He gave up nothing of the discipline of his own life and his passion for his work, but for her he made every concession. And she very sensibly was not jealous of his career but supported and indulged him in it. For her, too, the Army was inviolate. "It's no use, my dear," she would say to her friends. "I have reverted to type. All my children will be soldiers."

In part at least the long struggle against society was over. That taut nervous chain of resistance stretching back to his

MONTGOMERY, AGED 30

MRS. B. L. MONTGOMERY

childhood was softly broken and all his life was warmed and widened and made more tolerable. The role of father to his two step-sons suited him admirably; he adored this kind of patriarchal responsibility and the two boys responded willingly. The birth of his own son gratified a more than usual hunger for immortality. In every direction his life seemed to have been suddenly transformed. Even his career marched more swiftly ahead, and for the first time since the end of the war he began to glimpse the reality of the vision that never for an instant left him—authority and high command.

He was already a senior major. He was becoming a known man in the Army. More and more people were beginning to listen to him; or rather, as he himself put it, "resistance to my ideas was beginning to die down". Soon, perhaps, someone would die, someone retire, and he would get command of a battalion.

His marriage had broadened him, made him more tractable and more acceptable for promotion. Certainly he had still a long way to go before the men in higher command would docilely accept his acid criticisms. But he was learning patience and gathering followers around him.

Refreshed and exhilarated by three years of terrific work at Camberley he went back to his regiment, then stationed at Woking, and got the important job of acting as secretary of the committee which was to undertake one of the periodic re-writings of the Army's Infantry Training Manual. This was a big jump forward. At heart Montgomery was an infantryman and the focus of his interest in war lay in infantry tactics.

At Camberley he had become a notable lecturer on the subject. Once instead of taking his annual leave he accepted an invitation to go off to manoeuvres at Sheerness as an adviser on the infantry side. He had nothing to gain from this except gratification of his own enthusiasm. During the manoeuvres he propounded his ideas with such lucidity and vehemence that they were printed and distributed among senior commanders; and subsequently his notes became standard practice for the use and deployment of infantry.

It was a distinguished but not passionately active group of officers who sat on the War Office committee for the re-writing of the manual. Their secretary had not much difficulty in taking over most of the business himself. It was the old Montgomery tactics which he had employed steadily since his schooldays: get into the team and then run it. The manual, which was still current when the war against Hitler broke in 1939, was largely the output of Montgomery's own brain.

3*

When there were postponements in the printing of the book Montgomery protested to the War Office: "Why the delay in the publication of MY book?" He was told curtly that it was not HIS book, that the writing was poor and that his methods of taking over the committee for his own use were not approved.

Montgomery's reaction to this was quite simple. "This proves that the authorities are quite ga-ga." It never seriously crossed his mind that he himself might be wrong in a case like this. Eventually the manual was printed more or less as he wrote it. Describing it later on Montgomery said simply: "In it I dealt with the whole art of war".

4

At last in 1930 he cleared the hurdle which is of most importance in the life of a regular soldier: he was made lieutenant-colonel and given command of a battalion of the Warwicks. Slowly and painfully he had climbed back to the rank which he had held at the end of the war twelve years before. In January he sailed with his battalion for Palestine and his wife joined him there soon afterwards.

These were the days of the early simmering of the Arab-Jewish revolts. The full bitterness of the quarrel was yet to come, and for a year the battalion was disturbed by nothing much more than occasional sharpshooting. This one battalion was judged a sufficient force to garrison the whole country, and Montgomery, as Commanding Officer, Palestine, dwelt pleasantly at Jerusalem surrounded by the bare Biblical hills, the shepherds' flocks, the orange groves and the warm breezes of the eastern Mediterranean rolling up from Tel-Aviv.

Like his predecessor, Gordon of Khartoum, the Colonel was sometimes seen walking among the sights of Jerusalem and Bethlehem with his Bible and his guide books. He had grown into many strict habits of late. Each day he rose early—usually at dawn. He read the Bible regularly and was fond of quoting from it. More and more he was subduing his life to a strict and minute routine; half an hour for breakfast, so many minutes for dealing with reports and correspondence, so many hours for inspections. A light and very limited diet. His old wound in the lung did not trouble him but he looked after himself strictly. Drinks and tobacco were practically vanishing from his life. He was in bed by ten o'clock each night.

Now that he was advancing into middle age the influence of his father was growing more strongly upon him. The old Bishop, close upon ninety, had virtually retired to the family home at New Park in Ireland. He had seen the glories of the Church. He had risen to the rank of Prelate of the Order of St. Michael and St. George. He had embellished and decorated a fine chapel in St. Paul's. Each year it had been his custom to don his robes (amiably described by the Bishop as "my war-paint") and in a voice growing increasingly frail, read over the entire list of the illustrious names of the members of the Order. In the end he had himself been invested with the K.C.M.G. and now he was about to preach for the last time before his friends, the Duke and Duchess of York.

From Ireland, where he still strode about the country with his stick, the old man wrote letters and watched keenly the progress of his third son Bernard. He made him the trustee of his will. He sent him much advice. Almost alone of everyone in the world the Bishop was determined to believe that some great future was awaiting this boy who had begun life so restlessly and relentlessly in London.

And to Bernard, as he opened his father's letters in Palestine, the years rolled away and the old thunder came back : "Place your faith in God . . . you come of a family of gentlemen . . . remember that you must always be responsible for your actions . . . undiluted hell fire has done me a great deal of good . . . whatever you choose to do place God first in your life." To which Bernard added another phrase he was increasingly fond of using—"The Lord mighty in Battle".

There had been so much between them and so little expressed; in a strange way it seemed that their deep relation-ship had never been enough fulfilled, that each had a great deal more to give the other. But time and distance and the war and ambition had intervened. And now with that helpless terror and sudden tugging at the heart which one always feels at parting with someone who is dearly loved, Bernard began to realize that it was already too late.

There remained behind them the long stretch of photo-graphic memories; his father striding down the street in Hobart, the white beard, the upright figure, the air of radiating benevolence, and again the same scene in Irish villages where the peasants used to rise and touch their caps to him . . . the readings in the study on Sunday afternoons . . . the robes and the sermons and the music. Everything seemed to have gone by so quickly. His father had been so much the apostle of gentle-ness and peace and only now, at the very end, it was becoming apparent to Bernard that he might have made the complement to that idea of life by protecting it, by making the Lord mighty in Battle, himself the chosen soldier of the Church militant.

Of late he had been growing very like his father. Quite apart from this spiritual communion and the matching simplicity of their habits, a strong facial resemblance was developing between them. In reality their natures were basic opposites, the father bent upon personal negation and submission and a life of peace; the son riding a desperate craving for self-fulfilment in a world of struggle. But now, at the end, they were like two men who had reached the one goal on entirely different roads and they found their conflicting experiences had left them much the same.

Both appeared to have reached the same faith by the same method of excluding and despising the little human weaknesses of life; and in the keen and forthright look in the eyes of the old priest you could clearly read the future of the younger soldier in Palestine.

When at last the news came out to Montgomery in the Middle East that his father had died of heart failure at the age of eighty-nine, it was an overriding grief. Of the three great companions of his life—his father, his wife and his son—only two now remained. Writing of his father's death many years later Montgomery could only say, "I loved him".

In 1931 Montgomery and his battalion were ordered down to Egypt to take over the garrisoning of the port of Alexandria. He now came under the command of two unusual men. General Sir John Burnett-Stuart was the Commander-in-Chief, Egypt, and Montgomery's immediate superior was Brigadier Pile, who had set up his headquarters at Ismailia, a palm-tree oasis near the Bitter Lakes half-way along the Suez Canal.

Both men were keen regular soldiers, full of ideas of their own and ready to accept only a certain amount of independence and insubordination from a junior officer. Montgomery's reputation as an enthusiastic but tough customer had gone before him and he was watched curiously when he went to make his report on his first arrival. Trouble was not long coming.

Montgomery's job was not on the face of it very difficult. There was a long tradition of British soldiering in the Nile Delta, and Alexandria was a pleasant billet. He had merely to maintain a degree of smartness and discipline among his troops in the town, and from time to time lead them on manoeuvres in the desert. Rumbles and unwelcome reports began to emerge from Alexandria soon after Montgomery's battalion settled in. Senior officers were sent down from Cairo to investigate and were frankly annoyed by what they saw. It appeared at first that Colonel Montgomery was not popular in his battalion. Some of the officers disliked him outright and they were full of complaints. They said he was high-handed, ridiculously punctilious and autocratic. The men were uneasy. They were far from smart on parade. Under the eye of that weird heterogeneous population of Alexandria their discipline was lax. There were too many men locked in the guard-house and there was too much slovenliness round the barracks. Morale was bad.

Nor, after the first terse exchange of reports, did things greatly improve. Montgomery was on the telephone to Brigadier Pile at Ismailia: "Can you come down? A difficulty has arisen." The Brigadier began to dread those telephone calls. He would fly to Alexandria and demand of Montgomery, "Well, what is it this time?"

Usually it was some hopelessly involved affair beginning with a zealous but wholly unorthodox order of Montgomery's and ending in a mess that was far beyond the range of the Army text-books. Montgomery was running his battalion as though he were the head of a family back at Bishop's Court. Young officers who were apt to give up their leisure hours to the more earthly and exotic pleasures of Alexandria were suddenly finding themselves on the mat in front of the Colonel, their private lives most rudely exposed and the most unusual punishments forced upon them. This, they contended, was a little too much. A soldier's private life was his own affair. Montgomery usually took the opposite line. A soldier, he argued, was a soldier the whole time. If a soldier's private habits made him unfit for duty then he must be corrected.

Montgomery was also seriously concerned with the incidence of venereal disease among his soldiers. How, he asked himself, can we ever be fit for war if we take casualties behind the line before we start? It was a problem that he was going to meet in a much bigger way later on.

His approach to it was strictly practical and realistic. First, as a long-range strategic remedy, you must build up a sense of morals against the evil. Secondly, as a short-range tactical object, you must act on the best practical expedients available.

The Alexandria of the early nineteen-thirties was not much different from what it is now: a maze of sweltering streets teeming with every nationality in the Levant. Most of the coloured population was gripped by a garish and amoral poverty and immersed in the sordid struggle to escape from it by any method they could. Backsheesh. Piastres. These were the governing inspirations of life. In commerce there were no holds barred. Sell—sell anything so long as you sell—bath-tub gin, poisonous shellfish, fake jewellery, raddled women, drugs; ask ten times the market price, bargain for everything down to a toothpick. In that generous and fœtid heat obscure cafés and saloons with broken-down gramophones and women flourished along every other street, the residence of innumerable flies by day and innumerable pimps by night. The nightly murder was more or less routine; stabbing affrays barely worth attention.

All this was not, of course, the Alexandria that the tourist saw; the city of wide boulevards on the seafront, of white-robed servants in tarbooshes, of gin-slings on the terrace and bridge in the homes of the cotton millionaires. But it was the Alex-andria into which the soldier penetrated on his night out and inevitably he ran into trouble. A very great deal of the trouble originated in the brothels.

To combat this Montgomery, on his own initiative, broke entirely away from the old *laissez-faire* attitude of the Army. He introduced an enlightened scheme of personal hygiene among the men and, in a world where there was still no penicillin, gave them the chance of avoiding the worst evils of venereal disease.

Fortunately Montgomery had Burnett-Stuart and Pile as his superiors, and although they were often harassed by his experiments and innovations, they were able to see his side of the argument.

It was not so much *what* he did as the *way* he did it which was the upsetting thing—especially to the *amour propre* of Montgomery's younger officers. But to point this out to Montgomery was no easy thing: if he saw something he believed right he went bald-headed at it, convinced that his rightness alone would shine forth and explain all. He was still a long way from reaching the finer levels of a nice tact and diplomacy; perhaps he would never reach them.

It was not long before the telephone was ringing again at Ismailia. "Can you come down? A difficulty has arisen."

This time it was the regimental magazine. Montgomery had launched the paper as an improver of morale, as a means of inspiring the regimental spirit in the men. Then he *ordered* them to buy it. Inevitably a village Hampden and his followers arose in the regiment, in this case a non-commissioned officer and several privates. They would read the magazine willingly enough, they said, but they were damned if anyone was going to order them to do so. Into the guard-house they went.

It was an awkward knot to unravel. Clearly the men were

in the right. But how to release them without undermining Montgomery's authority? In the end a little quiet and reasonable talking settled the matter; the men were released, the order not enforced—and they bought the magazine.

For the regiment the incident was a little triumph in democracy. For Montgomery it was the sort of experience upon which the whole of his future career really depended. Outside of his own subject, the Army, he was no autocrat. Upon most of the issues of life he was as modest and willing to hear another man's point of view as anyone else. Although he did not drink or smoke he never forced others to conform with himself. They could stay up late, ignore the Bible, get drunk; in fact do anything they liked provided only this— they turned up fit for duty when they were needed. As soon as the Army was affected a rigid iron curtain came down in his mind. Here there must be no untidiness, no shilly-shallying with amateur ideas, no nonsense about the Army marching as slow as its slowest man and conforming to its weakest mind. Democracy in the Army—the stabilizing of things at the average level—this was out. There was a right and a wrong way to do things. Only the right way would do. Running an army and fighting a battle were matters as clearly defined and as technical as mending a bathroom tap. Montgomery felt like the plumber who arrives to find the amateur householder doing the wrong thing and making matters much worse.

It was because there were very few people in the world— still less in the Army—who were as sure of their skill as this that Montgomery ran into ninety per cent. of his quarrels. Very few people, especially at this time, were willing to believe that he was always right. He *said* he was always right. He behaved as if he thought he was always right. But was this not just an incredible conceit? And, anyway, could not the fellow occasionally behave with a little restraint instead of indulging in these outbursts of impatience and bluntness and ridiculous petulance?

For both sides the issue was extremely irritating. It was agony for Montgomery to admit that he was ever wrong—and he was wrong occasionally just as his mother before him had been sometimes wrong. Clearly whatever he had done in life he would have run into these brawls and misunderstandings. But in the Army it was especially so. The Army was still a repository of tradition. As at the turn of the century it still tended to attract the less brilliant minds of the nation. Many a mild drunk and incompetent had remained holding a commission after the war against the Kaiser. There had been no clean sweep through the regiments or the higher command. Indeed most of the best minds had got out of the Army directly the war finished. It has to be set down to Montgomery's account that every day he was up against inferior minds, lazy minds, pompous and silly minds; minds that were certainly much less enthusiastic than his own.

What he was learning now was that for better or for worse these were the people with whom he had to live, and only occasionally in his life would he have the luck to fall in with a superior like Hollond or Burnett-Stuart. He was learning—with what infinite pain—that he *had* to compromise and be tactful if he was going to get his way. One day perhaps he might sit at the top, a law unto himself, but he was a long way off that yet.

One other thing was becoming apparent to him: the best and surest way of getting obedience was to secure the men's liking. If they liked you and believed in you then you could get anything out of them. Deliberately he set about cultivating the men under his command. They reacted, he saw, to personal appearances and speeches: very well, they should have them. Montgomery was no snob. He was far too busy with what he wanted to do to clutter up his career with affectations of any kind. He genuinely enjoyed being with the men; it all fitted in very well. Little by little he believed he could gain their confidence and get them to see what he proposed was the best thing.

All this parading and loitering about Alexandria he disliked just as much as they did. There was no action to it. No smell of war. If they could go out on manœuvres he would show them what fun the whole thing could be.

5

At this time the Army penetrated no great distance beyond the Delta westward into the desert. Its principal duty was to guard the approaches and the flanks of the Suez Canal. Mussolini's Fascists were making excitable motions in Tripolitania, and lately they were constructing an absurd wire fence along their border with Egypt. But this was hundreds of miles away to the west. It was hardly credible that an army would cross the desert and attempt the invasion of the Delta and the Canal from the west. Some little mapping had been done as far west as Sollum—the heritage of the old war against the Turks and the Senussi tribesmen; there was a defensive position at Mersa Matruh; but this was about all. Manœuvres were held near at hand in the vicinity of the Great Pyramid and Mena House.

Montgomery was not a notable lover of nature. Scenery to him became interesting when it was properly mapped and marked out with possible defensive and offensive areas. There is no record of his responding in any marked way to the limitless spaces and the moving colours of the desert when he first led his men out of Alexandria. Yet something there evoked his special interest, and now, as later, from the moment he set foot on the open sand he stepped forward with absolute assurance.

Probably the desert appealed to him as being the perfect arena for war. Here as nowhere else you coul i join in a straight-out test of skill. There were no civilians to become mixed up in the fighting, no extraneous political matters to cloud the issue. War in the desert was as technical, as clear-cut and decisive as you could hope to get it.

Once in the desert there was no slackness any longer in the battalion. Both Burnett-Stuart and Pile began to realize that they had here a field commander of exceptional briskness and ingenuity. More than this he had a way of enthusing his men once they were in action which gave him remarkable results.

As for Montgomery himself, he was learning fast. There was one notable exercise against a rival force which was defending the Pyramids. Up to this point Montgomery had been a little chary of night actions; they were untidy, the formations were apt to get out of touch. But now it was essential if he was going to eliminate the enemy that they should be surprised. De Guingand, his old student from York, had now joined him, and the two men planned this, their first mock battle in the desert, togethei. Aircraft were sent out to discover where the enemy headquarters was lying. The first trip was blank. The time limit for the exercise was running out, but they decided to try again. This time the airmen came back with the news that they had discovered the enemy in a wadi. At once Montgomery gave the order to advance. His men rushed upon the rival encampment in the darkness, and under the light of flares dropped from the air they mopped up the whole position.

It is hardly likely that either Montgomery or de Guingand could have felt the touch of history at that moment. Yet before ten years were out the things they learned on this night were going to engulf a million men in one of the decisive struggles of the world; and all this was to happen in much the same way and not fifty miles from that same valley of the desert.

Things did not always go as well as this. There was another exercise wherein Montgomery, although a junior commander, calmly decided that the whole thing had got into such a hopeless muddle that it was not worth going on. He rode over to the rival's camp and managed to persuade the commander to agree with him. Light-heartedly they called off the manœuvre and sat down with their officers to a friendly meal.

Brigadier Pile was in charge of the manœuvre. Although a temperate man he became a little incoherent when this news was brought to him. Both commanders were summoned and reprimanded for their conduct with all the colour and vehemence which the Brigadier was able to produce. From Montgomery's rival there subsequently came an apology; from Montgomery himself, nothing.

Yet it was apparent now to anyone with half an eye that the Army had someone in Montgomery who was quite exceptional as a tactical leader in the field. All that unorthodoxy that made him an indifferent commander of a stationary garrison came brimming out once he was in action. He was persistent, he was lucid, and he had that rare quality that was painfully lacking in the higher ranks—the ability to think quickly *in terms of action*. As for the question of whether he had sufficient assurance to act on his ideas and on his responsibility—no one was greatly worried about that.

6

At home in Alexandria where his wife and baby were now installed, Montgomery's world was complete. That same glow with which the marriage began persisted here. Instantly Betty Montgomery had gathered friends around her. She had abandoned painting. ("My dear, it's impossible here. The atmosphere is steeped in two thousand years of pleasure.") And there were dinner parties, bridge, a life of servants and cars and good food. Montgomery organized everything; his wife embellished it, and both were happy. To guests and strangers Montgomery sometimes seemed a strange and remote figure in the amiable atmosphere that always surrounded his artistic wife. He insisted on punctuality at meals, he stayed only three-quarters of an hour for lunch, no matter what the weather was or who was being entertained. A telephone was always at his right hand at the table, and he was apt in the course of dinner to engage in the most startlingly blunt and vigorous conversations with officers at the other end of the line. Sometimes, too, guests playing bridge would suddenly find themselves bustled out of the house because some important business was on hand. But Montgomery and his wife understood one another: the Army was sacred. All the rest of his life was hers.

Montgomery was always at his best when he had responsibility, and in many ways it softened him. It was at these times that that streak of patriarchal kindness came out most strongly. Because he loved a younger brother, he was now paying for the boy's education, and this was not an easy thing to do out of a lieutenant-colonel's pay.

In Alexandria, too, many of his dealings were happier. There was the matter of the ceremonial church parade, always an irksome thing with the soldier not overly devout and certainly not anxious to give up valuable leisure time in going to church. Montgomery ordered the ceremonial parade to be cancelled. Irritable men, he argued, were in no condition to meet their God. In future they could go in mufti as civilians. He himself would read the lesson. The service was at once a success, but the inevitable reprimand came down from headquarters in Cairo. Who had given Colonel Montgomery the arbitrary power to do away with the ceremonial parade? Montgomery fought it. And this time he won.

By the time he came to take his battalion off to Poona, in India, he was developing fast as a popular commander "once you got to know him". His troops were a little lacking in spit and polish and they made no great show on the parade ground. But they knew their weapons and they were resourceful on manœuvres. They could fight.

On the whole it was rather bad luck they were going to Poona. In Poona the authorities reckoned on drill. Field experience was well enough, but unless a soldier had his buttons polished and was able to present arms with a certain amount of dispatch he was not much good to the Army. The garrison commander at Poona took one look at Montgomery's men and decided they simply would not do. Clearly the whole battalion would have to be reformed and re-trained. They were lax in their drill. Where was the ceremonial discipline? How could you send men on parade like that?

Montgomery, on his side, took one look at the garrison commander and applied for three months' leave. Poona very definitely was no place for him and he had better get out of it quickly before even worse rows ensued. In all Montgomery's long story this is probably the one prudent personal retreat he ever carried out.

Buoyantly he set off with his wife—for Japan. This was to be pure holiday. For two months they roamed about, shopping in Singapore, Hong Kong and Tokio. And while they were away things were moving in Montgomery's favour.

Both Burnett-Stuart and Pile had reported favourably upon him. "He is clever, energetic, ambitious and a very gifted instructor", wrote Burnett-Stuart. "But to do himself full justice he must cultivate tact, tolerance and discretion." Again, later, Burnett-Stuart describes him as "very refreshing to meet", and adds, "He revels in independence and responsibility".

Pile, too, had formed the same conclusions. "An officer of great military ability who delights in responsibility. He is very quick. He writes very clear memoranda . . . definitely above the average of his rank and should attain high rank in the Army. He can only fail to do so if a certain high-handedness, which occasionally overtakes him, becomes too pronounced." And again from Pile, "He has fertile and original thoughts which he expresses in the most inimitable way. He is really popular with his men whom he regards and treats as if they were his children."

Montgomery had been fortunate indeed in his superiors. Many a row and many a sore trial peeps out from those phrases; but handsomely, almost prophetically, the writers give him his due. And Montgomery, on his side, looked back with gratitude to those first years in the desert and the two men under whom he served there. Much later on he said, "I learned a very great deal from them. Burnett-Stuart was possibly the ablest soldier in the Army, a rebel against the old ideas."

There is a warm and prosperous aura over all these early years of the nineteen-thirties. Inevitably now Montgomery was booked for high command. There is an impetus behind him. The affair at Poona which would have been a major obstacle ten years earlier is now vaulted over lightly, almost gaily. Betty and the child David are with him everywhere; her other two sons are doing well at school in England. The whole family prospers and wherever Montgomery goes a home springs up around him. Now, in his late forties, the old loneliness has gone, at last the old hunger for recognition is being appeased. It has not been a spectacular career perhaps. There have been none of the great banners and the coloured lights of the adolescent dream; he has not set his age on fire, not led a new crusade for Christendom. But life has been a steady upward curve, he has made some mark on his contemporaries. It will be necessary always to struggle and work; but now surely there can be a little leisure in life and he can enter into his fifties watching his family and his career advancing steadily and evenly upwards. At last the unquiet spirit seems to have found a place to rest.

Back from his cherry blossom tour of Japan, Montgomery took his next bound upward with extraordinary ease: full colonel, General Staff Officer of the First Grade, senior instructor at the Military Staff College at Quetta. It has taken him sixteen years, but now he has regained not only the rank but the same authority that he had at the ending of the war. This time his rank is permanent and solidly founded on experience and a widening reputation.

Family, servants, luggage and furniture moved up to Quetta together and his three great years of teaching begins. This time there are no impediments. He has formed his philosophy of war. He has dotted all the "i's" and crossed the "t's" of his theory of training.

With the blackboard behind him, the rows of student-officers sitting in front, he explains tirelessly over and over again; should there be another war you have only to follow these rules and the whole thing will be perfectly simple.

1. Morale. Study the individual soldier. Create the atmosphere of success. Morale means everything.

2. Simplify the problem. Sort out the essentials which must form the basis of all future action; and once you have decided upon them ensure that those essentials stand firm and are not swept away in a mass of detail. As a commander, lay down the general framework of what you want done—and then within that framework allow great latitude to your subordinates. Explain the plan to them carefully and fully and then stand back yourself and avoid being encumbered with unessentials.

3. You must learn how to pick a good team of subordinates, and once you have got them stick to them and trust them. All men are different and all generals are different; so are brigades and divisions. But if you study human nature you will be able to fit them into the right places.

4. Make yourself know what you want and have the courage and determination to get it. You must have the will to win: it is much more important to fight well when things are going badly than when things are going well. Remember that battles seldom go completely as they are planned. Great patience is required and you have to keep on until the other fellow cracks. If you worry you merely go mad.

There is an *ex-cathedra*, an almost Biblical quality about these and all the many other pronouncements. Be wise. Be patient. Be brave. There is no explanation: they are simply flat statements of fact, flat commands requiring a simple act of faith. The dogma is almost Socratic. If you know the Right you will inevitably practise it.

The bulk of the lectures, of course, were concerned with Montgomery's own knowledge and ideas on the technical use of armour, artillery, air power and infantry. There were all the matters of administration and supply, signals and maintenance. He held forthright views about everything and these views were nearly all on the side of innovation. Air power, armour, mobility—these were the battle-winning factors, and even then, in that era of cavalry regiments and standardized drill, they did not sound so cut and dried as they do now.

But when the details were said and done with he came back again and again to the abstract and unalterable tenets of his creed: morale, morale, morale. Simplify everything. Let subordinates carry out the detail. Stick to the essentials and hang on until you win.

He was already, as a lecturer, developing certain tricks and mannerisms. He never raised his voice. But that thin incisive pitch of tone was getting a quality of conviction that was half missionary and almost fanatic. He always looked directly at his audience, fixing on one man's eyes, then another's, a clear, unblinking, concentrated stare. He went over the same points again and again. He developed the knack of picking out the most emphatic word in a sentence and repeating it several times over. Thus: "Never fail to win the air battle first: never . . . never (his voice getting softer) . . . never—(and then almost in a whisper) never".

You might disagree with him but you had to listen.

As a speaker he had long since ceased to feel nervous, because he was always engrossed in what he was saying and utterly determined to get himself believed. But at moments of listening or talking reflectively he had a habit of taking a little roll of flesh on his thin cheek between the thumb and first finger of his left hand and squeezing it gently in and out. This he would do for minutes together. It gave him an air of even deeper concentration and he was as a rule quite unconscious of the action. He had one other mannerism which he shared with the American Stonewall Jackson. In the act of explaining something, he threw out his left hand, its palm opened towards the man whom he was addressing, and he waved it gently and deprecatingly up and down to punctuate each point, raising his eyebrows at the same time. Every month he gained adherents. The more serious students gravitated to him at once, and there was a growing coterie of young men whom he deliberately sought out and befriended and pushed ahead in their careers. It was at this time that he warmly supported de Guingand's appointment to the Staff College at Camberley.

For the most part it was a sedentary life and, since teaching was a form of command, he talking, the others listening, he was happy. Even when disaster almost blotted out that whole community it passed him and his family by.

The Quetta earthquake came in May 1935 almost without warning. It was a sultry night. The horses in their stalls were nervous and restless. Montgomery and the British garrison were quartered outside the town and they heard in the distance a confused and unearthly roaring. After a while the noises stopped and again the night was ominously and unnaturally still. At 2 a.m. the earthquake suddenly struck with prodigious and terrifying force. The worst of it passed by the British encampment, but even here the ground was heaving and shuddering and people ran about in bewilderment in this monstrous insecurity, shouting reassurances and questions at one another. The real blow fell on the mud-hut native town of Quetta itself. As the city collapsed in smoke and dust awful cries and rumblings came out of the debris. Fires began and in the suddenness and completeness of the shock there was utter chaos among the Indian population. Streets disappeared into rubbish. Thousands of people were buried alive under the tumbling walls. Sewers burst, and when the morning came there was added to the appalling wreckage a violent stench and a thick acrid cloud of fumes that made men vomit.

The British soldiers mustered every ambulance and vehicle and climbed into the horrible rubble with their gas-masks on. But even so they could get no farther than the perimeter of the town. Amid so much smoke and dust the centre was in a complete confusion of dead and dying people pinned under the fallen roofs. For days and nights the survivors did what they could, but still they could make no headway among the wreckage and by now all human cries there were silenced. There was danger of disease. In the end the British cordoned off the whole city with barbed wire and left it, a vast mouldering grave, to be cleaned out by the scorching sun, the vultures and the jackals. Some thirty thousand people had died.

7

In the early summer of 1937, after three years at Quetta, Montgomery was posted to the command of the 9th Infantry Brigade at Portsmouth with the rank of brigadier. It was the floodtime of his life. It began to seem as if everything in the world was conspiring to his advantage. He had left England six years before, an untried and rather unpromising commander of a battalion. Now he was coming home, a man of influence, an acknowledged mentor in the Army.

General Sir Guy Williams, the Commandant at Quetta, had reported upon him: "He is a very fine teacher with decided views: fitted to be a major-general." The way ahead was clear.

Betty Montgomery was well. David was settled close by at his private school in Surrey. In all these years Betty had stayed beside her husband and now the marriage had gone beyond the point of success: it had become the interwoven basis of both their lives and neither could have conceived of their ever being apart. People had long since ceased to wonder at the union of two such opposite characters: they had become one of those married couples who are always spoken of together, who always appear together and who seem in the end to have become one person. At Quetta the devotion of Betty and Bernard Montgomery had been one of the things people smiled about and liked. Betty had been an unusual success as the Colonel's wife. She never played favourites, she never condescended to the "junior" wives and she never interfered with her husband's affairs. There was no gossip or angling for position in the Colonel's house; one went there to relax and listen to that infectious giggle, to talk painting or soldiering, whatever you pleased.

After all their wandering abroad the one thing now the Montgomerys wanted was something they had never really had before—a home of their own, a place where they could gather their children under one roof. In the Far East they had done much shopping. They had gathered a collection of Persian rugs from Kabul and Istanbul, from Bagdad and Jerusalem. They had bought silks and silverware and many other things. Now they wanted to unpack. For some time they had tired of the heat and the life abroad. And now at this very opportune moment had come Montgomery's appointment to senior command and in an ideal part of England, close to the children. On his brigadier's pay they could afford something pleasant in the way of a house, a car as well. 1937 was a marvellous year in their lives and they came home brimming with excitement at the long profitable days ahead.

There was an exuberant reunion with the boys, a whirl of shopping in London and the meeting with friends they had not seen for six years. Montgomery, with the three pips and the crown on his shoulder, his red tabs, looked over his brigade at Portsmouth. Something like five thousand men under his command now. Well, that was something. He would make them the finest fighting organization in England.

They were allotted a house by the Army close to Portsmouth—Ravelin House. It was a little large for them, perhaps a little too resplendent and expensive, but they liked it, and anyway the future stretched ahead. It would be ideal for David as he grew up. Together they worked eagerly on the making of this, their first real home. Montgomery took on this new piece of staff work with exuberance: furniture, carpets, books, garden—all just a matter of smooth organization. By midsummer the place was almost ready for them. Separate bedrooms for the boys, spare rooms for guests, the reception rooms and the study.

While the final touches were being added, Montgomery was called away to manœuvres with his new brigade, an event he was looking forward to with enthusiasm since it would be an opportunity to put some of his ideas into practice.

It was decided that Betty, at the same time, should take her summer holidays with David at Burnham-on-Sea. Then the whole family would unite in the new home at Portsmouth.

On the beach one day Betty suddenly felt unwell. Something had bitten her on the leg—an insect or an animal of some kind; she could not afterwards remember what it was. By the time she got home to her rooms with David the infection seemed to have spread, and she felt weak and faint. A doctor was called. A few hours later Montgomery, on manœuvres, was informed that his wife had been taken to hospital at Burnham-on-Sea. It was nothing seriously to worry about—an insect bite; but his wife had been rather run down with the excitement and the activity of coming home to England and it was thought best to have her in the hospital for observation.

Montgomery hurried over. He found his wife much worse. The infection was spreading fast and nothing seemed capable of retarding it. By now the leg was badly swollen. A second opinion was called in. The maddening thing was that no one could determine just what insect had made the bite or what the nature of the poison. It spread steadily and implacably.

At last the doctors could see no hope unless an amputation was carried out, and Montgomery was asked to agree to it. When the operation was performed and again there was some hope, Montgomery went off in a blaze of hunted energy for help. Very well. This was not the end. A life could be made for a cripple. There were special wheeled-chairs. There had been tremendous improvements in artificial limbs. They would work and practise together until she walked again. The rooms at Portsmouth were to be altered immediately. By rearranging things Betty should have a room that would catch the sun all day. There must be new furniture, bright and cheerful. The boys would be there. He would be there. He planned at a frantic pace. He talked it over with the specialists. Everything would be arranged. Betty should have a fine life when she came home.

In the hospital the patient grew worse. The pain was intense. The giggle stopped and the smile. Neither another amputation nor anything else would block the course of the poison. They waited. There was nothing more to do. On October 19th Montgomery was utterly and irrevocably beaten for the first time in his life, beaten beyond the chance of reprieve, beyond any power that he could hope to use. Betty Montgomery died, and at the inquest they found that it was due to septicæmia, accidentally incurred.

Montgomery went back to the empty house at Portsmouth with his son. Covers were placed over the furniture and the bright new carpets were rolled up. He locked the doors of the unwanted rooms. A male servant was engaged to look after David. No woman was allowed to come into that house.

CHAPTER SIX

MAD GENERAL

I

FOR five months Montgomery was alone in the great empty house at Portsmouth. Except for his work he would not come out. Each day he performed his job—precisely, punctually, industriously. Then back to the house.

He had no friends. His sister Una and members of his family tried to argue with him, tried to distract him from his solitude. It was useless. Almost angrily he turned them aside. He wanted simply to be alone. He felt no desire to discuss what had happened with anybody. Even when he returned from Burnham-on-Sea to his brigade he plunged at once into the military affairs on hand with the other officers. He said nothing of his loss, and in the face of that rigid outer indifference no one cared to offer sympathy.

If there is any mystery in Montgomery's life it probably lies here in these dark months in the winter of 1937. No one quite knows what he thought or did during the long hours when he was entirely alone in his house with his son. Clearly it was no ordinary struggle for reconciliation with life.

The marriage had lasted just ten years. He was not fifty. To a deeply religious mind the tragedy could only suggest one thing; the Lord had given and the Lord had taken away.

But this was an active and aggressive mind as well, and now it was opposed by something it had never admitted—utter defeat. There was nothing, absolutely nothing he could do about it.

The struggle dragged on for months. Referring to it later Montgomery said shortly, "My married life was absolute bliss. The death of my wife was a shattering blow from which I recovered with great difficulty, and very slowly."

In the end, as it had to be, the issues with himself were settled. Late in the spring of 1938 he emerged from his seclusion.

Outwardly it seemed as if he had simply chosen the obvious course: he would devote himself to the bringing up of his son and for the rest he would continue his career in the Army. Actually a much more fundamental change had taken place. The balance had gone out of his life. The old im-balance had returned, and with it a tremendous energy, almost, it seemed at times, a fanatical energy. With the Army at least he would not be defeated.

From now on the rocket accelerates at twice the earlier pace though perhaps on a more erratic course. There are no distractions whatever. It is almost as if he sees the end in view, almost as if he is saying to himself—"Get on, get on. Never let up, never weaken, never again let anything go beyond your reason into your heart. There is a future—something much higher than you have dreamed of yet. Get on. Get on."

We must take the next few years at a rush because that is how they were lived. Montgomery's story, like the story of so many others in the opening years of the war, suddenly loses most of its logical sequence, private life is submerged in public life, and we are raced almost haphazardly from scene to scene, now Palestine, now England, now France, now back to England again. From 1938 to 1942 there is hardly a moment to pause and examine a situation before it dissolves and is replaced by something quite different. Men pass rapidly to and fro in front of the moving backcloth apparently without volition of their own, and life is reduced to a matter of physical sensations, a series of superficial and immediate experiences having no definable pattern except that which falls out by luck and coincidence. It is like the stirring of an ant-heap. It is the precipice over which the river plunges headlong before it joins the calm ocean.

Although the second half of the war, from 1942 onwards, may appear in history to contain the greatest events, it was probably in the earlier period, from 1939 to 1942, that people suffered the most violent upheavals in their private lives. In the beginning everything was experimental and frightening, all the colours rendered more vivid by their newness. It was then that families were broken up for the first time, cities were bombed, men abruptly left their safe jobs, their tennis clubs and soft beds and vanished abroad. And on a larger plane it was the first shock of battle, the first experiences of enemy occupation, that disrupted the mind more than all the subsequent repetitions of the act of war. After 1942 we sailed in a broad and predictable ocean, the strategy was decided and the opposing forces distributed and arrayed according to a known order; we had the habit of war and people's minds had grown dulled and wearied by the struggle towards the known end.

The general pattern, then, of Montgomery's adventures during these next four years from 1938 is unextraordinary, and to obtain a correct perspective we have to hurry quickly through them until he reaches that point in 1942 when his course at last is definitely set.

2

In the 9th Brigade at the beginning of 1938 the soldiers began to feel an iron hand. On Salisbury Plain they swept everything before them.

In one manœuvre after another they were streets ahead of everyone else. Once again Montgomery's men made no great show on parade. There were arguments and difficulties. But in the field they raced in front of their rivals with many unexpected tactics and a most unusual enthusiasm for those peaceful days.

The Brigadier was seldom with the staff and usually with the soldiers. He had absorbed utterly his own teaching that "the soldier is the first weapon of war", and he entered into their lives with a curious persistence. The incident over the Welfare Fund is typical. The funds in the brigade were low, and Montgomery wanted money to provide his men with sports materials and other facilities. Opportunely the promoter of a fair approached him with an offer of £1000 for the rental of the Clarence Football Gound at Portsmouth for ten days over the August Bank Holiday period.

The ground was Government property, normally used by the military. Montgomery had no objection to giving it up for ten days at this rate of payment. He was urged by the Mayor to put the price up to £2000, and eventually a compromise at £1500 was agreed upon. But when the project was laid before the full Portsmouth City Council for approval it was turned down. Montgomery returned to the attack. If the Council would agree he would cut them in on the deal: they should have £500 for local charities. Upon this the Council changed its mind, the ground was let and the money paid over.

All these happy negotiations were put through without particular reference to Whitehall. It was not until everything was settled that the War Office learned with pained surprise that one of its junior brigadiers was going around letting Crown property—letting it, moreover, for the purpose of a common Bank Holiday fair. At once a letter was dispatched to Portsmouth. The proceedings were forbidden. In any event, if money had been collected for the rental of the ground it belonged to the War Office; and would Brigadier Montgomery oblige at once with his cheque for £1500?

"I can't", said Montgomery. "The ground is let and the money is spent." He was told that his promotion would be affected by these irregular proceedings. The row threatened at one point to reach one of those periodic crises in his career when the authorities were seriously thinking that for the good of all he ought to leave the Army. The correspondence went on for many months—indeed it may still be going on.

The brigade flourished. In 1938, a full year before the war began, it was chosen to carry out invasion exercises on the southern coast of England. The troops set out from Portsmouth in the cruiser *Southampton* and several destroyers, transferred to small boats, and assaulted the beaches in Dorset. Montgomery made the manœuvre as realistic as he possibly could. It was one of the first few glimmerings that England was awakening to the future. Precisely six years later another invasion fleet was going to set out in good earnest from Portsmouth.

Again, on Salisbury Plain, Montgomery's men were selected to carry out exhaustive trials in gas warfare. In secret they experimented with every known form of gas and gas equipment, and a plan was worked out for the general training of the Army. Montgomery in his report stressed the fact that in gas warfare more than in any other kind of fighting the onus lies upon the individual soldier; he alone could save himself.

At the end of the manœuvres General Wavell, then in the Southern Command, wrote: "Brigadier Montgomery is one of the clearest brains we have in the higher ranks, an excellent trainer of troops and an enthusiast in all he does. His work this year in the gas trials was of a very high order. He has some of the defects of an enthusiast, in an occasional impatience and intolerance when things cannot be done as quickly as he would like or when he meets brains less quick and clear than his own."

This, from such a notable selector of men as Wavell, was a remarkable tribute. Seldom had two such opposites been drawn together: yet Wavell, the humanist, the scholar, the man of infinite patience and infinite tact, had just this much in common with the angular and impatient Brigadier—he also was a rebel against the old ideas of drill and an enthusiast for unorthodox individualist effort. It was Wavell who had written "The soldier must be part gangster and part cat-burglar". And Wavell again who said, "You must care for a horse in the stable as though he were worth £500 and ride him in the field as though he were not worth half a crown".

Basically the two professionals were in agreement. And now not only Wavell but a few of the really outstanding men in the Army, like Alan Brooke, began to see a very likely horse and a very useful cat-burglar in the ardent trainer of the excellent 9th Brigade.

In Palestine the Jewish-Arab brawl was flaring strongly. Two divisions were to be sent out under the command of General Haining. One of the divisions was to go to an energetic little Irishman named Richard O'Connor. The other, the 8th Division, fell to Montgomery. It was a tremendous leap ahead. Wavell commented upon the new major-general from Portsmouth: "He will do extremely well".

Hurriedly Montgomery made his final arrangements for his son. For the last time he closed up the lonely house, and with his eyes fixed firmly ahead as though enclosed in blinkers he set sail for Palestine.

3

This was the nearest thing yet to war. The situation had got much worse in Palestine since Montgomery was last there in 1931. That rubbery declaration of Balfour's which at once defined and failed to define the British attitude to Palestine was bearing its rich ripe rotten fruit. The problem then was as simple and as insoluble as it is now—two people wanted the same small poor country and there was not enough room for both of them. For years the number of Jews legally entering the country on a fixed quota had been exasperating the Arabs already in possession. The Arabs had dwelt a long time in the hot sun. The Jews coming from Central Europe were educated, efficient, ruthlessly determined and some of them were fired with a holy zeal. They had no difficulty in creating and gaining markets; in ousting the Arabs from the best of the trade. More than this: they were developing a talent for the land. They farmed exceedingly well, they worked hard. Their communal groups were models in social behaviour to all mankind. They began to skim the cream of the dollars from the tourist.

Divided against themselves, relatively lazy and inefficient, the Arabs looked on in dark and helpless anger. They saw the whole of their land slipping away to the invader, and their protests took the form of unreasoning and hot-headed violence. The sniping began, the brawls by night. It was the outburst of the child who feels he is being treated unjustly. Unable to argue their case in high political courts they shot at the first Jew that came along. And the Jews rose to defend themselves.

By 1938 these brawls had created a state of national emergency. Things were really brought to open rebellion by the illegal Jewish arrivals. Crazy boatloads of desperate refugees were fleeing out of Nazi Europe down the Danube and the Black Sea. Each refugee paid fantastic sums to get aboard the boats. The conditions on the voyage were unbelievably squalid. But Palestine, sunlit, holy and free, shone in front of them. What did they care whether or not they were breaking some artificial British rule about quotas? There was death and torture behind them in Europe. Boatload after boatload ran the gauntlet of the British Mediterranean patrol and beached itself on the sandy coast between Tel-Aviv and the Syrian border. The refugees struggled ashore to the promised land through the waves as best they could. Once on land there was a Jewish organization to take care of them. These illegal landings of the Jews turned the Arab anger into outright revolt.

Inevitably both sides hated the British policeman. The policeman in his turn had only one recourse: to strengthen himself and keep the peace by force, while the politicians once again wrestled with that insoluble problem: "To whom does Palestine belong?"

By the time Montgomery arrived, the country was in a state of half-war. Travellers and traders wishing to journey between towns had to form up their vehicles in a column and await military escort—usually an armoured car posted at either end of the column. Even then, as the procession woured between the bare hills, it was likely that a shower of bullets would suddenly whizz down from the rocks. All that area of land out to the Dead Sea was forbidden ground, dangerous both day and night. All troops carried arms and were instructed to be ready to shoot.

Police headquarters scattered round the country were built in the form of forts with slit holes and parapets for rifles and machine-guns. Here and there sieges had to be withstood against the infuriated Arab tribesmen.

Trains were derailed. power-houses and signal-boxes blown up. Fierce and hysterical Jewish youths gathered arms secretly by night and went out on punitive expeditions. A curfew was imposed and still there was murder at night.

It was not the first time Montgomery had been ordered to settle rebellion by force, to use bullets to appease a mess of politics. The politics were of no special interest to him. He had his orders and that was enough. Here was a purely technical and practical job: to keep the peace; and he felt himself competent to be fair and just to both sides since he was profoundly unprejudiced in their quarrel. Anyone who illegally used a gun was an enemy, to be arrested and imprisoned. All the rest lay with the politicians.

The 8th Division was assigned to the northern half of the country and Montgomery set up his headquarters at Haifa by the sea. He knew the country well. He knew exactly what he wanted to do. And he controlled his division as though, in fact, it was in a state of open war. On his flank he had an equally resourceful commander in O'Connor, and the situation altered from the moment of their arrival. Each outburst from either Jew or Arab was followed by immediate reprisal. An efficient intelligence system began to operate. Villages being used as headquarters by insurgent tribesmen were suddenly surrounded in the night, their houses searched and burned and their illegal stores of arms and rifles seized. Murderers were promptly shot. It was the surgical method, which was probably the least bloody in the long run. For the first time in many a day Palestine came under a strong hand. Trade began to flow again. The basic problem was still entirely unsolved but the rebels were sucked dry, and at least, if general war should come, Palestine would from now on remain a safe base of operations for the Army and the Fleet.

Violent prejudice, especially in America, obscured the whole Palestine issue after the second world war. But it should be remembered that at this time, 1938–1939, the British spent a large part of their efforts in protecting the Jews from the Arabs. In the summer months of 1938 preceding Montgomery's arrival there existed only one brigade of British troops in the north and another brigade in the south. They had no real co-operation with the local Palestine police and they were working under a hopelessly milk-and-water policy. Palestine police were being murdered and shot up almost daily, but reprisals were forbidden. If a suspected village was to be searched the inhabitants were often informed the day before.

"Appeasement was rampant," one shrewd observer wrote, "and the whole situation was heading for complete disaster. While the army was there it was not being used and it certainly had no control.

"The arrival of Montgomery at the end of October 1938 coincided with a change of policy. The Army was to be in control. There was to be strict supervision of intelligence and movement. Military courts were to be made effective, co-operation with police put on a proper basis. The Army itself was strengthened by two brigades. The whole country was split up into sectors, and sub-area commanders were appointed.

4

The whole country became aware that Montgomery was in control in the north. This grip he kept and never relaxed until the end. The end came in sight towards the latter part of May 1939. By mid-August the rebellion was over."

One obtains a number of revealing glimpses of Montgomery at this time—glimpses which show him at the age of fifty-one developing into something a good deal more than the routine general. Once the Jews closed their shops for a day to express their disapproval of an army order. Montgomery sent for the Jewish leaders. He asked quietly when they intended to re-open their shops, and they said: "Next day." Montgomery replied: "No you don't; you close your shops for one day! I close them for seven." There was no closing of shops from that time forward.

Officers working under him at the time comment on the terseness and clarity of his orders, the "business-like feeling" about the command, and the direct and dynamic appeal to the soldiers on parade. This is a typical account from a contemporary:

"One Saturday evening he came to a boxing meeting which I had staged for the troops. He had supper first and then after the fights were over he presented the prizes and made a short address to the men; quiet simple talk but something with a meaning in it. He said he would make three prophecies—first that the rebellion would be over in three months, second that Portsmouth would win the cup and thirdly that there would be war before the end of 1939.

"We had this boxing meeting on the Saturday evening early in May and on the following Monday morning we heard with utmost consternation that he was very ill. First the report was that he had typhoid, then that he had scarlet fever, then diphtheria, then suppressed diphtheria or some disease like that. In fact the doctors were baffled, and he gradually got weaker and weaker, and eventually he had to go into the military hospital on the outskirts of Haifa, where his condition remained very serious.

"About the middle of June I was ordered to go home to the War Office and I went to say good-bye to him in hospital. There he was, pale and weak, in his pyjamas in bed, when he produced from beside his table a document and gave it to me to read. I found that it was a confidential report on me—even in his serious condition he was unwilling to leave work such as this to his successor. I remember I came away from him that afternoon thinking what a catastrophe it was that this illness had overtaken him. We were all quite sure that it was unlikely that he would ever soldier again."

Montgomery indeed was very near collapse. A spot had developed on his lung. Coming on top of his war wound this was an illness that refused to respond to treatment. His temperature stayed alarmingly high. He grew worse. In Palestine nothing more could be done for him and for the second time in a quarter of a century it was expected he would die.

At last, in the summer of 1939, a helpless cot case, he was flown down to Port Said in the care of two nursing sisters and an orderly. He was very feeble and quite unable to stir from his bed. On a Sunday night he was carried on board a P. and O. liner headed for England. Many tourists lined the decks to watch the strange arrival of the sick man. He was so tightly swathed in blankets on his stretcher that he appeared to be in a strait-jacket. As he reached the deck under so many curious eyes Montgomery heard one tourist say to another: "Who is he? What are they making all this fuss about?"

And the answer: "Haven't you heard? It's a mad general. They have to use a strait-jacket to keep him down."

It was a statement with which many people in the Army would have already at this time have found themselves in warm agreement.

At the height of his illness in Palestine Montgomery had been beset by an overmastering desire to go home to England. He had argued weakly with the doctors that if only he could go home he would recover. Beyond the obvious homing instinct of a sick man abroad there seemed to be no potent reason for this yearning; yet there it was, he had formed this fixed idea and he had reasoned with the doctors until they had let him go.

And now that he had got his way and he was at sea, steaming down the Mediterranean, he began to feel better at once. By the time the ship arrived at Malta he was strong enough to appear on deck. At Marseilles he was walking. At Tilbury Docks he had pretty well recovered. There could hardly have been a better argument for Christian Science. In a fever to get back to his command—a fever just as strong as his earlier desire to come home—he hurried through his official medical examination. They passed him. In a moment he was round at the War Office. When could he leave?

He was told he could not return to Palestine; the command had now been handed over to someone else. He must go to the pool in England and await posting.

This might have meant months delay, the loss of all the advantage in that valuable jump to command in Palestine. Montgomery argued, fumed and fretted. He would not go back to the pool. He must be given employment immediately.

If he could not go back to the 8th Division something else must be found. Looking around Montgomery fixed his eye on the 3rd Division. During his absence in Palestine he had already been named by the Selection Board as a future commander of the Division, but he felt that his illness had imperilled his chances of getting the appointment. He had seen the Third develop. It was one of the pitifully few English divisions fit for combat. In the last war the Third had been known as "The Iron Division", and who would be better suited to command it now, at this unsettled hour, than Montgomery himself?

He hurried back to the War Office. "There is only one man fit to take the Third into battle", he said. "That is myself."

To conceive this idea was to believe in it passionately and unequivocally. For ten days Montgomery repeated himself at the War Office *ad nauseam*. "I must have the 3rd Division. I am the only man fitted to command it."

At the end of ten days he got the 3rd Division.

4

The England of the summer of 1939 was a curious *mélange* of the ignorance, the shortcomings, the apathy and the unpreparedness of that other summer before the war of 1914.

Chamberlainism was dying hard. A virtue was found for Munich: it had given us "breathing space" (though not perhaps much space for those valuable Czech divisions which had been flung into Hitler's lap). A few serious officers like de Guingand had gone to Germany (at their own expense) and had come back appalled by what they had seen of the weight and efficiency of the Army there.

In England it is probably fair to say that the people were ahead of both their Government and their Army. They saw or sensed the coming cataclysm, and this time there was added to this realization a nameless dread of what war would mean. It was a dread that clogged coherent thought and, along with every other Government department, the War Office seemed to be gripped by a fatalistic apathy.

In tanks and guns and vehicles of every kind it was a repetition of the sad vicious story of 1914. For years professionals like Montgomery had raged and railed but none of them were at the top yet. In every regiment there were officers who had hung on simply because "soldiering was the thing to do". The reorganization and the clean sweep that might have been done twenty years earlier had never happened. To do the Higher Command justice, they had never been given the money to rebuild on a sound footing. But in some ways this small and hopelessly out-of-date professional army was worse even than a disorganized and enthusiastic citizen army might have been; when the money was poured at its feet there was no good machinery for using it and few who had the moral courage to break through the red tape and adopt innovations. The new system had to be encrusted on the old. Nearly everything that had happened in 1914 was about to happen again, with just this exception. By some extraordinary turn of fate three of the very ablest professional officers were actually in command of striking forces when the zero hour arrived.

Neither Brooke nor Alexander nor Montgomery was yet high enough to alter the broad tide of events. But at least they were senior enough to get to France together with a measure of tactical control. When six more years passed, when many others with equal and better chances had vanished from active service, those three were still going to be found together—at the top. After all the justifiable criticism of the Army is made it is only fair to remember that brilliant men did eventually emerge, and no fool or laggard held a high command in an active theatre for very long.

The war had already begun when Montgomery got command of the 3rd Division in October. There was time for little more than a cursory inspection before they were ordered across to France and given a sector in the north to hold.

All through that winter and the following spring of the "phoney war" Montgomery worked at his division with intense energy. For the first time on the field of war he was able to put into practice his theory of personal command. All details were handed over to the staff; the General himself spent most of his day with the men and commanders along the line. He seized every chance to show himself, to meet the soldiers and impress on them that he was their leader. When senior commanders called on the division no staff officers accompanied them on their inspections; Montgomery himself took them round. He had a remarkable knowledge of every corner of his command. It became a joke to try and ask him questions which he could not answer.

Through these eight months while the Allied war machine mumbled and bumbled along, there was not much doubt about the real issues in the minds of the junior commanders who were actually in the line. But they were mute. Regulations forbade them to say anything publicly, and their views as yet carried no great weight in Whitehall. In any event security made it impossible for them to speak openly.

And so a false and rosy optimism prevailed at home. The Prime Minister cried "Hitler has missed the bus". General Ironside gave an interview to an American newspaperman in which he confidently invited the Nazis to strike. Press releases were put out saying that the British Expeditionary Force was the finest equipped body of men ever to leave Britain. In France the hoardings were plastered with neat posters showing a map of the combined British and French empires, and underneath the caption ran: "We will win because we are strongest". In the streets and the pubs the people felt secure; many began to wonder whether the war was a serious affair after all. There were even rumours of "peace feelers". Unless the Germans were mad they must see that they were beaten before they started. For a long time before the war the Allied Press had published little or nothing about the German war machine. The Nuremberg rallies had been treated as just so much theatrical display. And now on the B.B.C. it was the fashion to jeer at the enemy, to remind him of how hungry he was and how well off we were.

This optimism did not reach as far as the front line in France. To the men who were about to accept the German assault when it came it was all too painfully clear that we were desperately inferior. In the training of the men and, above all, in the quality and quantity of the weapons we were far below the German standard. It was the purest sophistry to say that the B.E.F. was the best equipped force Britain had ever sent out. We had no tank the equal of the Mark III, no gun as deadly and versatile as the 88, nor had we a dive-bomber. But at this stage of the game it was the fashion to boast; boasting kept up morale and impressed one's friends like the Americans.

It was early decided that when Hitler struck, the B.E.F. should wheel into Belgium. This time the Channel ports had to be guaranteed, and Montgomery's division was chosen to perform a preparatory exercise. Under the eye of the Army commanders it wheeled backwards into France. It was a successful and impressive operation carried out by night. Some of the observers felt that the divisional general made a little too much of himself. He seemed to be forever hurrying about the place. He even attached a coloured light to his car, and when he was asked what it was for he replied with aplomb: "So that the soldiers will know I am there".

Then the spring and the invasion of Norway. The British expedition to Norway; the exclamations in London and Paris, "The best thing that could have happened. This time Hitler really has stuck his head out. How can he succeed without

command of the seas?" And, immediately afterwards, the
horrible awakening; the first of the British evacuations, and
the bitter evidence that the British soldiers had been hastily
and ill equipped, that they had been out-manœuvred as
though they were a mob of leaderless amateurs. And now,
before even the realization of all this could sink in, the first
monstrous and bewildering shock of the assault on the mainland
in Europe.

On May 10th, Montgomery's 3rd Division was in motion.
For months they had been trained in quick movement and
now they streamed across the border into Belgium. On the
following day they made contact, and the long shambles back
to Dunkirk began. For twenty days the division kept formation
in an arena where everything seemed to have gone mad—no
rest, no time for anything except retreat. One after another
the pathetic weapons crumbled up under an onslaught of
unthinkable power. The air assault alone seemed enough to
paralyse all action. In this awful emergency not only were
men dying at the front, but a violent reshuffle was going on
among their most senior officers in the rear. Brooke was
singled out for higher promotion as one of the few clear brains
in this madhouse. Alexander had the First Corps. The Second
Corps was now temporarily handed over to Montgomery,
and he was ordered to pass his soldiers out through Dunkirk
the best way he could. They suffered two thousand casualties
before they got to the boats.

Once back in England every possible priority was given to
the 3rd Division. They were the first of the British formations
to be re-equipped from that tragic little stock of spare weapons
in the home country; and now they were ordered immediately
to return to France by way of Cherbourg and take up the
hopeless struggle again. As Montgomery waited with his
soldiers to re-embark, France fell. There was no longer any
friendly port on the opposite side of the Channel. Italy was
in the war. Overnight the black hand of the Axis had closed
over Europe with utter finality and terrifying ease. The long
fumbling dream of peace was over. That clownish and
delirious propaganda no longer had any power to soothe.
Only two qualities counted now: one was character, and the
other was professional knowledge. And in their desperate
urgency the only thing the people wanted to hear was hard
fact. All this was underlined a thousand times when the bombs
came down on England and a wall was built against all past
experience by the hideous and meaningless barbarity of
explosion.

One of these bombs, falling at the height of the blitz on Portsmouth, burst upon Montgomery's storehouse. His clothes, his furniture, his books and his entire possessions gathered through a lifetime were lying there. In a second all these things were wiped off the face of the earth, everything down to the last photograph of his wife. For Montgomery nothing now remained of the bright and lighted time before the war except one thing: a quite cold, clear, unemotional and logical resolution that the Germans must be destroyed. He was not particularly seeking revenge nor even in the last resort was he seeking to protect anything or erect something new in the world. His was rather the attitude of the surgeon who, dealing with a malignant ulcer, decides unemotionally that it is evil and injurious, and cuts it out.

CHAPTER SEVEN

TELEPHONE FROM WHITEHALL

I

On the collapse of the British Army at Dunkirk, Brooke was made Commander-in-Chief of the Home Forces, General Auchinleck was given the Southern Command and Montgomery (largely as a result of Brooke's report upon him) was promoted to the Fifth Corps. He was still a long way down the scale, but at least he had charge of one of the vital sectors where the Germans were expected to land.

This was in September 1940, and a frenzy of digging was sweeping southern England. In an almost religious fervour gangs of men were throwing up earthworks, running trenches along the valleys and the hillsides, excavating anti-tank ditches, making air-raid shelters. Presently every village crossroads began to sprout dragons' teeth, and millions of yards of barbed wire spread like an evil and surrealist tropical creeper across the countryside. One after another the village tea-shops and the local banks began to disappear behind piles of sandbags. In tens of thousands mines were sown along the beaches, and a great tide of pillboxes, gun emplacements and barbed-wire entanglements began to spread inland up the cliff-face and across the counties of Kent and Sussex and Hampshire. The Home Guard arose; elderly country gentlemen got down their shot-guns and prepared to defend their land with great fierceness—as they undoubtedly would have done had the emergency arisen.

As usual Montgomery found himself in disagreement with a great deal of this. He said that everybody seemed to have become "concrete-minded". He had no belief in trenches or earthworks or permanent fixed lines of defence. The battle, he argued, was a fluid thing. Mobility was the vital factor in defence. Once men were stuck in garrisons they lost their initiative and they grew over-optimistic about the false security of their trenches. You had to come out and meet the enemy: all defence must be conducted offensively and a commander must have freedom of movement to strike at the best places at the right time. It was fatal to sit still and let the enemy pile up reserves against you. And then outflank you.

He stopped the digging within his command. He began to

4*

pull back his men from the beaches and out of the pillboxes. Let the enemy land, he said. The mobile reserves must be held in the rear ready to swoop down on the Germans in force once they disclosed their main lines of advance. If we disposed our men on the cliffs and that line was breached in the first assault, the enemy would fan out in the empty country behind—and then we might as well give up.

There was nothing startlingly original about this theory. Many successful commanders had adopted it before. But in 1940 that theory was not generally accepted. It seemed to the amateur to be the obvious and practical thing to turn every possible feature into a strongpoint, to throw up a barrier at every place where you had the labour and the materials, to stand guard on the sacred coast and hurl the invader back before he got a foothold. Montgomery's plan entailed immense risk. He was quite willing to sacrifice valuable towns at the outset; a point of view which did not suit the townspeople at all. Provided he kept certain arterial roads and railways open he was not concerned about the loss of large areas of ground; and this ran counter to the patriotic idea that not an inch of England's soil should be surrendered without a fight.

One can imagine the arguments Montgomery got into with his ideas of fluid defence. Men's feelings were running high at the time, and to believe in anything was to believe passionately. The placing—or the non-placing—of the smallest pillbox was regarded as a matter of life and death. And now for the first time he was coming under the eye of thousands of men and hundreds of equals and superiors. As the months of suspense went by, and more and more men tumbled out of their businesses and factories into uniform, queer stories began to circulate about the commander of the Fifth Corps.

Those who got close to the General found themselves confronted with an intense little man who never raised his voice, never used expletives or abuse. But when he was angry he spoke with a tight-lipped and waspish contempt. "Of course, you are useless", he would tell an erring subordinate. "Useless, quite useless." It was more than a sneer, it was a statement of contemptuous conviction. To the subordinate it sounded venomous. There was no argument with the General, not an earthly hope of appealing to any human weakness there. When you came before him it was like standing in the dock before a court of law.

With those he liked, and in doing normal business, Montgomery was affable and easy to get on with and startlingly clear in saying what he wanted. But even his senior officer would wait nervously for their interviews outside his room, and many of them came out later on with a sigh of relief. It was a headquarters without relaxation, and the place was dominated by the chilling and ascetic habits of the General.

Each morning soon after dawn his tea was brought to him. Then for something like half an hour or even longer he lay in bed thinking, planning each minute of the day. Every hour went by on a set routine: morning conference, correspondence (he liked to write in his own hand with a fountain-pen), interviews, round of inspections, evening conference, dinner in the mess, bed at nine-thirty to write his diary, read a little, think, and then to sleep.

Sleep, like everything else, was under command and subject to immediate obedience. He ordered himself to sleep, and sleep he did.

In his presence no one lit a cigarette unless they were expressly given permission. When he spoke the room fell silent. No one coughed, if he could avoid it. If, when addressing a group of officers, he found them unable to control their colds, he paused, ordered a three-minute interval for coughing, and the Staff sat through the rest of the talk in agony lest they should transgress again. Occasionally when a junior officer found himself unable to block a cough, he felt that cold grey eye on him, an appalling silence filled the room—and if he had any sense he rose with a mumbled apology and left.

There were sackings in the Fifth Corps: cold, electric and sudden dismissals. You were out. Degraded, expelled and banished—and there was no appeal. "I am sorry", the General would say. "But you are of no use to me. None whatever." That was the finish.

Very soon it became painfully apparent that the General was a fanatic for physical training. Elderly colonels who rarely stirred outside an office were appalled to receive orders instructing them to appear in suitable raiment on the parade ground, where they were obliged to go through the undignified procedure of marching at the double and jumping over hurdles. No one on the staff escaped. Often enough these proceedings took place at the crack of dawn. It was outrageous, it was ridiculous, it was Fascist. Inwardly and to one another they protested hotly. Montgomery fixed them with his cold eye and reminded them it was much worse for the men.

It was indeed. One division under his command marched forty miles in eighteen hours—and this at the end of ten days' manoeuvring and route marching. Another unit was marched fifty-six miles in fifty hours. In frightful weather, without food

for many hours at a stretch, tens of thousands of men grew
used to finding themselves benighted in the open countryside
in the depth of winter. There were many days of bitter hard-
ship on Salisbury Plain, and in camp the daily physical jerks
went on relentlessly. It began to seem that the General would
never rest until he had dragged the whole Army up to his own
cold level of austerity. The Fifth Corps could not fail to observe
that they were treated much more rigorously than others.
Once on manœuvres, when the day's work was done, a liaison
officer was dispatched from a rival headquarters with papers
for Montgomery. Reluctantly the young officer left the warmth
and lights of his mess and for some time was unable to find
Montgomery's camp. When he eventually discovered the
place it was in total darkness. All vehicles were widely dispersed and blacked out as though in imminent danger of air
attack. Sentries challenged him through the rain every few
yards. At length, very late at night, he found Montgomery
crouching over an oil lamp on the leeward side of a shed. He
was issuing orders for the following day.

Montgomery's austerity penetrated directly into the private
lives of his subordinates. While their husbands were still in
England it was the custom for the more fortunate of the officers'
wives to follow them and live in rooms or cottages in the
nearest town. To most people this appeared to be a harmless
and even beneficial proceeding. On their rare spells of leave
the officers would snatch a few hours' company with their
wives and sometimes their children—and who could tell
whether or not these moments would be the last to be spent
together? Most commanders winked at or even encouraged
the practice, and many of them kept their own wives close by.
Montgomery squashed all this outright. For one thing, he
said the ordinary enlisted men were unable to afford the
expense of taking their wives round England with them. For
another, it was distracting for the officers to have their wives
close by. All wives were banished forthwith; none were permitted to live anywhere near their husbands. There were
bitter complaints and some protests. Montgomery was adamant.
This was war. All through these months whenever he was
moved to a new command, a doleful trainload of wives would
set out the day before he arrived. For this he was hated at
times, and hated thoroughly.

There were also his personal oddities which were the
constant unending subject of conversation wherever he went.
Some of the incidents had a quite inexpressible flavour about
them. There was, for example, the day he was addressing a

meeting of Home Guard officers. Those who arrived sixty seconds late (including one general) found the doors bolted against them. Indignant and hostile, they were admitted at half-time and sat down to hear an hour's brilliant exposition (I quote the indignant general) of defensive tactics. At the end of his lecture Montgomery announced that he would present a play which he had written himself. While the audience waited fascinated, four soldiers dressed in German uniforms entered carrying umbrellas. As they opened the umbrellas a loud report echoed through the hall, and this, apparently, was to illustrate the arrival of parachutists in England. The four soldiers then lined up on the platform and announced solemnly: "We'll cut the throat of that bastard Montgomery". Finish of play.

Even across the years the mind still reels as it contemplates this exhibition. And yet and yet: 1940. Invasion expected at any moment; perhaps there was something in it. At all events few people in that hall forgot the lecture. Or Montgomery.

2

One might reasonably have expected that, given time, Montgomery would have become the most unpopular general in England. Yet it was not so. 1940 and 1941 were the years of crisis, and under that unthinkable menace of invasion most Englishmen were willing to follow a strong leader anywhere. His dismissals of officers were not nearly so numerous as they were reported to be, and for the most part his decisions were not unjust. The more intelligent and enthusiastic soldiers— especially those who had come into the Army from civilian life—realized that Montgomery was simply doing something which ought to have been done by the Higher Command long ago. The deadwood had to be cut out: the fools and the drunks, the shirkers and the playboys, had no right to authority at this dangerous moment.

As for the men, the majority liked a colourful and eccentric leader. They liked the absence of brass-hattery and pomposity in Montgomery. They appreciated the fact that the bulk of their work went, not into useless ceremonial parades, but into very definite exercises in the trade of war. Deliberately Montgomery cultivated their friendship.

More and more through these years he was growing into a resemblance of that other "soldiers' general" who was born in Virginia, in the United States of America, some hundred years

earlier. The careers of Stonewall Jackson and Montgomery
have an astonishing similarity. Both families sprang from the
neighbourhood of Londonderry, in Northern Ireland (a
breeding-ground of generals). Jackson, too, had his early days
of free country life, and at school he was the leader in all the
sports. Then West Point. As a cadet of eighteen he was a
simple, serious and not very sociable young man, but he had
that same deadly earnestness, that inability to compromise;
the power of concentration and the unquestioning religious
faith.

In his twenties (as with Montgomery) we find Jackson
plunging into battle for the first time as a young officer. There
is the surf-boat landing on the Mexican coast, the bloody march
on the capital, the same rapid promotion—and then the long
peaceful years of teaching at the Virginia Military Academy at
Lexington.

Stonewall Jackson was belatedly baptized at the age of
twenty-five, and straightway he enters an ascetic life of simple
and unbounded devotion. His health compels him to a simple
diet (for years he does not even drink tea or coffee). He is a
confirmed early riser. There is no dancing, no smoking or
drinking in his house. He never misses the daily Bible readings,
the regular services. A prayer precedes every act in his life.
Both his wives are the daughters of churchmen. He adores
children. When he comes to command he treats his soldiers as
his children and he rules with the same ease and missionary
purpose. For Stonewall Jackson the soldier is everything in
battle.

Even his military ideas are the same. Simplicity, mobility,
trust your subordinates. We find him saying to one of his
officers, "I neither ask nor desire to know anything of your plans.
Take the responsibility and act, and call on me for assistance."

With the outbreak of the awful massacre of the Civil War
Jackson goes into battle with fire and enthusiasm and stealthy
cunning. There are no fixed lines of defence in his philosophy;
to attack, to outflank, to march by night, to hit and steal away:
that is the way to defend. He deals harshly and ruthlessly with
fools and cowards; he works his men unendurably, and they
love him. An emotional and inspirational current runs between
the soldiers and the leader. They feel they are not only in the
right but they can also do the impossible. And "Old Jack"
moves among them in an aura of devotion and admiration
which is probably quite incomprehensible to anyone who has
not experienced such a thing nor felt the elemental simplicity
of life on the battlefield.

Of the two men Jackson's is possibly the more saintly and selfless life; but we must place him somewhere in Montgomery's spiritual background. There was much less bitterness in Jackson's career, and fewer complications; but that sense of touch in devotional leadership did not quite go out at Bull Run and in the fields around Richmond. It begins to revive here eighty years later in England.

3

In 1941 Montgomery was removed from the command of the Fifth Corps to the Twelfth Corps, and finally in 1942 to the command of the South-Eastern Army with the rank of lieut.-general. Already in 1940 he had been made a Companion of the Bath and, in the gathering momentum of his life, it was obvious that he was now headed towards greater honours. He had gone beyond the point where he could be set back through minor eccentricities; now he had the power to impose them upon other people. The rocket was nearing the end of its long, laborious climb from the ground to the point where it could become a law unto itself.

He was beginning to come in contact with people who were really in control of affairs. There had already been a first meeting with Churchill shortly after Dunkirk, when Montgomery took him on a tour of the coastal defences. As they watched a group of Guardsmen dismantling Brighton pier, Churchill remarked sadly that they were hacking away the place where he used to be taken to see the performing fleas as a child.

Cabinet Ministers found the new general docile and obedient in all things except military matters. Then he spoke up strongly and sometimes with insubordination. In all the areas under his command he considered himself master. There was the incident of the Archbishop of Canterbury, who came under Montgomery's care when he was given the South-Eastern Command. The Archbishop declared that if the Germans landed in Kent he would not move. Montgomery had air-raid shelters dug round the Cathedral and declared that the Archbishop would certainly move. Brushing all protests aside he issued strict orders that if the crisis came the Archbishop was to be placed on a train and conveyed northwards.

But in regard to the policy of scorching English earth Montgomery would not listen to it. He would not accept the idea that the Germans would succeed in their invasion. Fruitlessly the Board of Trade wrote to him suggesting urgent meetings to discuss the demolition of supplies and transport centres. He declined to discuss the matter. Finally Sir Edward Crowe, an old friend from his Switzerland days, approached him. Surely it was plain that this was an elementary precaution? Montgomery replied: "There is no need for 'scorching earth' whatever. We are not going to retreat. We will attack."

This was in 1942. For some time it had been apparent that, at least as far as England was concerned, the worst of the crisis had passed. It was Montgomery's opinion that (granted their preliminary victory in the air) a German invasion could not have been withstood either in 1940 or 1941. England was utterly unprepared and for most of the time without allies beyond the Empire. Had the German Navy been able to keep up supplies he believed that with fifteen divisions the enemy could have "pinched off London" and brought the whole of the island's war potential to a standstill. But by the summer of 1942 there were immense numbers of strongly equipped men in arms in southern England. Coherent and practical plans for meeting invasion at all points were ready. England for the time being was safe.

Indeed, the war-centre had shifted from the west to the east. The focus now was not upon England but on the wastes around Stalingrad and on the Western Desert of Egypt. The desert was, in fact, the only British land front with the enemy. Most of the ablest British commanders and the strongest divisions up till now had been concentrated on the urgent job of protecting the mother country. With the spring of 1942 it was apparent to the senior commanders at home that they were at a temporary dead-end. The job of preparing England was largely finished. There was nothing for them now but to await idly the Allied invasion of the Continent or some other operation in the west. Meanwhile reputations were being made and great issues were being decided in Egypt.

For two years the pendulum had swung maddeningly back and forth across the Cyrenaican bulge of Libya. The first Italian onset had been flung back by Wavell as far as the Gulf of Sirte. Then Rommel had come in on the returning tide. Montgomery's old friend General O'Connor had been lost, a prisoner of war, and Wavell had been replaced by Auchinleck as C.-in-C. Middle East. Auchinleck had made his thrust, had succeeded, and then failed. And now, most dangerously, in the full summer of 1942 Rommel was coming on again.

In June the most disastrous news was arriving from Egypt.

The Gazala Line, with its series of strong-points or "boxes", was in a state of disintegration. This was followed by the abysmal and almost incomprehensible collapse of the stronghold of Tobruk in a single day. All cohesion seemed to have vanished from the British command, and even veterans like General Gott were temporarily out of touch. In one widening and chaotic tide the British Army was streaming in disorder back into Egypt.

This time the pendulum was heavily weighted. It swung past the Egyptian border, past Buq Buq and Sidi Barrani, paused at Mersa Matruh and then came on again. At Alamein, the last defensive box before the Nile, a handful of weary and dispirited soldiers were clinging to their positions in early July without much hope of staying there. In Washington Churchill was asking for—and getting—the immediate dispatch of new arms to Egypt. But weeks would elapse before they arrived and in the meantime it appeared most likely that Egypt would fall. The fall of Egypt could mean anything—the loss of Palestine and the Persian oil; perhaps even the linking of the German and Japanese armies (now advancing through Burma) and the collapse of India.

In Cairo wisps of smoke hung over G.H.Q. and the British Embassy, where secret documents were being burned. Already evacuation had begun. Auchinleck started to devise a plan for splitting his armies—one force to remain at Alamein as long as possible and eventually fight its way back to the Suez Canal through the Nile Delta; other forces to save what they could of the wreckage by marshalling in the far south at Khartoum and in the east in Palestine. In Rome Mussolini got out his ceremonial white horse, and a medal was struck to commemorate the expected Axis entry into Alexandria and Cairo.

For a few days the pendulum teetered at Alamein. Then it stuck, unable to swing farther forward—and there was no power to push it back. British, Australian and New Zealand reinforcements struggling up to the line were just able to hold the position and no more. Auchinleck at this time exhibited a generalship for which he has been given little credit. It was certainly he, more than any other man, who stopped the rot at Alamein. But the Army's convalescence from its crisis was proving alarmingly slow.

Through July a series of indecisive attacks and counter-attacks continued along the Alamein Line; and still the enemy were entrenched in great strength a few hours' drive from Cairo. Worse still, there were reports of enemy reinforcements. Malta was on the point of starvation; ship after ship endeavouring to reach the island was sunk. It was an impossible situation. The stalemate could not continue.

Churchill, arriving in Egypt from America, found that British morale was at an ominously low ebb. Even with the arrival of reinforcements and new tanks from America the situation was extremely dangerous. The desert war had gone on so long and so fruitlessly, so many had died, so many attacks had been made only to end in failure, and now the men were listless and indifferent. They were tired. No one was able to see clearly ahead through the endless sandstorms, the heat, the ennui, the unending menace of the enemy. A wave of homesickness and dispiritedness was sweeping through the Army. Everyone, from general to privates, talked of the possibility of a new attack from Rommel. It was the atmosphere of retreat, the mood of defeat, or at least of stalemate.

Great plans had been made in Washington for the Mediterranean war. A combined British and American force was to land in the French possessions in North-west Africa and its object was ultimately to link up with the British Eighth Army coming from Egypt. Already the troops were gathering in England and in the United States. Malta was to be saved, the Mediterranean opened up, an attack made upon the mainland of Europe from the south.

This was the plan. And now it was apparent that the whole project was likely to founder here in the desert where the Eighth Army was too tired and too listless to accomplish any more.

Surveying the dreary scene in the desert Churchill arrived at one definite decision: the Eighth Army must have a new leader to replace General Ritchie. Two names had already been suggested to Auchinleck as his desert commander: one was General Slim, the other was General Montgomery. But already Churchill had taken his own decision. His choice fell on Gott, who was by far the ablest and most versatile of the Corps commanders in the desert, a man greatly loved by the troops for his daring and his calmness. Gott accepted the promotion. It was hoped at least he would be able to hold Rommel's fresh onslaught when it came.

Back in England the generals waiting impatiently for an opportunity to show their skill in active service in the desert began to realize that once more promotion had slipped by. They must continue to sit and wait.

4

On August 7th Montgomery was in Scotland with General Paget watching a most secret force at its manœuvres. This was the British First Army and its mission was the invasion of French Algeria on the North African coast. Already General Eisenhower was in England preparing to take command of the operation. General Alexander, back from his campaign in Burma, had been nominated to serve under him as the leader of the First Army.

An urgent telephone call came through for Montgomery from London: he must report to the War Office immediately. It was a bad flying day and Montgomery took the night train down from Scotland. At the War Office he was told by General Nye, the Vice-Chief of the Imperial General Staff, that there had been a change in the arrangement for the high command. Alexander would replace Auchinleck as C.-in-C. of the Middle East. Montgomery would take Alexander's place as the commander of the First Army on the North Africa invasion. He was to interview General Eisenhower the following morning.

Montgomery returned to his headquarters at Reigate and went to bed. He was shaving at seven-thirty the following morning when his A.D.C. hurried in. The War Office had telephoned. General Montgomery was to disregard the conversation of the previous night. Instead he was to stand by to proceed immediately to Egypt to take command of the Eighth Army.

General Gott was dead. His aircraft had been shot down by the Germans at the moment of taking up his appointment.

Montgomery rushed through his arrangements. He did not see the War Office again, and a Liberator was placed at his disposal to leave England the same night. There was just time to say goodbye to his son David and arrange for him to stay at his old school in Surrey. A bedroll was brought; tropical gear. He did not need very much equipment. One A.D.C. was to travel with him.

Again that night the weather was bad and it was decided to delay another twenty-four hours. At nightfall on August 10th the Liberator took off from England with its strange freight: a roll of bedding, an A.D.C., and a general on probation, a thin and unimposing little figure in battledress and a peaked cap ringed with red, a man unknown to the public and the world—

another candidate for command in the desert where so many had set out and ended in utter failure.

They arrived on the airstrip at Gibraltar the following morning for breakfast and waited there all day—at this time Axis aircraft were ranging the Mediterranean and it was forbidden for transport aircraft to travel by day.

At dusk on August 11th they set off again straight down the Mediterranean for Cairo.

Sitting hour after hour looking out into the black space, Montgomery was under no delusions. This was his chance. Now at the age of fifty-four it had come at last. He was going out to "a bit of a dog's breakfast". He had followed the intelligence reports of the desert war and this was clearly the low-water mark for the British there.

What was wrong? Organization. Training. Leadership. Those were the three essentials. Apart from all the technicalities and the questions of equipment and reinforcement, those were the fundamental things: a definite plan and a tight control of it. A proper grouping of the men and a clear explanation of what was wanted of them. And finally, a leader. Yes. He could be the leader. Now, just this once—and for the first time in his life—let them listen and do what he ordered: then they should see; then they would discover how battles should be fought.

Intently and positively as the plane flew on he made his plans.

The rocket had struggled up to the zenith of its launching flight. It had been a long way with many halts and set-backs; once or twice it had faltered and nearly expired. Now at last it was bursting out into the stratosphere.

CHAPTER EIGHT

FORTY HOURS

I

At 9 a.m. on August 12th, 1942, Montgomery's aircraft put down on the desert outside Cairo. One must consider now, quite separately and distinctly, the next forty hours in this life: they contain the expression of a mind working at the limit of its capacity and the consummation of a long career. This was the moment of the flood-tide, and, just as an expert surf-rider will launch himself on a wave at the precise moment of its breaking and ride on with it in absolute assurance to the shore, so now one can watch this adventurer from hour to hour follow his inspiration quite consciously until it brings him to a conscious and inevitable goal.

From the airport Montgomery drove straight to G.H.Q. in Cairo, a large block of flats called Gray Pillars which had been ringed with barbed wire and converted into a military headquarters. Auchinleck was waiting for him in an office on the third floor.

For Auchinleck, the out-going general, it could hardly be other than a bitter moment. He had worked in a frenzy to the point of exhaustion in these last few tragic months, and almost everything had turned to defeat and disaster as soon as he touched it. Having dismissed one general from the command of the desert army he had appointed another. And when this second general had failed he had delayed too long in taking over himself. True, he had succeeded in holding the Alamein Line and restoring the situation, but by then it was too late to save himself.

Now in the summer of 1942 Auchinleck was facing the same fate as Wavell had twelve months before, only his position was worse. No acceptable job had been found for him. He was simply banished. His crime, perhaps, was that he had tried over hard. He had been unable to appoint an efficient staff and trust it. All his efforts had been drowned in detail. Even at the height of the crisis he had made an abortive attempt to institute an austerity campaign at his headquarters: officers in the desert were reduced to the roughest food, the barest simplicities. Those in Cairo had been ordered to abandon their city offices and live in tents near the Pyramids. There could hardly have been a plan more calculated to create confusion at that critical moment when telephones and quick communications were vital. It had failed along with so many other things. Now it was too late. Alexander had arrived to take his job. And here was Montgomery ready to go down to the desert to attempt the thing that Auchinleck could not do—defeat Rommel.

These matters had brought Auchinleck very near to breaking point, but he had still two more days of his command to run—until August 15th—and he was determined to go out with dignity. He said simply to Montgomery:

"You know I'm going?"

"Yes. I know", Montgomery said.

Auchinleck then suggested that Montgomery should go down to the desert for a couple of days before he took over command on the 15th and the interview closed.

Once outside the room Montgomery sought out one of his old pupils, Major-General John Harding, who was in charge of the training of troops and, in Montgomery's opinion, one of the ablest commanders then in the Army. Harding was astonished to see him and even more astonished when he heard what Montgomery wanted:

"Can you create a panzer army? Can you get together an armoured corps of three divisions capable of being used as a striking force?"

Harding demurred. Montgomery's visit at this time was a close secret. Harding had no notion of what he was doing in the Middle East. How could he take orders from Montgomery? In any event you could not produce panzer armies out of your hat. Montgomery pressed him. "I want to know whether there are in Egypt at this moment sufficient forces to create an armoured corps."

In the end Harding agreed to go off and find out what he could. It was arranged that he should present his report at six o'clock that night.

Good. That was one hurdle taken. Montgomery turned to the next thing. He met Alexander. Their friendship went back far beyond Dunkirk to the student days in Camberley.

"Hello, Alex."

"Hello, Monty." They were both very much incognito and the meeting was vaguely reminiscent of two elated but slightly guilty schoolboys.

"Let's go somewhere and talk it over."

Montgomery suggested Shepheard's. Their two A.D.C.s should go ahead, select a quiet corner table, and then leave them.

In Cairo at this time there were four main places where
officers went to talk, to gossip and meet one another: the Turf
Club, the Gezira Sporting Club on an island in the Nile, the
Continental-Savoy and Shepheard's Hotel. The terrace and the
lounge of Shepheard's were particularly crowded with officers
on leave. They stared with great curiosity when two unknown
senior generals came walking through the crowds of suffragis
and street vendors and passed into the dingy and mosque-like
splendour of the inner lounge.

Except for their mutual enthusiasm for soldiering there
was hardly a point in common between the two men. Montgomery was at the full stretch of his intensity and unequivocal
eagerness: a quivering reed. Alexander remained as he always
was: bland, interested, patient. He was one of those very few
men who are inevitably destined for the inner and the higher
circles of any society in which they move. In many ways it was
a charmed life. Born in the midst of wealth and assured position, the younger son of a titled family, he had passed easily
through the best schools and the best regiments. As a young
man he was full of natural talents, an excellent horseman, an
intelligent and ready conversationalist. He was neither lazy
nor insensitive (as he might easily have been). He painted well.
He had an Irish sense of humour, an easy manner. And, as if
it were not enough that he should have had his charm, his
naturalness, his health and rather jaunty good looks, something
else had been given him as well: an apparent absence of any
physical fear whatever. At Dunkirk, in Burma, and again on
many days after this meeting at Shepheard's many people
marvelled at his entire disregard of personal danger, the poise
and balance of his mind at a crisis when all around high
explosive was bursting and men were dying.

Inevitably he was popular. Without bombast or personal
exertion of any kind he was sure of himself and his position in
life. He was modest and undemonstrative because it would
never have occurred to him that it was necessary to thrust
himself forward or emphasize his standing . . . and it never
was necessary. He was accepted. Wherever he went he enjoyed
the intimate liking of the best minds. For the same reason—
the fact that his status was assured—he was liberal in his
outlook; he could listen with patience and infinite good
humour to any argument or dispute; and make a disinterested
judgment at the end of it. And, beyond all else, Alexander
was no fool. When he applied himself to a thing, as he was
applying himself now to the war and this special job in Egypt,
he could make shrewd and steady decisions. His absence of

vanity made him particularly susceptible to advice, and he had the character to act on it with enthusiasm and great determination.

In all the Army, Montgomery could not have found a more fortunate superior. Jealousy had no part in Alexander's make-up (a rare virtue among senior generals). If Montgomery had a plan for defeating Rommel, well and good, let him get on with it; he could have his head, and there would be no interference.

Looking back long after an event, one sees, if not with clarity, at least from new angles. It is apparent now that had the roles been reversed, had Alexander gone down to the desert and Montgomery stayed behind in the High Command in Cairo, a hopeless confusion might have developed, and very quickly. Montgomery as C.-in-C. would have been entirely unable to prevent himself from interfering. Almost certainly he would have had disputes around the conference table with his allies (the Australians, New Zealanders, South Africans, Greeks, Czechs and Poles). Alexander's talents, moreover, lay far less in the tactical fighting of a battle than in the general management and organization of men in a wide strategic field. At Alamein he would have been wasted.

Montgomery himself summed up the matter: "We had totally different mentalities," he said. "I ruffled people's feelings. Alex smoothed them down."

And now in this dark corner of the lounge at Shepheard's the two men took up their exact positions. Alexander issued the one and only order he had for Montgomery throughout the entire campaign: "Go down to the desert and defeat Rommel."

Quickly and vehemently Montgomery sketched his plans. The Germans had a panzer army: we must have one too. The issue had to be fought out in the desert and nowhere else. Morale must be entirely revived. There must be a considerable regrouping of the whole Army, probably the replacement of certain commanders. Would Alexander give him a free hand?

Yes.

Would he stand behind Montgomery in Cairo and back him up, endeavour to fulfil all reasonable requests from the desert.

Yes.

Looking across the table Montgomery saw that he was trusted completely. He also saw that this trust and his freedom of action would go on just so long as he was successful. If he failed, he was out. While he was trying, Alexander would support him to the limit; but he would have to try very hard indeed. The bargain between them was never broken.

In the afternoon Harding came with his report: Yes, an armoured striking corps could be got together.

"Then go ahead with it", Montgomery said.

The next thing was to get in touch with one more old pupil. De Guingand was in the desert acting as Chief of Staff to the field force. Already he had been for some time in the Middle East, at first in the intelligence branch and latterly in this new position. It was arranged over the long-distance telephone that de Guingand should rendezvous early the following morning at the "Alexandria cross-roads"—the point where the road from Cairo turned west into the open desert.

Montgomery never saw Auchinleck again. Nor was he again to see Cairo until this, his biggest adventure, was resolved one way or the other. He slept that night at the British Embassy on the Nile, and at 5 a.m. on August 13th he left by car with his bedroll on the five-hour drive to the front.

De Guingand, brown and thin, wearing khaki shorts and an open shirt, was waiting at the cross-roads at 8 a.m. They looked at one another curiously, each estimating the other after this absence of years. Up to this point there had been nothing more between them than a few brief meetings, a warm but not hearty mutual esteem; and de Guingand was still well down in the hierarchy of generals. He jumped into Montgomery's car and as they drove on over that particularly vile stretch of the desert road known as "The Ripples" he outlined the situation.

The line was holding and not much more. All counter-attacks had failed to achieve anything definite. Morale was very definitely low. Rommel was expected to attack again at any moment and it would be extremely dangerous. He might even penetrate to Cairo. In that case the Army was under orders to fall back on to the Delta and, if necessary, abandon Egypt.

They spread the map out in the car as they jolted along. The British line ran from the Mediterranean for a distance of some thirty miles due south to the Qattara Depression, a tangle of rocky cliffs and loose sand impassable to armour. It was not expected that Rommel would attempt to go round the Depression through the open desert to the south; to reach the Delta he would have to break the existing line near the coast. This front stretched across flat open desert and was broken

by three low ridges running at right angles to the line: one was
Tel el Eisa, Hill on the Coast; another was the Ruweisat feature
and the third was the Himeimat—Alam Halfa feature. Something like half a million soldiers, Germans, Italians and British,
were encamped on either side of the line.

Here at the north, on the sea, Australians and South Africans
were holding the front. Then came British and Indian troops,
and finally New Zealanders in the south. The British armour
was dispersed about ready to move to points of urgency.
Plans? Nothing very definite in view of the critical situation.
There were several schemes for charging the enemy with tanks
for limited objectives. The enemy had been recently building
up with a new division from Crete. Their tank workshops were
going at full blast. More aircraft and guns were arriving. Clearly
there was going to be an attack, and we had no reserves to meet
a determined effort.

Towards 10 a.m. the car left the macadam road and turned
south across the loose yellow sand to the Army headquarters. It
was hardly an inspiring sight. Apart from the fact that it was
grotesquely inaccessible both to the main road and to the front,
a rigid austerity reigned. There were no sleeping-quarters:
officers and men slept on the open sand or at the foot of their
trucks dispersed about the desolate landscape. A good deal of
their business was likewise conducted in the open under the
blazing sun. In the handful of command vehicles there was a
shortage of clerks, signallers, typewriters and most of the office
equipment usually found in a headquarters. Meals of cold bully
beef and sandy cheese were eaten in the open. Even Auchinleck
slept beside his caravan. Occasional dust-storms, hot, choking
and all-penetrating, swept across the encampment. As these
passed, innumerable swarms of flies settled upon every living
thing, and on the mess tables there was a gradually deepening
layer of dead black insect bodies clustering round the plates of
rancid and melting margarine.

Montgomery was no sybarite but he gazed at this scene
with fascinated astonishment. Where was the Air Force headquarters? Where the war rooms, the maps, the offices?—
where indeed in the midst of this isolated wilderness was the
war?

General Ramsden was acting as Army Commander.
Montgomery asked him to return to his corps and immediately
sent out a radio message to the Middle East Command saying
that he, Montgomery, had from that instant assumed command
of the Eighth Army. This was at 2 p.m., August 13th.

He then set out by car to visit the most relentless and

redoubtable fighting soldier then commanding in either army
in the desert. General Freyberg, V.C., and his New Zealanders
were some distance away. Once you left the main road in the
desert there were a thousand tracks but none you could trust.
The method of proceeding from one place to another was, as
at sea, on a compass bearing. The desert was new to Montgomery but he could not help observing after a time as the car
bounced and swayed over the rocks that his guide, an A.D.C.,
looked nervous.

"Do you know where we are?"

The boy was frank—"No, sir". Then after a bit he
added dubiously: "I think we are in the middle of a minefield,
sir". For the first time that day Montgomery seemed a little
restless.

"Then get out of it", he blazed. "Get out of it at once." They
drove out over the warning trip-wire without coming to harm,
found their bearings and pushed on.

Freyberg eyed his new commander with compassion; it was
their first meeting.

"I feel terribly sorry for you," he said kindly. "This is the
grave of lieutenant-generals. None of them stay here more than
a few months."

Upon the general situation Freyberg was gloomy. This was
the atmosphere everywhere Montgomery went that day. When
was Rommel going to attack? Where? Were we going to hold him?

Soon after 5 p.m. Montgomery was back at his desert
headquarters and he got on to the telephone to Alexander.
Two new divisions, the 51st Highland and the 44th, had arrived
from England. They were earmarked for the defence of the
Delta. Could he have them, instead, in the desert and at all
possible speed? "Yes", Alexander said.

In the operations quarters Montgomery asked the staff
officers what they were doing. They told him their orders: At
all costs the Eighth Army was not to be destroyed *in situ*. If
hard pressed they were to make a fighting withdrawal through
the Canal and re-establish headquarters south of Cairo. Those
were the plans upon which they were working.

At 6 p.m. under the new commander's orders de Guingand
had assembled all available staff officers in a little amphi-
theatre of sand close to the headquarters. As they sat in a semi-
circle in the evening light, the empty desert on every side,
Montgomery stood up and addressed them.

"The defence of Egypt lies here at Alamein and on Ruweisat
Ridge", he said. "I have cancelled the plan for withdrawal. If
we are attacked, then there will be no retreat. If we cannot stay

here alive, then we will stay here dead. These orders have already gone out."

There was no call for oratory, no need for emphasis. They listened to him breathlessly as the extraordinary series of flat statements went on.

"Two new divisions have arrived in Egypt and I have asked for them to be dispatched here immediately. With this support our task is easy. Given a week the situation will be steady. Given fourteen days we will be sitting pretty. In three weeks the issue will be certain. In due course we ourselves will attack. We will then finish with Rommel once and for all."

So many commanders (now lying in limbo) had come down to the desert full of pep talks and rousing orders of the day; but in sheer audacity and unblushing assurance none had gone as far as this.

Who was this man? How could he talk like this? How could he know what would happen? If this was just one more piece of bombast from a raw and ambitious fool sent out by the War Office, then it was a bitter and a monstrous joke. Fool or no fool they would have to obey his orders. And die because of them probably. All around them the desert stretched out interminably: an empty, a beautiful and forbidding space that could fill so suddenly and easily with enemy tanks and high explosive; enemy coming out of nowhere, suddenly appearing on the horizon behind, and to the left and the right, trucks racing madly back, straggling and bewildered men, signals going silent, and then the rout and the confusion, the line breaking up and no one knowing where to go or what to do. It had all happened before more than once. Everything for two years seemed to have ended in just that way. And the only thing to show for it was this same interminable desert, the same implacable resistance of the enemy coming on and on, bouncing back, impervious to counter-attack. Was the bloody place worth fighting for anyhow? Had they not all been stranded and neglected here far too long? Now here was this fresh brass-hat out from England talking as if he knew all about it, talking preposterously as though the whole thing were cut and dried, as though these past two weary years had never happened. And still the thin insistent voice persisted:

"There will be no retreat. We will stand here. This is where we fight. We remain here either dead or alive."

Well, at least this was something definite after the unending indecisions and hesitations and doubts of the past few months. At least everyone knew where he stood. But how could anyone have this colossal assurance?

"It will be quite easy. No doubt about it whatever. We will finish with Rommel once and for all."

Possibly he did have something up his sleeve: the arrival of two fresh divisions was certainly some sort of a guarantee.

Calmly, picking his phrases slowly, Montgomery told them his plan. A new British panzer army would be created. The line would hold until it was ready. There would be a certain regrouping. There would be reinforcement in every department. At the right moment the British would assault in main force— and the panzer corps would follow through.

No one now was missing a syllable. Quite clearly all this was something quite different to anything that had happened before. This was action—clear and uncompromising.

"I will now explain my methods", Montgomery said; and he proceeded to turn upside down half the accepted ideas of running an army command. De Guingand was nominated Chief of Staff. From now on the Army would be managed through the Chief of Staff. He had complete authority. They were to understand that whatever came from de Guingand was Montgomery's order and to be obeyed immediately.

Senior commanders would have the right of coming directly to Montgomery and he would send for them from time to time. At these meetings they would have to be prepared to state their business inside ten minutes. He would listen to no details. All these would go to the Chief of Staff. As C.-in-C. he himself would live apart and devote himself to the study of the general picture. Memoranda and papers were out. From this night onwards they would have to get used to receiving and transmitting orders by word of mouth. Where papers were necessary they must go to the Chief of Staff.

Montgomery himself would lay down the general plan. They and all their men would be thoroughly briefed on it before the Army went into action. But they themselves must handle the details. They would have great latitude inside the general framework laid down by Montgomery. They could do things their own way, provided only this—that they succeeded.

And finally, the one governing, overriding factor they must fix in their minds was this: No retreat. No withdrawal. Resistance. Then the complete smashing of Rommel.

Montgomery stepped down and walked away to his sleeping-quarters. He left behind him an atmosphere that was electric, a hope and an enthusiasm that many thought had died out of the desert forever.

All that night while the C.-in-C. slept peacefully from his usual hour the message was going round the Army. No retreat.

No withdrawal. We stand here alive or dead. By the morning thousands of men were beginning to look at themselves and the desert and the enemy as though some strange transfiguration had happened in the night. Perversely, the first effect of the new order was a sense of relief. In the end men probably fear the unknown more than anything else in life. In war—especially at any crisis—a steady and positive fact, no matter how hard to take, brings with it a sense of sanity. At least it is something firm and unchangeable to cling to in a changing and chaotic world where everything is in rudderless motion, where all the rest is anarchy and luck and ungovernable chance. And so this wave of relief began to sweep through the Army. Here at last after so many conflicting half-hearted orders was something utterly clear and inescapable. They were all in it. Every officer, every man. Stand fast.

More subtly the order had something else in it as well. The desert forces had begun to feel a thing which I can only describe as mass loneliness. The men in those days were isolated by many months from their homes. Some had had no home leave for years. The war stretched interminably ahead and the victory was most uncertain. Living in this stark world of blinding sunlight and limitless sand everyone sooner or later acquired the feeling that he was forgotten and neglected—that his family had forgotten him, that the war leaders had begun to regard this as a dead and profitless front where men could be left to lie and rot. It was a kind of *cafard*, and in the desert there was little except the presence of danger to distract the mind from any fixation.

Now, abruptly, this new order revealed that this front was a very important place indeed. The issue was regarded as vital. In the eyes of the world this was a struggle in which a man might risk his life to some purpose. The soldiers were eager to see the new general behind the new order. They were agreeably surprised and stimulated. Montgomery was very early on the move the following morning and he did not look like a brass-hat, nor did he behave like one. A queer little bloke who stood up in his car and waved at every passing group of soldiers as though he had known them for a long time. No saluting, none of that beefy, red-blooded look usually associated with red tabs. He was constantly getting out of his car and talking in a casual way to anyone who happened to be there. He appeared to have no blood-and-thunder-and-glory attitudes: it was simply, "We've got to hit them for six". He wore an Australian slouch hat and, grinning, he accepted badges from the men and stuck them in the crown. If this was a pre-arranged act to gain popularity then no one felt it was so, and it did not appear to be so to those who were watching at the time. From the Australian 9th Division which had been attacking desperately around Tel el Eisa in the north he had a particularly good reception.

Very soon Montgomery had visited all the important sectors along the line and had told all senior commanders and their staffs the rough outline of how he proposed to make good his promises.

Then back at his headquarters with his own staff he fixed his plan and began issuing a stream of orders which transformed that tranquil place into feverish activity. First, the present site of the headquarters was banned. Austerity and the Spartan life were out. They would move at once to Burg el Arab so that there could be close liaison with the Air Force headquarters already established there. The place had excellent road, rail and air communications.

Officers were to have tents and proper equipment. Clerks and typewriters were to be sent down at once from Cairo with additional vehicles, including a caravan and a bath for the C.-in-C. The staff was to eat in a properly run mess.

Next, certain high officers were forthwith dismissed from their posts and they were to be replaced by new men sent out from England. Signals were to be dispatched asking for General Horrocks to fly out at once to command the Thirteenth Corps, and General Leese to replace General Ramsden in the Thirtieth Corps. General Lumsden was to have command of the Tenth Corps—the new panzer force. General Harding was to have the picked division—the Seventh.

Next, a general programme of training was to be started at once. It was nonsense to say that the soldiers learned all they wanted to know in the actual fighting; their leaders got killed and wounded and the new men had to be trained.

Next, the battle. The three vital points on the line were Tel el Eisa, on the sea in the north; Ruweisat Ridge in the centre and Alam Halfa in the south. Rommel would certainly attempt to strike near Halfa in the south; that was the critical point. At present the British forces were disposed more or less evenly along the whole line. This must be altered at once. In the north and the centre the line must stand fast: to the south of Halfa it must give way—at first. The gap must be mined and the 7th Armoured Division sent to the danger spot at once and kept mobile. As soon as Rommel attacked, the Seventh must retire before the enemy, shooting him up as he came on; in fact the Seventh must be ready to do everything to lure the enemy tanks forward. The real British line, instead of continuing on to the Qattara Depression as at present, would stop at Alam Halfa and turn sharply at right-angles away from the enemy. This would leave a corridor for the enemy between the Depression and the rising ground of Alam Halfa. Once Rommel was in the corridor, the 7th Armoured Division retreating in front of him, tremendously heavy British fire was to open from the northern flank on Alam Halfa. One of the new divisions—the Forty-fourth—was to be entrenched on the Halfa position as soon as it arrived in the desert. In addition, artillery and tanks under the command of two very able officers, General Gatehouse and Brigadier Roberts, were to be dug into the hillside there.

Rommel would never dare to by-pass Halfa and proceed directly towards Cairo. He would try to subdue the hill first. As soon as he came under the flanking fire he would attempt to rush the hill—and find the British had their heaviest forces there.

That was the plan which Montgomery, with the aid of de Guingand, began to propound and shape on this second morning in the desert. He felt absolutely certain that Rommel would attack in that particular place in the south: he said he was equally certain that Rommel would be defeated there. All this, coming from a man who had never seen the country, never fought a battle in the desert and who had had barely time to go thoroughly into the maps and dispositions, was a little startling. It was particularly startling because under this plan Montgomery deliberately proposed to allow the enemy to penetrate his line with all the danger of an out-flanking movement ensuing. Suppose the new division did not get into place in time, suppose they failed to hold the hill? Montgomery would not consider it. They had to hold; therefore they would hold. They would squeeze the life out of Rommel's thrust in the gap there between Halfa and Qattara.

In his philosophy he told them there was only one way to plan a battle—to make a plan, stick to it and make the enemy conform. In this and in every other battle no matter what happened the enemy must never be allowed to fight according to his own plan; always according to Montgomery's plan. Then the result was certain. Montgomery was going to repeat this point a good deal later on.

On one matter the C.-in-C. was especially emphatic. This was to be a static battle. Except in the fluid gap in the south no one was to budge an inch in any direction. It did not

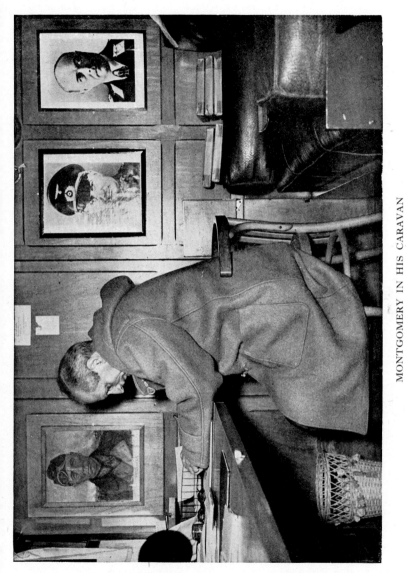

MONTGOMERY IN HIS CARAVAN

Behind him (*left to right*) : Rommel, Model, Kesselring

MONTGOMERY WITH HIS LIAISON OFFICERS

Major John Poston standing second from the left

matter if the enemy were routed; there was to be no pursuit. Everyone must stand fast. The enemy must be beaten off and then left alone.

The reason for this was that the real conflict with Rommel was going to follow later on when everything was ready. The defensive battle of Alam Halfa must do nothing to dislocate or disturb the building up of the Tenth Armoured Corps in the rear. No reserves must at this stage be committed to a limited and indecisive pursuit. Everything must await the mass struggle which would start some weeks later when Montgomery judged things ready, not before.

Insistently and steadily, hour after hour the orders went out, and a great commotion spread across the desert. Thousands of men and vehicles on the backward trek were suddenly halted and turned round. Tens of thousands of men, new guns, new tanks and new vehicles began to pour down towards the front from the Nile Delta. Liaison officers in jeeps were dashing about from unit to unit; *Cancel the previous orders, here are the new—for immediate action.* Headquarters abruptly began to pack their trucks, strike their encampments and set off across the open sand. Huge columns were preparing to move, some going south, some north, some towards the front and others away from it. Isolated convoys carrying land-mines and signals, tanks workshops and camouflage gear, hospitals and petrol, barbed wire and food, ammunition and tentage, water and clothing, artillery and spare parts—all the paraphernalia of this strange expedition in the sand—began to chart their courses and drive off through the dust. Everywhere men were digging or on the march. Officers in staff cars were constantly careering by.

To a newcomer the scene would have presented an impression of the wildest confusion, a disordered scramble through the waves of heat and blown sand. Indeed, to the majority of soldiers at this stage this sudden upheaval had no logical pattern. But what was apparent to everyone was that something new and dramatic had happened in the desert. It had come up with the suddenness of a storm and just as inexplicably; but it was a storm blowing from the east, from their own side. It was an act not forced upon them by the enemy but something done of their own volition by their own commanders. And this in itself was a thing to blow a spark of hope.

In his camp Montgomery issued one more order. The use of the word "box", meaning defensive position, was henceforth banned in the Eighth Army. In future there would be no

5

"boxes" and no suggestion that any man could shelter behind barbed wire. From now on the war was to be out in the open.

Just six days had elapsed since Montgomery had heard in England that he was to have command of the Eighth Army. Two days had gone by since he had arrived in Egypt, and he had been in the desert some twenty hours, more than a third of which he had passed in sound sleep.

CHAPTER NINE

THE LORD MIGHTY IN BATTLE

I

No ONE ever knows the truth while a war is being fought. Even after a successful battle the high commanders and the politicians have no time to examine what they have learned from the enemy and themselves before they are plunged again into a new situation full of uncertainties and doubts. As for the general public, a wall of enforced ignorance grows up between them and the actual events, and in a world maddened by its own prejudices and hatreds very few people would be capable of seeing the truth even if they had the knowledge. The men in the inner tactical councils and at the hot anvil of the event, they too can scarcely hope to have a complete and balanced view since they are bounded by the harsh and narrow spotlight of their own experience.

Even years afterwards it is not possible to extract the complete truth because by then the falsehoods of war have been repeated many times and become entrenched; documents are lost, the men who together had a special intricate pattern of knowledge at some special place and time become dispersed and memory grows uncertain.

Probably to this day the majority of people believe that Field-Marshal Alexander and his staff planned and conducted the Battle of Alamein and the subsequent march across the desert to Tripoli. But this was not so. Alexander has never suggested it was so; nevertheless the idea grew and persisted, and in England particularly it was felt that while Montgomery supplied the somewhat egotistical heroics and dramatics at the front, Alexander was the calculating and organizing brain behind.

In actual fact Montgomery was never in any really imminent danger of his life at the Battle of Alamein, and from his headquarters behind the line he probably had a more complete and detached view of the fighting than any other man. This was because Montgomery himself and his staff fashioned the entire plan of the battle in the desert many weeks beforehand. They changed their tactics half-way through the battle and organized the ensuing pursuit. And a great deal of this was done without previous reference to either Field-

Marshal Alexander's headquarters in Cairo or the British Cabinet in London. Indeed at various times both Cairo and London were opposed to and worried about certain measures taken by Montgomery. They offered advice but they did not interfere.

To suggest that Alexander played merely a passive part in the battle and the pursuit to Tripoli would also be the wildest inaccuracy. But for Alexander neither Alamein nor any of the other battles could have been fought. He delivered the men and materials, he gave Montgomery his strategic direction, he controlled in a skilful way all the vast and intricate organization behind the lines without which Montgomery would have collapsed at once. Alexander at the same time dealt with great issues beyond the desert—the saving of Malta, the garrisoning of the Middle East, the clandestine war in the Balkans. He consistently supported Montgomery in the Cabinet Defence Committee and settled in Cairo many great difficulties which would otherwise have gone down to the desert. Wherever Montgomery chose to go he had Alexander behind him offering encouragement, smoothing things out, keeping a balance. In the last resort Alexander was throughout the whole period a vital back-stop, an insurance, a clear brain ready to come forward and take up the reins had anything gone wrong. And while he waited and watched and kept the whole huge machine turning over he never interposed his will except to offer more support.

It was an atmosphere of freedom which Montgomery was going to enjoy only once or twice more—and again at a vital time—in the whole course of the war. He flourished in these circumstances. His brain worked at immense speed and with a certainty that at times seemed mystical. That touch, that buoyant sureness, diminished whenever a restricting hand was placed on him; then, given the rein again he suddenly bursts forth with the same clarity and decision. For Montgomery's superiors it was the old problem of the racing stable—how often could you put the high-spirited horse to the jump? How far would he go if you did not curb him? Would he not plunge into some disastrous folly unless you held him in check from time to time?

At this moment of time, from the autumn of 1942 to the spring of 1943, he was given the free rein and to such an extent that he was allowed to buffet other horses from the course and go against the will of his superiors.

Churchill and the War Cabinet were deeply concerned about the fate of Malta, then approaching starvation and under the imminent threat of invasion from Italian and German airborne forces in Sicily. They put it to Alexander. Could not the attack at Alamein be launched in September? Alexander sent on the message to Montgomery. No, Montgomery replied, I am not ready yet. Again the Cabinet pressed, and this time it was more like an order. Montgomery finally replied to Churchill through Alexander with these three points:

1. If the attack starts in September it will fail.
2. If we wait until October I will personally guarantee great success and the destruction of Rommel's army.
3. Am I to attack in September?

It was a polite form of blackmail. The Cabinet gave in. In many ways it was an extraordinary truculence in a junior commander, but Montgomery had one solid factor to back his judgment: the Battle of Alam Halfa had begun on August 31st and it had gone precisely as Montgomery had planned and predicted it. Rommel had attacked in the south, had been sucked into the corridor at Halfa, had been mercilessly bombarded while he was in the British minefield, had turned to assault Halfa itself and been destroyed on the new British positions there. Eventually after six days of intense fighting, when wave after wave of the enemy had been beaten off, Rommel had ordered the retreat, and now the gap had been sealed off with a new minefield linking Halfa to the Qattara Depression.

As a curtain raiser, as a promise of his skill and foresight, Montgomery could not have a better start. Many experts regard Alam Halfa as his greatest battle. The swiftness of the planning, the soundness of the dispositions, the intelligence of the anticipation, the clarity of the orders—all these things had an electric result in the desert.

The British troops had not been permitted to pursue, but their elation at standing firm, at wreaking such damage, and now the sight of so many reinforcements pouring into the desert—all this began to fan the spark of morale into a flame.

Then, too, Montgomery had been fortunate. Rommel's attack had come a full fortnight after his (Montgomery's) arrival in the desert. He had had time to get his two new divisions into position. On the other hand, it would be grossly incorrect to say that Montgomery was bound to succeed because of the reinforcements. This is another delusion which has been persisted in since Alamein. It was said that he had the rare good fortune to take over a highly trained army and at a time when two fresh divisions and many extra guns and tanks were being delivered. Any commander (so the argument runs) could have succeeded in these circumstances.

In actual fact the reinforcements were very little more than those which the opposing army had been building up, and they constituted only a small part of the entire force. Other commanders in the desert before Montgomery had been given larger reinforcement than this and come to grief. As for the highly skilled nature of the Eighth Army, this was to a great extent overborne at the time of the new commander's appearance by the lowness of morale and the lack of existing direction. The skill existed no doubt in the Army but it was badly disposed. Above everything else the soldiers were crying for intelligent and inspiring leadership. They were critically in need of a success.

Methodically and precisely Montgomery planned for the success. Even while Alam Halfa was being fought his panzer corps was being built up behind the lines. Everything was done with a minuteness and thoroughness which one does not usually associate with a colourful and piratical leader. But all this went on in secrecy. Neither during nor after the Battle of Alamein did the public hear anything of Montgomery's planning, or of his re-organisation of the Army's supply service, or of his re-grouping of the divisions, or his new methods of handling artillery and tanks, or of his dovetailing the Army with the Air, or of his new technique of staff command, or of any of the fifty other wearisome technicalities. Above all, they knew nothing of the *gradualness* of his preparation and of his refusal to be hurried. And so when the victory was won and the people came to regard the successful general, they were allowed to see nothing beyond the black beret, the caravans and the lurid and simple declarations of faith. These personal things were photographic and colourful, and out of them was built up a popular figure which had very little to do with Montgomery as he actually was.

The business of planning a battle had, by 1942, become a very intricate thing indeed, involving the pooling of many minds. Montgomery's method, adopted for the first time in full before Alamein and in all the subsequent actions, was this: he stated in general terms what he wanted to do—to destroy such and such forces, to make such and such an advance or capture such and such an objective. His planning staff then went off and prepared several alternative schemes. Returning with these they argued the various merits and demerits of each proposal and it was left to the C.-in-C. to make his own choice of which one he preferred.

Once the plan was selected a series of intensive interviews followed with the commanders of the various Army branches and units. One by one the heads of supply, intelligence, artillery, armour and signals were called. The head of artillery, for example, might be asked to reduce things to the simplest form: "How many guns have you got? How long will it take you to bring the total up to a thousand? How many rounds of ammunition will you want to maintain a barrage of two hours' rapid fire?" And to the controller of the armour: "How many tanks? How long to proceed from A to B? How much petrol wanted?" Each man had to be prepared to answer clearly, simply and rapidly—and then make his word good. Very soon commanders learned it was stupid to boast, worse than stupid to underestimate: Montgomery was particularly severe on those who he felt were not doing enough. To everyone it was painfully clear that mistakes and miscalculations were followed by only one thing: instant dismissal.

With his controller of supplies Montgomery went into a careful examination. "When could he deliver? And once the battle became fluid for how long could he keep up delivering and at what rate?"

With the intelligence branch a different game was played. "Imagine yourself the enemy", Montgomery said. "Suppose I did this and this. What would you do?" It was up to the intelligence officer to carry in his head the latest dispositions of the Axis Army, to know its strength from day to day in guns, aircraft, men and tanks, to have information on expected reinforcements. In front of him the dispositions of the coming battle were spread out on a map and he was expected to play against Montgomery a strange and fascinating parlour game, making move for move against the British.

Much of this was, of course, accepted practice in planning. Montgomery's special contribution was that he heightened and centralized and streamlined the whole procedure. Having chosen his plan he discarded the alternatives. All his eggs were put into the one basket. Consequently his orders were very few, very simple and very definite; everyone knew exactly what he had to do. This was the very reverse of what had happened at the fall of Tobruk.

The Air Force was a much more intricate problem, over which the leaders had been quarrelling for years. The air marshals—many of them trained in the old Royal Flying Corps —insisted that for efficiency they must remain a separate unit. Against this the Army argued hotly; Air Force and Army, they said, must be combined as in the Russian, German and

American Armies. In the same way as artillery and reconnaissance units, groups of aircraft must be attached to each division and act under the divisional command.

Montgomery took up a middle position. The idea of splitting up the Air Force piecemeal among the divisions was, he said, nonsense. The Air Force must be flexible; it must be ready to throw its whole weight into a point of emergency, and quickly. The only way to achieve this was through central control. And such control was best exercised through the Air Force leaders. If they and the Army planners lived together, slept, ate and worked together, then you would get an efficient machine. Hence the rapid move of his headquarters to the Air Force camp at Burg el Arab prior to the battles of Alamein and Alam Halfa. No doubt the rival commanders were feeling their way to this solution before Montgomery arrived, but it was he and men like Coningham and Tedder who definitely fixed the matter in the autumn of 1942. At one stroke the controversy was silenced. The co-operation between the Army and the Air Force, starting here in the desert, was to continue to expand until the end of the war in Germany.

At this time Montgomery was paying particular attention to the Germans. Rommel had an especial fascination for him. He acquired a photograph of him, pinned it above his desk in his caravan, and whenever it caught his eye it was his practice to ask himself: "Now what would Rommel do about it? Suppose I were Rommel. What would *I* do?" He studied the photograph intimately, the determined chin, the rugged mouth, the shaded confident eyes, the thick neck, the bullish set of the head. Scraps of information about the rival commander always interested him intensely. In some curious way he felt that by looking at the picture, by trying to project himself into the other man's personality, he would grow to know his failings and his weaknesses. From the first he envisaged this as a personal struggle, a conflict of wits between Rommel and himself, and quite simply and openly he discussed the battle in this way.

With all the broader issues of supply and man- and firepower, it was the job of the Chief of Staff to synchronize the information and the possibilities, to keep moulding the plan along Montgomery's line; and little by little, as the days after Alam Halfa went by, all the threads of the pattern were drawn together and they began to work towards a definite date.

Montgomery had decided to introduce several new features at Alamein. Across the intervening ten years he and de Guingand remembered that old manœuvre at the Pyramids and he determined to attack by night. At this period of the war there was no such thing in use as artificial moonlight, created by shining searchlights into the sky, and so they needed a moon—preferably a waxing moon. The meteorologists told them that this and other necessary conditions would occur on October 23rd.

The advantages of a night attack were obvious: the infantry could find cover in the darkness but it would not be so dark under the moon that they lost contact with one another. For the last few hours before dawn they would be able to pick up mines, dig into the sand and remain there under cover to repel daylight counter-attacks until the following night. Then they would advance again.

Up till now the artillery had been dispersed along the line. Montgomery decided to bunch it together so that it should strike with one concentrated blow. This was part of the general over-all scheme that attack should always be delivered on a narrow front with tremendous driving power behind it.

Further, he discarded the theory that a gap must be made by the infantry in the opposing minefields and fixed defences: the infantry at Alamein would start the gap and then the armour was to blast its way through the remainder. In this case they would be led by the newly invented flails—tanks which exploded mines harmlessly by threshing the ground before them with long chains.

Years before, General Wavell and General O'Connor had established the principle that you must encircle the enemy by penetrating deep into the unprotected desert to the south and then wheeling north to the coast. At Alamein Montgomery temporarily abandoned this theory. He argued that if we attacked in the south—admittedly the weakest part of Rommel's line—then our southern flank would be closed by the Qattara Depression and the thrust would have only one alternative—to wheel northwards. He determined to put his main thrust into the north-centre of the line so that he would be able to wheel either north or south according to how the battle developed.

Finally, there was an elaborate scheme of deception under which tanks were camouflaged as trucks, and fake encampments with fake tanks were secretly built to deceive the enemy reconnaissance aircraft.

For his initial strike Montgomery had upwards of a thousand guns and seven divisions of infantry: the Australians, New Zealanders, South Africans, Indians and the 51st Highland Division. There were also the British 50th and 44th Divisions. With these he would force a "pocket" in the enemy line in the neighbourhood of Ruweisat and Tel el Eisa on the night of

5*

October 23rd. The armour, comprising the 1st and 10th Divisions under Lumsden, would move up to the front in the night and enter the battle at dawn.

2

On the morning of October 23rd there was a momentous and awful quiet in the Army. In that unbearable strain of waiting it was apparent to everyone that this was to be a major battle, that many would be killed and wounded and that all the future was intensely doubtful. The preparation had been so methodical, so secure, so painfully slow; and now everything was suddenly to be squandered, suddenly committed as though all the carefully tended tanks and guns and the men themselves were not worth anything at all. This is the maddest moment of war: the eve of the battle when men can still cling to their reason and the rational habits of life and yet implacably they are committed to an anarchy, a negation of all the reasoned preparation, and almost, but not quite, a negation of hope. It is the moment of absolute loneliness when all a man's life is focused down upon himself, when he feels that nothing in the world can save him, when all the intelligence, the kindness and capacity for enjoyment in mankind is put away out of reach and that nothing is so important as the fact that this rifle lock must slide, this trigger must give to the finger, and that these legs somehow must find the strength to take him up from the protecting earth and carry him into the open chaos.

By now the soldiers had been told the plan and what they had to do. To this Montgomery added the first of his orders of the day. "When I assumed command of the Eighth Army", he declared, "I said that the mandate was to destroy ROMMEL and his army, and that it would be done as soon as we were ready.

"We are ready NOW.

"The battle which is about to begin will be one of the decisive battles of history. It will be the turning-point of the war. The eyes of the world will be on us, watching anxiously which way the battle will swing.

"We can give them their answer at once: 'It will swing our way'.

"We have first-class equipment; good tanks; good anti-tank guns; plenty of artillery and plenty of ammunition; and we are backed by the finest air striking force in the world.

"All that is necessary is that each one of us, every officer

and man, should enter the battle with the determination to
see it through—to fight and to kill—and finally, to win.

"If we do this there can only be one result—together we
will hit the enemy for 'six', right out of North Africa.

"The sooner we win this battle, which will be the turning-
point of the war, the sooner we shall all get back to our families.

"Therefore let every officer and man enter the battle with
a stout heart, and the determination to do his duty so long as
he has breath in his body.

"AND LET NO MAN SURRENDER SO LONG AS HE IS UNWOUNDED
AND CAN FIGHT.

"Let us all pray that 'the Lord mighty in battle' will give
us the victory."

And then the thick aggressive scrawl beneath this declaration:

"B. L. MONTGOMERY,
"Lieutenant-General, G.O.C.-in-C.,
"Eighth Army."

It was the formula which, just as unconsciously and
instinctively, he was going to use again and again: the "I" and
the "we"; the emphasis—the prophetic emphasis—that this
was a battle in which it was worth a man's risking his life,
indeed a battle that was going to shake the earth and alter the
course of the war; the boisterous and personal reference to the
enemy; the comforting reassurance that the soldier was not
alone—he had the Air Force behind him and good weapons:
the mention of reward in the soldier returning to his family;
and finally the commitment of the whole issue to God.

3

In general outline the Battle of Alamein was fought
according to Montgomery's plan. At no time in that violent
fortnight did the enemy regain the initiative.

It was fortunate indeed that Rommel was absent at the
outset; fortunate that he did not get back until it was too late
to stop the rout. For the result all the credit must go to the
planning and handling of the men and more particularly to
the men themselves.

Outwardly Montgomery remained entirely unmoved
throughout; he went to bed at his usual hour each night and
slept well. If he was shaken at the several crises he gave no
evidence of it whatever.

When commanders came to argue with him that to con-

tinue was impossible he blandly opposed a "no", and it was
clear that he would maintain the offensive until, if need be,
half his men were dead, including himself. Many subordinates
found in him through these days an almost surgical coldness
and callousness. When he came up to the front each morning
early and the weary officers met him after the night's fighting
they were startled by the almost fanatical look in the thin hard
face and the staring and penetrating appearance of the eyes.

The battle continued more bitterly than Montgomery or
anyone else could have imagined. When the armour followed
the infantry into the northern gap on the 24th it became
jammed and much immobilized in the enemy minefields.
An intensely heavy fire came down and it was impossible to
break through. In vain Lumsden argued with Montgomery
that the manœuvre was impossible; the tanks were forced to
remain there fighting it out.

The original plan was to wheel the thrust southward from
the gap but this came under such opposition that it had to be
abandoned. Montgomery now struck due west and north, and
to the north some headway was made; the Australians began
to pinch the enemy out from the coast. By now most of the
German armour which had been held mobile along the line
was banked opposite the gap.

Half-way through the battle Montgomery suddenly withdrew part of his armour for thirty-six hours' rest, regrouping,
re-tanking and re-manning with new soldiers. It was a move
which created the darkest forebodings in London and at headquarters. Was not Montgomery throwing his chances to the
wind by withdrawing at this vital moment when he should have
been putting reserves in instead of bringing men out? Richard
Casey, then Minister of State in the Middle East, came down
to Eighth Army headquarters and gently sounded things out.
But Montgomery was adamant. The armour must be regrouped
for the final thrust and to it would be added Freyberg and his
New Zealanders, also withdrawn from the line.

The real issue now was the direction of this final thrust,
and the break-through. Already there were signs of the Axis
weakening. Everything depended upon the disposition of the
German forces who formed the hard core of the opposing army,
and a tremendous responsibility rested on Intelligence to
discover just where the Italian and German divisions were
placed and how they were moving. There were signs that the
entire German force was moving to the north, leaving the
south weakly held by the Italians—but as yet no one could be
sure.

At first Montgomery favoured the coastal road for the break-through; it was the shortest route through the line, and once opened the road would offer speed and mobility for the pursuit. An opposing school of thought favoured the centre since there would be fewer obstacles, thinner minefields and space to manœuvre. While the armour rested, the issues were debated anxiously. Those who opposed the use of the coast road began to feel that it was hopeless to argue with Montgomery any further; he appeared absolutely fixed on the northern route.

At this point the Intelligence Staff presented a hard-and-fast report: the entire German force had moved to the north. Their point of juncture with their allies—nearly always the weakest point of any line—lay just below the bloody battle-field in the gap. It was the turning-point. At once Montgomery cancelled the plan to break through along the road. The rested British divisions now fell upon the Axis point of juncture, smashed it open, and flowed through: the Seventh heading straight across the open desert for Sollum, on the Egyptian border, some 250 miles away, the New Zealanders and the First for Mersa Matruh, the coastal hamlet and Axis supply point nearer at hand on the coast, and the Tenth for Daba just behind the enemy lines.

The Italians were left for General Horrocks to demolish. With one final shattering and cataclysmic blow the entire Axis army collapsed and fell to pieces. Thousands upon thousands of exhausted and bewildered Italians simply gave themselves up. The rest, with the Germans in the van (because they grabbed most of the vehicles) set off pell-mell in wild disorder down the coast road in the long and dangerous attempt to escape into Libya.

On November 5th, when this happy result was far from clear and still the awful clash of artillery was exploding along the line and many were too numbed and broken to think of anything but rest, Montgomery called his war correspondents together to make his announcement to the world. He toyed with his cap. He exchanged light-heartedly a few banalities, and suddenly he said, "Gentlemen. This is complete and absolute victory." His audience stared at him incredulously. They had been prepared to hear a tense discussion of the difficulties, an admission even of partial defeat, so close had been the fighting. But this flat and arrogant assertion was a bombshell. Returning hastily to the front the men found the pursuit had begun.

It was indeed going so fast that Montgomery himself,

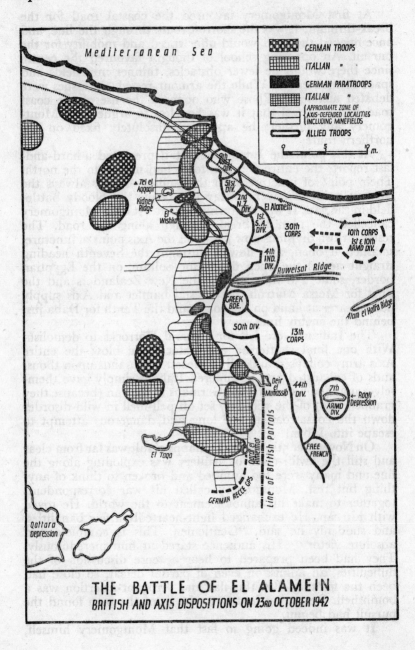

Mediterranean Sea

GERMAN TROOPS
ITALIAN   "
GERMAN PARATROOPS
ITALIAN   "
APPROXIMATE ZONE OF
AXIS-DEFENDED LOCALITIES
INCLUDING MINEFIELDS
ALLIED TROOPS

0   5   10 m.

9th
AUST.
DIV.

51st
DIV.

2nd
N.Z.
DIV.

1st
S.A.
DIV.

El Alamein

30th
CORPS

10th CORPS
1st & 10th
ARMD DIV.

▲ Tel el
Aqqaqir

Kidney
Ridge

El
Wishka

4th
IND.
DIV.

Ruweisat Ridge

Alam el Halfa Ridge

GREEK
BDE.

50th DIV.

13th
CORPS

Deir
el
Munassib

44th
DIV.

7th
ARMD
DIV.

Ragil
Depression

El Taqa

Qarat el
Abeinhot

Line of British Patrols

GERMAN RECCE GPS.

FREE
FRENCH

Qattara
Depression

THE BATTLE OF EL ALAMEIN
BRITISH AND AXIS DISPOSITIONS ON 23rd OCTOBER 1942

paradoxically, was nearly captured a day or two later. Riding
in the van in an open car he sent two officers down the coastal
road to Mersa Matruh to site a new headquarters, and was
about to follow when shooting broke out. The officers (who
included Montgomery's stepson, Richard Carver) were
ambushed by a German rearguard and were captured.
Montgomery himself turned back just in time.

And now at the moment when the British were about to
snatch the entire prize, fortune suddenly swung to the Germans.
A violent and unseasonable storm began. The rain streamed
down. Presently the pursuing columns were reporting back
that their tanks were bogged. Vehicles heavily laden with
petrol and ammunition were delayed for days. Pursuing
aircraft were grounded. Hour by hour the momentum slowed
down. At this news Montgomery revealed the first sign of
weakness he had shown since his arrival in the desert. Discussing the matter later he said: "I nearly burst into tears in
front of my staff".

But the prize if diminished (and lacking the capture of
Rommel) was still immense and still the pursuit struggled on
across the seaboard of northern Africa for hundreds of miles.
Tobruk was avenged on November 11th. Martuba fell on the
15th. Racing across the base of the Cyrenaican bulge the
British tanks and armoured cars arrived in Benghazi just too
late—the Germans had slipped in and slipped out again on
their desperate journey south and west around the Gulf of
Sirte.

The taking of the Martuba airfields was probably the most
vital date in this headlong race. Montgomery had been told
that the plight of Malta was now critical: either a convoy with
oil and food had to get through from Alexandria or it was the
end of the island. To give the convoy any chance it had to be
protected by land-based fighters, especially through the narrows
between Crete and Africa, and the only place on which the
fighters could be based for the task was at Martuba. On
November 17th the convoy set out from Alexandria, and
simultaneously fighter maintenance crews, working at speed at
Martuba, got their aircraft off the captured airfield. More
fighters came out from Malta for the last stage of the journey.
The convoy got through and the island was never again in
danger.

On the land the Eighth Army streamed on to that critical
point at El Agheila, south of Benghazi, where two British
armies before them had been halted and flung back. General
Miles Dempsey had flown out from England to take over the

command of the Thirteenth Corps. Everything now was bent towards the task of maintaining the striking spearhead long enough until it could be reinforced, until the spring could be re-coiled for another strike.

Montgomery issued his second order of the day to the troops: "I said that together we would hit the Germans and Italians for six right out of North Africa", he wrote. "In three weeks we have completely smashed the German and Italian Army, and pushed the remnants out of Egypt, having advanced ourselves nearly 300 miles up to and beyond the frontier. The prisoners captured number 30,000, including nine generals . . . the enemy is completely crippled.

" I feel that our great victory was brought about by the good fighting qualities of the soldiers of the Empire rather than anything I may have been able to do myself.

"I know you will all realize how greatly we were helped in our task by the R.A.F.

"There is some good hunting to be had farther to the west, in Libya; and our leading troops are now in Libya ready to begin. AND THIS TIME, HAVING REACHED BENGHAZI AND BEYOND, WE SHALL NOT COME BACK.

"On with the task and good hunting to you all. As in all pursuits some have to remain behind to start with, but we shall all be in it before the finish."

Christmas was near. Except for the feverish activity along the lines of communication stretching back to the Nile Delta, there was a temporary pause along the fluid front. Back at Alamein British soldiers selected a tranquil hollow in the desert and began the work of digging graves and erecting some seven thousand crosses there. And, slowly and inexorably the sand began to blow across the empty battlefield, tearing the paint off the broken, rusting tanks, filling the dug-outs, banking up around the many thousand land-mines, obliterating the million tyre tracks and the impression of a million feet. Soon it would all go back to the desert and there would be nothing left except the white crosses and an occasional bedouin camel picking its way through the mines which no one had had the time to gather up.

4

The desert affected everyone in a different way. Some people—the extrovert, the individualist and the frankly physical—loved it. Others loathed it and pined for the cities and civilization. The majority felt physically healthy and, so long as there was fast action, they were willing to accept this kind of war as well as any other.

The problems of sex, of neurosis, of *cafard* did not often arise. In the absence of nearly all the ordinary amenities and pleasures of life most men developed personalities which were at least superficially new. There were no cinemas, no advertisements, very few radios and newspapers to remind them of women, and women themselves were never seen from one month's end to another. To a great extent sex was sublimated in the intense comradeship of the men, a thing that is almost wholly unknown on this scale in peace. There was no alcohol, but the soldiers talked endlessly over their thick and sticky tea, and the desert gave the mind a sense of spaciousness so that the talk, like the talk of undergraduates, ranged endlessly and experimentally over heaven and earth unfettered for the most part by taboos, by special knowledge, by custom or by superstition or fear.

Very soon the Eighth Army became a private expeditionary force, a crusade, remote from all the world. The men *felt* different to other men. The atmosphere was that of a boys camp: physical, communistic, exuberant and determined. They developed a new argot of their own, a new style of dress (among the officers it was desert boots, coloured scarves, corduroy trousers). Like chameleons, the Army—the men and their vehicles too—turned the colour of the desert; red-browns and whitish-browns. They grew lean and hard. In this life there was no money and no commercial value upon anything, no scheme of social grades, not very much personal ambition. All the real values rested upon the man himself, upon human life, upon the daily accomplishment of some practical thing. By this you were assessed, not upon your background, and each man felt himself to be a separate individual fulfilling an essential part in the machine.

All this Montgomery encouraged strongly. He had great shrewdness in reacting to an atmosphere and the emotions of men in the mass, but it was largely an unconscious shrewdness, more a sense of touch. And thus occurred the matter of the black beret.

One day during the Battle of Alamein he climbed into a tank in order to go up nearer the fighting. A member of the crew offered the General his beret as something more comfortable and convenient to wear in that confined space. Montgomery added his general's badge to the Royal Tank Corps insignia already on the beret, and he continued wearing it throughout the battle. By this time the soldiers everywhere had grown used to looking for it; it became the sign by which they recognized the General and they waved and shouted to him—and he waved and shouted back. Montgomery had no special liking for berets, but it was clear to him that this particular beret was becoming a notable morale builder, since soldiers always liked to see their generals at the front. Moreover, he enjoyed being looked at and recognized. He was convinced that he was a good general, a man most likely to win victories, and therefore the more the men saw him and recognized him as their leader the better it would be for everyone. He was aware that some people accused him of cheap personal vanity. Twice he was officially asked to discard the beret as something which he was not then entitled to wear and which, moreover, was hardly consonant with the dignity of a commanding general. He refused flatly. "I don't give two hoots what anyone says", he declared. "This beret is worth two divisions." By the time he got to Tripoli he had decided he would never again wear any other official headgear in his life. To the whole Army now he was known simply as "Monty".

There was, further, the matter of von Thoma, the German commander who was captured at Alamein. Montgomery shook hands with him, took him to supper at his headquarters —and this was photographed. There was astonishment and incomprehension in England when the picture was published. Montgomery was asked to explain. What was he doing— making friends with enemy generals? It looked like treachery. Was not von Thoma another of the Nazi beasts who was murdering women and children? Montgomery's duty was to strike him down with loathing—not fête him with buns and marmalade. In England the war was a war of emotion, a war of hating.

To Montgomery it was quite different. Nothing so untidy as emotion should distract the General. Soldiering was a professional job to be conducted coldly and clearly. Once his opponent was defeated in battle he ceased to be of any interest; no point in hating him or getting excited about him—especially if he had fought hard. He was finished, and that was that. But in one way he could be of considerable use (Montgomery argued): he could assist in making a check on the errors and successes of the battle tactics.

Accordingly, as soon as von Thoma was seated at the supper-table, Montgomery began aiming questions at him. Had the Germans expected attack? And in what place? What did the Germans think of the use of the British armour? How was

Rommel affected by it all? Maps were brought in and they began to fight the battle over again, two professionals discussing a championship match. Montgomery explained his plan; von Thoma responded. By the time the meeting broke up the British general was in possession of a great deal of information about how the enemy fought; more than this, he had discovered something of the mystery he was always probing—the mentality of his opponents, especially the arch-opponent Rommel's. To Montgomery the rumpus over his talk with von Thoma was sheer nonsense. He felt he had done well out of it; he had gathered a number of valuable points for the next battle.

The incident gave him one other thing as well—a stronger awareness of the role of the Press and propaganda in warfare. As with most British generals the Press and the Radio had been to Montgomery a closed book: they fulfilled somewhat the same functions as the strolling troubadour in olden days who, after the battle was over, sat by the camp-fire with his guitar and wove pleasant and romantic stories around the heroic deeds of the soldiers. They were the light appendages of civilization but not to be confused with the serious business of making war.

Latterly as a general he had shifted his ground somewhat: the Press was valuable in maintaining morale. It could be used. Of itself the Press had no validity, no entity, no mission any more than the Morse Code had a mission: it was simply a signalling set for transmitting news to the people at large according to the desires and requirements of the commanders and the leaders. Accordingly it was necessary for the Press to function efficiently. He issued orders that the war correspondents must be kept fully informed and given all possible facilities.

Thus at one stroke, without any real sympathy with or understanding of the Press (as the Press regarded itself), Montgomery cut straight to the heart of the matter. He never questioned the loyalty or the goodwill of the Press. Again it was his Socratic approach: the Press had only to report the activities of the Eighth Army and morale would improve and all would be well. And in point of fact this turned out to be so. By an altogether foreign method of reasoning the General had arrived at the conclusion that pleased everyone. The dangerous question of the freedom of the Press, the right of the Press to criticize and publish conflicting points of view, never arose because the issues in war are simple, one-sided issues and Montgomery was always winning victories.

Napoleon, on leaving Paris to command in Italy, is reported to have said to a journalist: "In the accounts of our victories be careful not to speak of anyone but *me*, always *me*, you understand". Nothing of that sort ever happened with Montgomery. No correspondent was ever obliged to write to order in Montgomery's armies, none was ever dismissed or even disciplined by his orders. Actually Montgomery held only two Press conferences in the African campaign, and he saw the journalists much less frequently than the other Allied commanders. It was simply that he was one of those few people who inevitably of themselves are news.

As with the Press, so with most of the other technical departments under Montgomery's command. He did not possess a notably detailed knowledge of engineering, of signaliing, of medicine, of ballistics or logistics or any of the other intensely intricate departments of a modern army, except possibly infantry tactics. His knowledge was general and he deliberately kept it general. As soon as he was confronted with a technicality he at once demanded, "Who is the expert? Bring him here." On the arrival of the expert he looked him over shrewdly. Moving on the presumption that a man of character and decision will be good at whatever job he is doing he looked for these virtues in the expert. Finding them he would say shortly: "Very well. You know all about it. You take charge." Which was stimulating for the expert and made him work keenly. This was why Montgomery was so exceptionally successful in the selection of his subordinates.

About this time he formed his Army staff and in many ways it was the oddest group of men who were ever put into an army command. It included two Oxford dons, a particularly shrewd business man, a group of quite untutored adolescents and one or two most irregular regular soldiers. Some of them were undoubtedly Montgomery's intellectual superiors, but, as with everyone else who worked close to him, they were devoted. They were the experts and they were allowed to work without interference. Consequently they found Montgomery the best of masters. Few of them ever left him so long as the war continued. As the months went by they were close knit together under de Guingand into a highly skilled team. A very great deal of Montgomery's success lay in his headquarters. At any crisis he had the enormous advantage of simply taking his decision and handing it over for its implementation to this smoothly running organization.

It was one of Montgomery's ideas that as soon as you have picked your team you must stick to it. And so he carried this team with him wherever he went. Thus he was never a "one-man" general such as the public imagined him to be. His word was law at his headquarters, but at the same time he was entirely dependent on his subordinates and he was intensely loyal to them to the end. As they followed his star upwards he saw to it that they shared the honours and the promotions.

In one other respect this headquarters was a break with tradition. For a very long time up to and including this war it had been the practice of British generals to appoint to their staffs wealthy and influential young men, the sons of dukes and earls and baronets. And sometimes these young men, especially when they entered politics, were useful to the generals in later life. One does not suggest that there was any bribery and corruption about this, but the fact remained that many generals were to be found in the fashionable houses of England after their wars were done. It was simply an extension of the "old school tie" system, the system of a social class looking after its own.

With this business Montgomery would have no truck at all. No one with a title got on to his staff. Pure merit was the only way of getting there and staying there. He was entirely devoid of snobbery, entirely uninterested in money and not at all concerned about his future career outside the Army.

At the time he took over the Army command Montgomery decided on one more innovation. He created a Tactical Head-quarters where he lived quite apart from and some miles forward (*i.e.* nearer the front) of his Main Headquarters where de Guingand presided.

The object of this was to give the C.-in-C. "time to think". He already possessed unusual powers of mental detachment and this was a move to take this meditative process one step further. Tactical and Main Headquarters seldom linked up until the Army reached the Baltic in Germany at the end of the war.

Tactical Headquarters was a tiny camp. Montgomery lived there with his cook, his batman, his chauffeurs and a small group of young men who were his aides, his secretaries and his liaison officers. Together they formed a kind of personal body-guard and information corps. No one approaching Mont-gomery's own age, no other general or commander, ever lived with him ; he was entirely surrounded by very young men. Except for senior officers no one without previous authorization was allowed within the precincts of the camp. All visitors except Royalty and those of Cabinet level were usually for-bidden. Usually, if a general wished to see the C.-in-C. he had first to go to de Guingand. It was rare even for de Guingand to spend more than a night or two at Tactical Head-quarters.

Within this isolation and seclusion Montgomery lived according to his strict routine: the 6 a.m. cup of tea, the hour of lying in bed and thinking, then breakfast and out in his car at 8.30. Most of the day he spent along the front and he was back in his headquarters for tea. From tea until dinner he was telephoning de Guingand and the Corps commanders, receiving information and laying down orders and plans for the next day. Following this, de Guingand would hold his own evening conference at Main Headquarters. After dinner Montgomery would listen to the reports of his liaison officers. Then to bed at 9 p.m. to write his diary, to read a novel and to think again. He was very healthy, he never overworked and he never worried about anything without immediately translating his thoughts into action and so getting done with the matter.

He lived comfortably in three motorized caravans which followed him wherever he went. Two of them were captured from the Italian generals Messe and Bergonzoli and the other was sent out from England. One vehicle contained his bed and his bath, another was his office, his personal "war room" fitted with maps, and the third was for the use of his overnight guests. All three vehicles were comfortably fitted with coconut mats, stoves, fans, radio, and canvas chairs.

Life in the camp was far from being the ascetic régime that most people imagined. The food was excellent. His aides and young officers had their own mess, their bar, and they gambled and amused themselves with games much as any other men would. At times there was a large collection of pets, even cows and horses, around the caravans.

Montgomery's attitude towards his personal staff was very much that of a father or a housemaster. He was deeply inter-ested in all their affairs: their girl friends, their escapades and their occasional outbursts of misconduct. One of them, a lad named John Poston, who had been with him since his first days in the desert, he loved deeply. They were all athletic young soldiers chosen for their bravery, their initiative, their manners and their independence.

On the face of it this little *corps d'élite* around the com-mander was a most dangerous experiment. They received particular favours, they had unusual powers. They were "the eyes and ears" of the C.-in-C. Each morning they drove out to the farthermost parts of the front, checked the maps, gathered and transmitted information and then returned to report to Montgomery in the late afternoon. From his point of view the scheme was most valuable, since each evening he was put in possession of the latest first-hand news from the entire front.

The commanders of the soldiers in the field might not have looked upon the arrangement so favourably. These young men had the ear of the C.-in-C. They were his agents. They had *carte blanche* to travel everywhere and see everything. They were on nodding terms with all the senior generals and even some of the politicians who visited Montgomery's camp. Clearly the system was open to abuse.

In actual practice nothing of the sort occurred. The men were very junior, they were modest and they did not gossip; Montgomery drove them hard, at crises tremendously hard. In their jeeps each day they often had to chart their courses through no-man's-land in order to get to the outlying pickets and they were constantly in danger, which is probably the final purifier of venality and materialism.

They lived in a world where they had to expect death, and as time went on a shockingly high percentage of them did die.

All of them were utterly devoted to Montgomery. They accepted the paternal arrangement as a thing quite natural and spontaneous, and presently there grew up in the camp an atmosphere of curiously monastic obedience and affection, the atmosphere of a large Victorian family house, such as, let us say, Bishop's Court in Tasmania or Bishopsbourne at Chiswick. It was the final keynote in this latest pattern of Montgomery's life.

Five years had now elapsed since the death of his wife: years for the most part of bitterness and private grief, the years of renouncement and isolation and defiance; and also the years of professional disappointment in Palestine and Dunkirk; the years without kindness or a home.

But now at the Christmas of 1942 he had pitted himself in an immense gamble and won. He had vindicated in front of all the world the ideas of a lifetime. After Alamein he had been made a Knight and created a full General. Honours had flowed upon him in an avalanche. Messages had come from his King, from his Prime Minister and from all over the Empire. The struggle for recognition was over.

True he jeopardized his reputation in the risk of each new battle, but now he was more certain of himself than ever and now he had the power and the freedom. And something else had arrived, possibly the most important thing of all. The balance was coming back into his life again: the lost affection was returning. This time it was the affection not of one person but of a hundred thousand. He had performed the extraordinary process of making his private life entirely public. It was almost as if he had contracted a public marriage with his Army.

Every hour of the day he was surrounded by men who respected him, admired him and perhaps even loved him. Every time he drove out in his car he was confronted by soldiers; all looking towards him, knowing him, standing ready to obey orders. Could he regard them as anything else but his family? Here they were alone in the desert together. This was their pilgrimage. Could he do any other but lead them, look after them, take them on from one success to another? He had lost one great and private affection. A host of others had flowed in upon him. He was no longer a private individual. He belonged to the soldiers. This was HIS Army and he was THEIR General. Together, he and they would see this thing through to the end.

Thus went the orders of the day and the little impromptu speeches to the soldiers along the desert tracks. And just at the stage where the atmosphere might have become delirious and sentimental to the point of mysticism, that hard, clear, shrewd Protestant brain cracked down and the Commander-in-Chief addressed himself to the problem of getting up sufficient ammunition to undertake the next engagement.

5

Rommel's situation after the Battle of Alamein was, as the saying goes, hopeless but not critical. He had only one resource —to retreat. He retreated fighting, laying minefields as he went. In that immense desolation, with seven hundred miles of desert behind them and another seven hundred miles to go before they reached Tripoli, the war for the British became a quartermaster's war. How to get the supplies to the front? That was the governing and overriding question behind every move.

Just before Christmas the Eighth Army advanced on the Agheila position.

The New Zealanders made a forced march across the desert—a "left hook"—and laid a net around the Axis Army, but Rommel slipped through in the dark and again the chase went on. The psychological effect on the British, when they had passed this point where two armies before them had been flung back, was immense. Now they were certain they could succeed, and at Christmas Montgomery sent out a message to the troops :

"It is wonderful what has been achieved since the 23rd October, when we started the Battle of Egypt.

"I have received a Christmas greeting from Hull, in Yorkshire. It is quite the nicest I have ever received: 'Dear Sir, to wish you and our lads of the Eighth Army a very happy Christmas. Good health. Good luck. And by the Grace of God, VICTORY in 1943. Keep 'em on the run, Monty. Best wishes from a Yorkshire lass with a lad in the Eighth Army.'

"What better Christmas greeting can I send on to you than the one from the Yorkshire lass?"

And again he urged them to hasten on towards Tripoli. But now, for the second time, in the first week in January the weather came in on the Axis side. An immense storm flooded and sank the British ships in Benghazi harbour, the principal, indeed the only supply port of the British. By now they were six hundred miles from Benghazi and the Nile was another six hundred miles farther back; Tripoli was two hundred miles in front of them. Montgomery admits that this was the moment in the campaign when he almost lost heart. The risks were immense. War in the desert could react like an electrical storm. Overnight a victory could be turned into complete disaster. In this exposed position thirst and the lack of petrol could wipe out the soldiers by the tens of thousand. Either Montgomery had to get to the port of Tripoli quickly or turn back. He demanded ten days' supplies from his quartermasters. They said it was impossible; Benghazi was useless. He suggested Tobruk, two hundred and fifty miles farther back, as a supply port. Too far, he was told, no transport to bring the supplies on overland—a week's drive for an army truck. Montgomery abandoned half his Army. The entire Tenth Corps was grounded at Benghazi and its vehicles were handed over to the supply corps for the long haul between Tobruk and the front.

The General waited until he had just ten days' supplies and then on January 15th attacked Rommel's position at Wadi Zem Zem. It was realized that if it failed to get through to Tripoli by January 25th the Army was finished. Concealing his anxiety Montgomery raised another battle-cry to his soldiers. "Nothing has stopped us since the Battle of Egypt", he exclaimed. "Nothing will stop us now. ON TO TRIPOLI."

Again it was a battle of the left hook followed by the punch along the coast. While half his slender force made an inland wheeling march across fantastically difficult country where vehicles had to be jacked across ravines and quicksands, Montgomery himself took command on the coast. Both forces broke through to Tripoli on January 23rd with just two days to spare.

It was a victory to stretch the imagination. After years of defeat Alamein had turned the course of the war. And now that success had been sealed with a desert march of 1400 miles —a march that no general in history had ever accomplished before. The casualties were extraordinarily light, although some of the best leaders like Harding were wounded, others dead. Tripoli fell precisely three months after Alamein. Montgomery had been in the desert just under a hundred and fifty days. From Tripoli he spoke to the troops—"Once again I thank you from the bottom of my heart".

Back in August, Churchill, then staying for the night at the headquarters at Burg el Arab, had written in Montgomery's autograph book: "May the anniversary of Blenheim, which marks the opening of the new command, bring to the Commander-in-Chief of the Eighth Army and his troops the fame and fortune they will surely deserve".

Now, flying down to Tripoli from England in the first week of February to congratulate the Desert Army, the Prime Minister added another page which he headed "Chapter Two".

"On this night in Tripoli the Desert Army reported the completion of all its tasks hitherto set them, the enemy being driven out of Egypt, Cyrenaica and Tripolitania and all his establishments captured or destroyed.

"These memorable events fulfil the wish I expressed on an earlier page and are, I trust, the prelude to a still more glorious chapter."

6

The chapter followed almost at once. With Tripoli in his hands and rapidly opening up as a supply port, Montgomery headed straight for Tunisia where the British First Army and several American divisions were already fighting. By now he had the measure of Rommel and the technique of desert fighting. Four months earlier (before Alamein) he had told Wendell Willkie that he admired Rommel but that the German commander had one grave fault in that he "tended to repeat his tactics". This was true enough since there are not many novel tactics one can employ when one has lost the initiative and is in retreat.

Up to now war in the desert had fallen into a neat and comprehensive design. For the most part the armies were very evenly matched and battles tended to repeat themselves. There was even a certain equilibrium in the swaying mobility of it all.

In that vast and empty space commanders moved their forces as though they were playing some monstrous game of chess; and Montgomery emerged as the successful player, not because he broke the rules of war or invented new ones, but because he paid the most painstaking attention to the rules and because he had that kind of professional patience which never gives way to an emotional impulse, but waits for the eventual loosening of the will in the opponent. While Montgomery was enjoying at home the reputation of being a daring and unorthodox commander, he was pursuing his campaign in Africa in the most practical and level-headed way.

The outward appearance was showy and dramatic; the core was unromantic logic. And now the pendulum of the desert war was about to be swung back forever.

Rommel (who had achieved a parallel reputation in Germany) was an entirely different sort of leader. Unlike Montgomery, he could never leave the details to his subordinates. He was forever jumping into his car or his tank and driving from unit to unit at the height of an engagement, altering his orders, trying experiments, shifting his ground. It was to a great extent an emotional leadership based on flair, an *ad hoc* inspiration. He was not really an Army general: a Corps command was nearer his level and at that level he was extremely resourceful and dangerous. But he was ill-equippd for this long waiting game, and a set-piece battle with all its hundred complications was foreign to his temperament. Even more than Montgomery he was a worshipper of mobility and he had a gambler's instinct for daring innovation. And now as both Allied Armies ground down upon him—the First from Tunisia and the Eighth from the desert—the opportunities for innovation became less and less. He was ill with desert sores. His *will* was wounded. Sooner or later he was bound to commit some act of folly.

About a month before the fall of Tripoli, Montgomery's staff began to plan the battle of Mareth. It was foreseen that, if Tripoli fell, Rommel would no doubt continue his retreat directly to the Tunisian border and there entrench himself in the old French fortifications. Except that this time it was the British who were at the end of a long line of communication, the situation resembled Alamein, and the ensuing battle followed roughly the same course. All February went by in preparation. Then, on March 6th, Rommel committed his act of folly: as at Alam Halfa he struck first, and precisely at a moment when Montgomery had got his reserves into the line. The Germans came on in a massed charge of tanks.

Montgomery was almost conversational in his address which was read out to the troops:

"I did not expect for one moment that the enemy would attack us", he said. "It seemed absurd. But he has done it and we must show our gratitude in no uncertain way."

Yet the moment was critical, and he insisted, "There must be NO WITHDRAWAL anywhere, and, of course, NO SURRENDER". Let the Army just stand firm; Rommel would be crippled and "THEN IT WILL BE OUR TURN TO ATTACK HIM". Once again there was to be no pursuit of the enemy after the assault was beaten off. By this time Montgomery had a magnificent instrument to play with in the Eighth Army. Morale was at its zenith. In an extraordinary outburst of courage the gunners withstood the charge, demolished fifty German tanks outright and the whole attack was flung off balance.

Then a fortnight later the British released the coiled spring again: a heavy direct punch to involve the enemy on the coast and then a circular flanking movement through the inland desert. It looked at first as though things were going wrong. The coastal attack was rolled back. General Leese came to the C.-in-C. at two in the morning with the alarming news that the soldiers had foundered in a wadi; there had been no time to get the anti-tank guns across before the enemy counter-attacked with tanks. Relentlessly Montgomery dismissed the general in charge, plugged the breakage with reserves and sent forty thousand men and two hundred tanks round on the left hook. At the time it seemed a hazardous move to fling all the weight into the left while the right was being hard pressed, but Montgomery was determined to fight the battle according to his own plan and not Rommel's. Success was almost instantaneous. In many ways it was due to the Air Force. Although Montgomery had achieved a closer liaison with the Air than any commander before him, there had been some bickering over the question of whether or not the fliers should come down low to blitz the ground in front of the advancing troops. One group of Air Force leaders believed that low flying was too expensive in pilots and machines and opposed Montgomery in the matter. Air Vice-Marshal Broadhurst, however, was on the spot and was persuaded that the risk was worth while at Mareth—and so it turned out. Nevertheless the happy issue of the affair did not endear Montgomery to his opponents.

The pursuit streamed on again, this time heading northwards up the coast towards Tunis. Within a fortnight the Eighth Army had reached Gabes Gap, the last defensive position in the south. Again the coiling of the spring, again the sudden strike. This time the assault went in under a black moonless night. Rommel by now had given up. Sick and disillusioned he had flown off to Germany, and there remained in Africa no enemy commander of sufficient calibre to delay the onrush of the Allies. Gabes was a snap success against a collapsing foe. The Eighth Army raced across the battlefield and on past Sfax and Sousse, another hundred miles to the north. And there at last in the spring, within six months of their departure from Alamein and after a march of nearly two thousand miles, they struck the mountains. Of the original German Afrika Korps virtually nothing remained. It was the first decisive victory of the British in the war. It was the last time the British were to be asked to fight alone.

CHAPTER TEN

TOWARDS THE GATES OF ROME

I

IN the late spring of 1943 Montgomery flew home to England for a few days to discover that, after a lifetime of anonymity in the Army, he had become a national hero.

His family and his intimate friends who had known him since he was a young man were astonished at his success. It almost seemed as if some trick had been played. Whatever could have happened to Bernard? Whoever would have dreamed that he had it in him? He had been rather difficult at times and very keen on his job, but there had certainly been nothing remarkable about him before this. Very definitely he was not a prodigy as a child. He was never really brilliant at school and he never seemed to take much interest in books or politics or making speeches.

They were even more astonished when they observed the aplomb with which Bernard accepted all the honours and the assurance with which he moved in his new exalted circles. Here he was making speeches. Visiting Buckingham Palace to receive his Knighthood, paying calls at Downing Street. Whatever could have happened to Bernard?

A few leaders in the Army, like Wavell, who had appraised Montgomery's military ability long ago, could say they were not surprised. A few, like Burnett-Stuart, could remark sagely: "Genius never shows itself until it is given the opportunity"; or perhaps more aptly, "Genius is the capacity for taking infinite pains, and that is the one thing Montgomery has done all his life". But for the rest, Montgomery's sudden rise was a startling piece of evidence that many of us pass through life without making any real contact with the people around us, even those by whom we are intimately known and loved. It might seem to us that we pass on to others all our hopes and fears, that they understand us and accept our own valuation of ourselves, or at least a valuation that is fair and reasonable; and that, at the end of life, we have said nearly all we had to say, and done nearly all that we could have done within the scope of the luck allotted to us. But then, in the course of things, some tragedy or disappointment intervenes and suddenly we discover then how much we are alone and unable to communicate. A vague and frightening loneliness ensues when nothing in the world seems of interest, and this persists until we are rescued by routine habits and the little hedonistic pleasures of life.

Perhaps this despair presses most heavily in adolescence when we have so few habits and when the vision of what we might do in life is strongest and our capacity for disappointment is most acute. But then the adolescent dream is thrust down by the material necessity of making a living. It is appeased a little by a love affair or the distraction of pleasure or the illusory sense of power as we advance in our careers or even in our hopes for our children, and in the end it is forgotten: all that we might have been, all that we really hoped for and all our inmost desires in life become as strange to us as they would be to other people. And we accept what we have become as inevitable and true to ourselves. Yet might it not be that we are no more than a mass of habits and adjustments to society, that we have imprisoned our real individuality which nevertheless goes on living somewhere in the background, growing weaker and weaker until we die? Just occasionally and with a few people the true individuality suddenly bursts out, and because we do not know the intimate and secret history in these people's lives we are amazed at what they do.

Montgomery, far less than most people, had revealed himself to the outside world. His life had been lived in very definite separate compartments. His family saw him as the strong-willed and boisterous little boy. They knew very little of the military side of his career where he exhibited a quite different character. To his wife again he showed another side of his nature, something analogous perhaps to his relationship to his father. And, remote from his family, the Army and even from his marriage, there was clearly something else which he had never been able to share with anyone, a certain intensely serious determination to impose his will on other people.

These four attributes, his capacity for struggling, for working, for affection and for power, like an unruly team of horses, had been pulling for a long time in different directions or unequal combinations, never achieving a balance. Now in his middle fifties, by a combination of persistence and good luck, the whole team pulls together and Montgomery alone was unastonished by what was happening to him. This was one of the easier parts of the road.

His visit to England was a military secret, but it was soon learned that he was staying at Claridge's Hotel in London, and crowds began gathering round the doors to watch him pass by.

Ever since the beginning of the war the people had been hungry for a military hero to balance the political hero they had found in Churchill. Here was one ready-made and, moreover, a general full of delightful idiosyncrasies, a man who responded to admiration. When he went to the theatre in his beret he stopped the show. When he appeared in the streets, people rushed forward to shout "Monty". The usual number of witless women wrote letters offering marriage. In the desert Montgomery had personally answered his letters in his own handwriting (except the marriage offers which were not answered at all). Now the correspondence became overwhelming and his A.D.C.s were forced to struggle with it each day.

It had only to be known that he wanted something—a dog, an article of clothing, a car—for gifts to come pouring in from all over England. Many people eagerly offered to replace the books he had lost in his bombed house at Portsmouth. Oceans of bad verse were written about him. Publishers offered him large sums for his memoirs (one offer from America was for £25,000). Charities besieged him to make personal appearances, or confer his patronage. Many millions of words were written about him in the newspapers. His mother and his family were interviewed. Every day his photograph appeared somewhere and presently all Britain and the Empire knew that thin ascetic face. He was a public character and the accent was on the character.

Numberless funny stories about him went the rounds of the pubs and the clubs, most of them variations on the theme of his abstemiousness, his severity and his overwhelming self-confidence. Anyone who had known him from any distance in the past raked up some yarn, some colourful tit-bit. There was the time he had ruthlessly flung civilians out of their houses in the Southern Command and filled the windows with cement. There was the officer whom Montgomery had court-martialled for speaking to his wife while he was on parade. There was the description of the lives of his staff who were forbidden to smoke or drink alcoholic liquor or consort with women, a chastened and fearful little group of prisoners who were compelled to attend morning and evening prayers and dared not cough while Montgomery read the lesson. There were the oppressed Army clerks who took one puff of their cigarettes—and then kicked the butts under the mat when Montgomery came into the room. There were the stories of the sackings, the stories of rows between Montgomery and Alexander.

TALKING TO CANADIAN TROOPS IN SICILY

AT ALGIERS, 1943

Left to right : Mr. Anthony Eden, Sir Alan Brooke, Air Chief Marshal Tedder, Admiral Sir Andrew Cunningham, General Marshall, General Eisenhower, General Montgomery, Mr. Churchill in centre

"How is the battle going?" someone is reported to have asked. The reply: "According to schedule. It started at six and Monty sacked the brigadier at ten."

To Churchill was ascribed the line about him: "In defeat unthinkable, in victory insufferable". And it was related with glee how Montgomery had been appalled at the billows of cigar smoke and alcoholic fumes with which Churchill had filled his tent in the desert. Montgomery's "You and I will see this thing through together" became a catch-line for the wits, and there were half a dozen after-dinner stories of how he had ascended to heaven to dethrone the Almighty.

Montgomery was now "placed" irrevocably in the public mind as a martinet, an eccentric and something of a braggart of the Cyrano de Bergerac variety. Yet perversely he was liked and admired for these qualities, and no one ever questioned his honesty, his piety, his simplicity or the palpable facts of his military success. There was something in this make-up, perhaps the absence of snobbery and military formality, which appealed strongly to the crowds and they loved him. The slight touch of malice in the funny stories tended if anything to increase his popularity.

The genuine opposition came almost entirely from the top and from Whitehall and the West End of London. Uneasy politicians scented an autocrat, a military dictator who was getting too big for his boots. What would happen if he entered politics? The General returning home at the head of a successful army had been a menace since the days of Rome. In the Regular Army there were dark misgivings. Elderly generals saw in him the upstart, the bombastic and reckless wrecker of tradition. In the Navy and the Air Force too there were many who regarded him as vulgarly flamboyant, a film-star commander who was all too ready to seize the credit. Was not Alexander really the man? Was not Alexander the actual brain behind the success?

From the top of the American command there was also some slight coldness. This guy seemed to think he knew everything. It was felt that too much limelight was being grabbed by the British Eighth Army and its unblushing commander.

For the moment this antagonism was not strong; the facts of Montgomery's extraordinary success could hardly be brooked. In the face of the cold and pressing danger of the war it was seen in the Cabinet Defence Committee that this horse must be allowed to gallop on a little longer, although from now on the curb might be usefully applied from time to time.

6

2

For the next nine months, from the spring of 1943 until the end of the year, Montgomery was principally engaged in fighting the Sicilian and Italian campaigns. Throughout this period he was acting under orders: the plans for the most part were not his own. Consequently it was a period of argument and dissension. He believed neither in the strategy nor in the tactics as laid down by Allied Headquarters. Sometimes he got his own way; sometimes he failed. Outwardly he continued in the same way, an inspirational general leading his men to the conquest of one city after another, always advancing, always successful in the battle. Unknown to the public and the Army itself he was carrying on with some gusto a guerrilla campaign against his superiors. There was nothing very personal or acrimonious about it, but great issues were at stake and the memoranda flew thick and fast between Eisenhower's base at Algiers and Eighth Army Headquarters.

After the fall of Tripoli and the successful landing of the Allied Forces in North Africa, an entirely new and experimental chain of command was set up, and it persisted until the end of the European war. One must recall it briefly to clarify Montgomery's position. It was a three-decker structure. On the first stage sat Roosevelt and General Marshall in Washington and Churchill and Field-Marshal Alan Brooke in London. Theirs was the world to play with. Assisted by their retinues of experts they decided such momentous questions as where the United States should first commit her main effort—in Europe or the Pacific. On the next stage sat Eisenhower and Alexander at their combined Anglo-American headquarters, and theirs was the responsibility of carrying out the strategy in Europe. Upon the third stage were the operational generals like Patton and Montgomery whose duty was to fight the actual battles.

Inevitably the three stages overlapped. Hardly anyone was willing to stay in his place. Churchill particularly (as in the previous war) was apt to go shooting up and down the scale at a bewildering rate, at one moment urging on the soldiers at the front, at the next carrying out delicate negotiations with the ambassadors in London. Both Eisenhower and Alexander also were prone to step down from the strategy and take a hand at the tactics. Patton and Montgomery, having no convenient stages below them, reversed the current and expressed strong views on the general conduct of the war.

Unavoidably, since they lay in the centre, Eisenhower and Alexander became sandwiched between the upper and the nether layers. While Washington and London kept tugging them this way and that for political reasons, Montgomery and Patton were demanding more power and greater freedom of action in the field. Fortunately both Eisenhower and Alexander had the ideal temperaments to withstand this two-way barrage, but they walked a thin tight-rope at times. They stood between the politics and the battle. They were the governors who simultaneously regulated the driver and the motor. They were the translators who explained the politician to the soldier and the soldier to the politician. On the whole it is remarkable that there were so few quarrels. It was only when Eisenhower and Alexander stepped off the dividing line, when they encroached on the actual fighting (as in Italy) or on the politics (as at Algiers), when they abandoned the generality for the detail on either side, that, occasionally, the results were not so happy.

Montgomery's first contact with the Americans had passed off very well indeed. At Tripoli he had lectured a group of visiting generals on how he had won the desert war, and since the generals were new to war he made a considerable impression.

At Gabes Eisenhower had flown down to spend a night at Tactical Headquarters, and the charm, the modesty and the honesty of the Allied Commander-in-Chief had done its work. There followed the incident of the Flying Fortress which, though it irritated the Allied Command at the time, was not very serious. In a light-hearted moment General Bedell Smith, Eisenhower's Chief of Staff, had promised Montgomery a Fortress for his personal use if he got to Sfax on April 15th. Montgomery arrived five days ahead of schedule and demanded his prize. This was embarrassing to the Americans; they were hardly entitled to go betting with Flying Fortresses, and in any event every machine was wanted at that moment for the subjection of Tunis. This was pointed out to Montgomery. He replied that a bet was a bet and insisted on the delivery of the plane. Understandably nettled, the Americans paid up eventually and the Fortress with its crew of eight (to be maintained at the expense of the United States) arrived at Tactical Headquarters. For some months Montgomery flew about in it between Africa and England. At Allied Headquarters one or two people began to put Montgomery down as a pretty tough dealer.

The bad feeling between the British Eighth and First Armies went a good deal further. For months, while the Eighth Army was making its prodigious advance across the desert, the First

Army under General Anderson had been stuck in the mud and
the mountains of Tunisia. In addition, the desert soldiers were
veterans, while many of Anderson's men were new to fighting.
Inevitably Montgomery's Army captured the headlines in the
Press, and a few of the Eighth Army soldiers no doubt behaved
a little arrogantly when they arrived at Tunisia. It was bitterly
galling for the First Army soldiers who had had so much hard
fighting and so many casualties in the mountains. A good deal
of this bad feeling was directed against Montgomery himself,
indeed it took him many months to overcome.

Some of the First Army units like the 78th Division were
very fine formations, but until Alexander arrived to take
command there was a lack of cohesion in Tunisia. With all its
tremendous experience and morale the Eighth Army itself found
the mountains a formidable obstacle when at last it arrived
at Enfidaville to the north of Sousse. A useless battering against
the heights began and, with a good deal of grim satisfaction,
the First Army saw the desert soldiers turned back.

But Enfidaville was, in fact, an impossible proposition.
Montgomery and de Guingand very soon suggested that they
should desist and instead divert four of their best divisions to
the First Army command where they could be used for the easier
assault upon Tunis along the Majerda Valley. Time was pressing. The remainder of the Eighth Army was due to regroup
for the landing in Sicily. The offer was accepted and Tunis fell
on May 7th.

Meanwhile the first real difference of opinion between
Montgomery and the Allied Command had arisen over the
Sicilian invasion. In April, while his Tactical Headquarters
were still at Enfidaville, Montgomery sent de Guingand back
to the Nile Delta with a planning staff to work out the details
of the operation. De Guingand, on receiving the Allied Headquarters' plan, quickly made up his mind that it would not do.
It was proposed to make two separate landings: Montgomery
with the Eighth at Gela on the southern coast, and the Americans under Patton far away to the west near Palermo. To
Montgomery (who warmly agreed with de Guingand) the
whole essence of a landing was concentration. If you sent your
armies ashore at different places they were in danger of being
destroyed piecemeal before they could link up. He believed
that during the early critical period you must make one concentrated blow. The two armies should land side by side at
Gela; then the Americans could wheel north-west to the capture
of Palermo and the British north-east to seize Catania, the
second biggest city. Signals and messages began to flow briskly

back and forth between Montgomery and the Allied Command. Things were running fast towards a deadlock when Eisenhower wisely decided that he would listen to the rival arguments in Algiers.

De Guingand, deputed as Montgomery's spokesman, set off by air from Egypt armed with his dossier—and crashed in the desert near El Adem. Weakened by months of overwork, injured in the crash, he was taken away to hospital. Hurriedly, General Leese was put into his place and flown to Algiers. For some time the arguments flowed back and forth, but in the end, in this first contest with the Higher Command, Montgomery won his point: the two armies would land side by side.

On July 11th, under the full midsummer heat of the Mediterranean sun, the adventure began.

3

In Sicily the oranges were on the trees. The street barrows were laden with melons and peaches and vivid flowers. In the crumbling villages and among the unending olive groves the peasants were driving their ox-carts, spreading out their tomatoes to dry in the brilliant sun, gossiping in the shade of the church, gossiping round the water wells. There was ice-cream for sale, chickens and eggs and wine. Girls in gay colours were hanging out of the upper windows among the flowering creepers; on the cobblestones below priests trotted by on dusty donkeys. All the ox-carts were painted with allegorical pictures full of bright and bulbous angels and swarthy shepherds.

Like the Israelites coming out of the desert the Eighth Army gazed on the scene with delight. And Montgomery, like a prophet, kept riding among the soldiers urging them to keep their eyes off these pleasures and get on with the battle. The first landing had come through with a rush but a choppy sea was running and the boat commanders were protesting that they could not get the heavy equipment ashore. Montgomery sent for the commanders on the beach. They *had* to get their cargoes ashore. He did not care how they did it but the equipment had to be delivered within twenty-four hours. That was the deadline. No excuses would be acceptable. Angrily he went off in search of others who needed bullying.

It was usually the same during a critical moment: he would listen to no arguments; he seemed oblivious of any losses he took and he was quite capable of dismissing anyone—even a general—on the spot. Then when the peak of the crisis passed

most of his irritation and unreasonableness passed as well.
These outbursts were reserved for the senior officers; the
soldiers knew nothing of them and quite possibly, as they
cheered him along the road, they would have relished the
information that he had just been extremely insulting to one of
their commanding officers.

And now, as they pitched the Germans off the Primasole
Bridge and ran on across the malarial plains of Lentini to
Catania, that same crusading atmosphere of the desert came
back into the Eighth Army. There were many newcomers, the
Canadians, the 5th and the 78th Divisions and the French
Goums who cheerfully went about behind the enemy lines
cutting people's throats without particular reference to
whether or not the victims were enemies. The combining
element of the Army staff remained the same. In addition to
de Guingand there were Richards who controlled the armour,
White the signals, Graham the supplies, Williams the intelligence, and Belchem and a group of others the operations. It
was growing into a large headquarters now and there were
many young colonels and majors and captains who had become
avid disciples of the Montgomery technique. General Dempsey
was among the new commanders who had come out from
England, and a particularly able young Canadian, General
Simmonds. Of the old desert divisions the Australians had gone
out to the Pacific, and the New Zealanders, South Africans and
the Indians were due to arrive later, but the British 50th had
come in with the assault along with the 51st Highlanders.
These were a *corps d'élite* who, with such commanders as
Horrocks and Dempsey, were going to persist with Montgomery
until the end of the war.

The Eighth Army was an extraordinarily water-tight
combine, almost a private club. Here and there it fell on bad
days and bad country in bad weather. Occasionally for short
periods it came up against better combinations of soldiers and
from time to time it grew tired. But it was forever renewing
itself with new members, and by the end of 1943 nearly every
part of the Empire had sent contingents into its ranks. To wear
the Africa Star, to carry the Eighth Army Shield on one's
jacket, had become a matter of some pride; and when General
Graham came to write to Montgomery at the end of it all he
said simply: "Under your command I have never been asked
to do anything but advance".

In the last resort the Eighth Army (and subsequently
21 Army Group) succeeded not perhaps so much because it
contained such ruthless and determined leaders as Freyberg,

but because of its continuity under the one command, its one continuing purpose.

Essentially it was a professional army with an elaborate network of empirical habits. To be a member of it gave one a sense not only of security but a sense of privilege as well. Montgomery described it as "a family", and in the simple acceptance of that idea he went about administering blame and punishment, encouragement and damnation, as though he were a feudal Irish landlord.

It was an extraordinary experience to go riding out with him along the dusty Sicilian roads. He would set out in an open car soon after breakfast with one of his A.D.C.s, either Poston, Henderson or Chavasse. His pennant fluttered on the bonnet and a large parcel of cigarettes was perched beside him on the back seat. Motor-cycles ran ahead to clear the road of the ox-carts and incredible numbers of Italian children. High on the left rose the stupendous jet-black peak of Etna, smoking quietly, all around spread the vineyards and the orchards rising tier on tier to the overhanging villages; and here on the coast itself the vivid colours of the sea, the ancient fishing hamlets, the flowers and the mouldering churches in the hot sun.

Montgomery had eyes for none of these things. A group of soldiers mending a bridge would catch his notice and as they looked up and shouted to one another, "There's Monty", he would order the car to stop.

"What unit is this?"

Such and such a company of field engineers.

"When will the job be finished?"

To-morrow night or the night after.

"Why not to-night?"

Because they were waiting for a load of girders to come up. Then, to the young officer who had hurried up perspiring as he gripped himself to attention, "Got to hurry on with the job, you know. Keep these fellows' eyes off the girls."

Grin from the soldiers, who were now joined by many others running across the fields.

"Do they smoke?"

"Yes, sir."

"Better hand some of these out."

A dozen hands reach up to take the parcel and the car drives on again. The chances are that the bridge will be finished when Montgomery returns that night.

It was not difficult to do this once. But to do it thirty or forty times in the course of a day was something even beyond the strength of a seasoned politician. The smallest things caught his attention. A sudden ululation of school children standing on the steps of the village church; at once Montgomery whips round in his seat and waves. As he rides past a convoy of lorries on the road he stands up in the car acknowledging the cheers from every vehicle. More cigarettes at the river-crossing. More again at the regimental aid-post. An exuberant Italian mayor comes rushing out from the *Municipio* scattering *benissimos* and *ben venutos* as he advances. Great God, the British General! A crowd comes running, children and asses and fruit-vendors. Poston tries to head them off. Montgomery delivers a two-sentence speech through his interpreter and passes on again through an outburst of *vivas* and clapping hands. Always, at every turn in the road, the staring faces, the shouts, the clapping, the cries, "There's Monty", the salutes and the reaching hands.

Wherever the Eighth Army goes, in the desert or here among the orchards, it creates a village atmosphere where every sign means something to the members of the club and everyone knows everyone else. You have only to proceed along the Army's line of march to gather all the day's news and see everyone you want to see.

From time to time Montgomery holds up his hand as he looks ahead into the traffic. "Stop that car." It is General Smith or perhaps Brigadier Brown. They pull into the side, Montgomery jumps out and the maps are spread across the bonnet of the car. While the Italians look down delightedly from the housetops, there is a rapid conference: half a dozen questions from Montgomery, two orders, a flurry of salutes and the cars move on again.

In the divisional and Corps headquarters there is no fuss as the C.-in-C. drives in. He spends half an hour in the commander's caravan, another half hour at an observation post overlooking the enemy lines across the vineyards, ducks for shelter there when stray shells come by, and then comes back to the rearward areas to address a parade. The men sit round in a circle on the ground while he stands up in a jeep: "We are going to have a bit of a party . . . good party too . . . hit them for six this time. . . . I would say that this division is second to none . . . one of the very finest members of the team. . . . Americans on our left putting up very good show . . . no doubt about the result, no doubt whatever. . . . I would say the end is in sight . . . not over yet, got to keep going . . . but the score is adding up our way . . . got to finish the match. . . . Now, I don't know if you fellows smoke . . . some cigarettes here will be handed out afterwards . . . very good luck to each one of you."

One could never really analyse a Montgomery speech. Perhaps it was what was left out, perhaps it was the very banality and simplicity of the words, perhaps the way they were spoken, or perhaps merely the fact that he was Montgomery the commanding general who held powers of life and death over everyone who heard him. Yet the effect was always the same, the same breathless interest that had nothing to do with discipline. Just for a moment of time here in the orchard or on the beach the General and the soldiers were completely at ease with one another, and all the frightening chances of war were reduced to a simple and sane community of friendship.

In the afternoon Montgomery drove back to his camp, sometimes a distance of fifty miles, and again it was the same spontaneous parade. At home at four or five o'clock (he had pitched his headquarters near Lentini) he took his tea with his visitors and the A.D.C.s and then got down to the planning of the next day's or the next month's fighting.

This routine seldom varied. It was an extraordinary ebullition of sustained effort, and in this atmosphere at once parochial, feudal, exciting and dangerous, one was irrevocably drawn in so that after a few weeks one felt that this life was the only life, that it was exact and correct and that it well might continue for ever.

4

By August 1st the Italians were negotiating for a general surrender and the Germans were driven into the north-east corner of Sicily. By the middle of August—five weeks after the beginning of the campaign—the Germans had been ejected entirely from the island.

Montgomery moved now to a lavish palazzo high on the cliffs of Taormina where he could look directly across the Straits of Messina on to the mainland of Italy itself. It was a moment of hiatus in the war and his feelings were a sharp mixture of black and white. On the credit side he could look back on one more campaign that had been planned, launched, fought and won. On July 30th he had noted in a message to the troops: "The enemy is now hemmed in . . . we have knocked Mussolini off his perch. We will now drive the Germans out of Sicily."

On August 17th he had added: "In February last the

6*

Italian Overseas Empire had ceased to exist. To-day we have captured our first slice of the Italian home country.

"It is difficult to find words to tell you my true feelings. Since I assumed command of the Eighth Army, in August 1942, exactly one year ago, you have given me your confidence and you have never failed to respond to all the calls I have made on you. . . . Well done. Well done indeed."

And now he was writing in his round clear hand another message: "The time has come to carry the battle on to the mainland of Italy.

"To the Eighth Army has been given the great honour of being the first troops of the Allied Armies to land on the continent of Europe.

"There can only be one end to this next battle, and that is: ANOTHER SUCCESS.

"Forward to Victory. Let us knock Italy out of the war."

The Allied Headquarters' plan for the invasion of Italy was a curious mixture of over-insurance, over-confidence and political ignorance. To understand it at all one has to cast back one's mind to the summer of 1943 when it was planned in Algiers. There were three possible places on which to assault the "soft under-belly" of German Europe: France, Italy and the Balkans. The Balkans route was discarded because no one was able to foresee either the success of the Russian drive through Rumania or the extent of Tito's partisan movement in Jugo-Slavia. It was also judged that the ports and roads were not adequate. The French route was negatived because we lacked sufficient ships and the necessary air cover.

Everything seemed to beckon us on to Italy. It was near— you could even look at the place with the naked eye across the Straits from Sicily, and see the enemy vehicles moving about in Reggio. Mussolini was on the point of collapsing. And the Air Forces were clamouring to gain control of the vast air-fields around Foggia, so that they could bomb Germany from the south. No one envisaged the necessity for fighting a pro-tracted campaign against the Germans during the coming winter (let alone the succeeding winter as well). Negotiations for an armistice with the Italians were already far advanced in August, and it was confidently hoped in Algiers that as soon as this armistice was announced the Italian Army would turn round and assist us in ejecting the Germans from Italy. In the face of the general opposition it was hoped that the Germans would withdraw at once to the Po Valley in the north. This was the error of over-confidence.

As for the landing itself the utmost caution prevailed. The

Montgomery creed of a deception plan backed by one concentrated thrust was discarded: it was decided that we should have several landings so that we would split the enemy concentrations: Salerno on the ankle of the Italian foot, Reggio on the toe and Taranto on the base of the foot were the selected points.

Even after the landings had taken place it was not judged necessary that we should concentrate the forces: the Fifth and the Eighth Armies were to make their way separately northwards on either side of the Apennines, presumably until they reached the Plain of Lombardy.

The objects then were threefold—

1. To knock Italy out of the war.
2. To seize the Foggia landing-fields with the adjacent ports such as Bari and Naples.
3. To pursue the enemy through Rome to the Plain of Lombardy.

The Salerno landing was to be called "Avalanche", and the Reggio landing "Baytown".

Montgomery's small role was defined thus: "Your task is to secure a bridgehead on the toe of Italy to enable our naval forces to operate through the Straits of Messina. In the event of the enemy withdrawing from the toe you will follow him up with such force as you can make available, bearing in mind that the greater the extent to which you can engage enemy forces in the southern toe of Italy the more assistance you will be giving to 'Avalanche'."

From the beginning Montgomery was opposed to both the general plan and his own part in it. Quite apart from his temperamental dislike to carrying out an operation which he had not designed himself, and in which he did not have a leading part, he believed his own forces were too small for what they were being asked to do. Two of his best divisions— the Fiftieth and the Fifty-first—were going home on leave. Others, like the Seventh Armoured, which normally lay in the Eighth Army command, had been taken away from him and given to the Americans. The curb was on.

Brooding darkly on all this in his palazzo at Taormina he saw that on this occasion he was not going to have much choice: he was bound to obey orders. Nevertheless he was determined to raise what opposition he could, and in this spirit he crossed over to the conference of the commanders-in-chief in Algiers on August 23rd. First he asked for—and got—additional forces and landing-craft for the Baytown operation. He then expressed the view that it was by no means certain that the

Italians would turn round and help us once the armistice was announced. There were some fifteen German divisions in Italy. The splitting of the Allied forces laid us open to serious counter-attack.

But by now it was far too late to consider any such sweeping changes in the plan. Forced to be satisfied with the reinforcement of his own front, Montgomery flew back to Sicily and went out to rouse the men. At least he would be the first to put his foot on the mainland—and this on the anniversary of the beginning of Germany's war against Britain. Tactical Headquarters was moved down to a convenient spot among the olive groves on the coast, and a launch with the General's pennant was ordered to stand ready.

There was an unreal, almost a pantomime atmosphere about that day of the landing on September 3rd, 1943. When Montgomery called for his early cup of tea and the first reports, the assault troops had been ashore for some hours. There had been a heavy bombardment across the Straits by the British guns the night before and when the first soldiers grounded their boats on the shingle they were met by nothing much more than a few terrified Italian peasants and disorganized soldiers whose one thought was to surrender. The German rearguard bolted rapidly to the hills, blowing up the bridges behind them.

Montgomery read through the reports, issued a few orders, made a broadcast for the B.B.C., and called for his boat much as one would set out for a picnic on the Thames. Indeed the scene was like some monstrous naval regatta. On the Sicilian beaches Italian girls were offering fruit and flowers to the soldiers as they clambered on board.

Hundreds of boats of every kind, from motor launches to steamers and warships, were swarming back and forth on the placid water of the Straits like so many gnats on a pond. The sun streamed down on the beautiful scene but the smoke of many fires and bursting shells still obscured the mainland around Reggio.

There were only three or four miles to steam. Montgomery stood on the prow of his launch taking coffee and biscuits, discoursing on the art of making war and admiring the view. Every few minutes a boat laden with soldiers passed by and they roared their greetings across the water. Only once the idyllic atmosphere was shattered when a German aircraft dived out of the clouds scattering bombs and Montgomery flung himself full length on the deck.

A few hundred yards off the beach he transhipped to a duck (which was already loaded with cigarettes) and motored ashore. A thousand men rose to meet him with yells and shouts. And behind them another thousand. And another and another. Appearing suddenly like this, on the heels of the successful landing, Montgomery seemed more than a successful general— it seemed as if he was inspired and that everything he touched was bound to turn into a victory.

In actual fact Montgomery was beginning to wonder whether he was running into his first failure. True enough the initial landing had been carried off with barely a casualty, and on the evening of September 8th the armistice with the Italians was duly announced. But there was no sign whatever of the German Army turning tail and running for the north. The Salerno landing was meeting with the bitterest resistance. Indeed, on September 10th, barely twenty-four hours after it had gone in, Montgomery received a message from Alexander urging him to maintain all pressure in the south so as to relieve the strain at Salerno. Later these messages become more pressing. Could not Montgomery make an immediate junction to strengthen the Salerno bridgehead?

It was a crisis for which we had hardly bargained. Apart from the eight thousand men now landing at Taranto (where they had their hands full) Montgomery commanded barely three divisions. They were separated from the Salerno battle by some two hundred miles of immense ravines, rocky coasts and mountain passes many thousands of feet above sea-level. As the Germans retreated up the toe they tore away the railway tracks, they lay in ambush for the British bridge-builders, they exploded the viaducts and the culverts. Furthermore, no resources had been granted to Montgomery for a forced march of this nature. The lack of petrol alone made it impossible for any but the lightest forces to press forward.

Despite these difficulties it is possible that Montgomery might have effected a link-up more rapidly than he did. Possibly he underestimated the psychological power of the Eighth Army's name and did not realize what a galvanizing effect the mere appearance of a handful of his troops would have made among the tired defenders at Salerno.

What was apparent to him was that he could never hope seriously to buttress the man-power at Salerno in the space of a day or two, and he did not propose to jeopardize his own position hopelessly in trying to do so.

Nevertheless the junction was made on September 16th, the tide turned at Salerno and things began to march forward rapidly.

Confidently and professionally the Eighth Army spread out

over the southern mountains. Brindisi, Bari, Catanzaro and Potenza fell one after another and the troops marched forward along the Adriatic towards the all-important Foggia air-fields. The Eighth Army was a club again, a private expedition wandering off into the mountains, always advancing, always Montgomery leading them on to one more conquest. It was summer. The vines were dripping with grapes. The villagers, smiling and waving, disgorged unending chickens and eggs. In the first week of October Termoli, on the Adriatic north of Foggia, was seized by a sea landing and Foggia itself fell almost without a blow. The Fifth Army entered Naples on the other side of the mountains.

So far so good. But was it good? Far from evacuating Italy, the Germans were reinforcing. Here and there, especially in the north, Italian partisans rose heroically but sporadically, and there was no real sign whatever of the Italian Army *en bloc* joining our ranks. The Italian Army was disintegrating. In a state of hopeless disorganization the soldiers were vanishing to their homes. It began to look as if we would have to fight every mile of the way up the Italian peninsula.

And now winter came down with an extraordinary abruptness. At one moment it seemed there was dust and hot sunshine; then suddenly it was mud and snow. And with the winter the fighting began, not skirmishes but pitched battle: the Biferno . . . the Trigno . . . the Sangro. Not death in packets of a dozen but hundreds dying and the corroding cold making life hellish for those who survived. It made no difference if you captured one river valley; another lay just beyond. And beyond that more mountains, more valleys, more impossibly entrenched positions. Huge convoys were bogged along the roads and sometimes were halted altogether for hours or even days. A piercing wind kept sweeping down from the Apennines, and the Adriatic turned from cobalt blue into a sullen grey. The private expedition was not such fun any more. There was still no sign of the Germans retreating to the Plain of Lombardy; they preferred to snipe down on the Allies from the rocks and the ravines. Somewhere, somehow, the campaign had gone wrong. And this was evident to the soldiers as they climbed slowly northwards with that kind of blind resolution which is somewhere between bigotry and divinity.

Looking back on the Italian campaign one sees there was a chimerical quality about the whole operation. Success seemed to be forever just round the corner. Each time the commanders reached forward to grasp it something went wrong, the light died out—and then suddenly flickered up again in some other place. Off we went in pursuit of the new hope until that too, in its turn, died away. By mid-October the whole character of the campaign had changed. The original conception—the rapid withdrawal of the Germans—had proved false and now we found ourselves, twisting and turning and compromising, with a series of short-term objectives. Having got one thing with much pain and effort we were lured on to try something else and in the maze of minor operations the over-all plan lost its clear purpose.

Had we been content with the capture of Foggia and Naples and gone into winter quarters, no doubt many lives would have been saved. But to Alexander (who had now set up his headquarters in Italy) and Eisenhower in Algiers it seemed that we had to secure these two places from counter-attack by further advances to the north. And having made these advances it was then judged necessary that we should capture Rome itself. This was an impossible project in the mountains in midwinter, but it did not appear to be impossible at the time. The feeling was —one more effort and we shall do it. And so Clarke on the left and Montgomery on the right were constantly urged to push on. The general idea was that, by fighting both sides of the mountains, we would split the German opposition. Montgomery, by advancing on Pescara, would protect Clarke's flank while Clarke himself marched on the capital.

Montgomery's opposition to this project was threefold. In the first place he did not believe that we were splitting the German forces by attacking along both sides of the mountains: the Germans simply moved their mobile units from side to side as the point of danger shifted. The way to advance, Montgomery believed, was to concentrate all our forces for a concentrated blow on one side of the Apennines.[1]

Secondly, he argued that we were running a losing race against the winter. He agreed in October and November that it was worth while making one more effort, but he also said that unless Rome fell by Christmas the wisest plan was to abandon all hope of getting there until the rivers subsided in the following spring.[2]

Finally he protested that our resources were not strong enough to continue with the winter battle. Already much material and many men were being drawn off for the Normandy landing in France. "We became involved in a major campaign," he said later, "and we lacked a pre-determined plan of action. The result was that the administrative machine

[1] This was eventually done the following spring, and Rome fell as the result.
[2] Rome fell in the first week of June in the following year.

became unable to keep pace with the widening scope of our operational commitments."

However, in the late autumn of 1943 none of this was yet clear. So we kept on. Montgomery's actions along the Adriatic are not especially interesting. As the weather worsened the pace got slower and slower and the opposition stronger and stronger. Sometimes when there was an especially heavy downpour in the mountains the river levels altered by six or seven feet. Bridges were carried away, roads turned into impassable quagmires, and the mud and the cold continued with a persistence that seemed to go beyond ill-luck into positive and conscious malignance.

At last, in early November, the Eighth Army struggled wearily up to the Sangro River at a point opposite Rome on an east-west axis. Here the Germans had established their "Winter Line". They did not defend the river itself but the ridge beyond overlooking the river valley; and so the Battle of the Sangro was really a battle for this ridge.

Four or five times Montgomery had to alter his plan of assault. As soon as one scheme was drawn up the rain pelted down in a series of cloudbursts, transport was bogged, supplies were lost and it became impossible to poise the assaulting divisions on the start-line. For a great part of the time the Allied Air Force was unable to operate. Tanks played a steadily decreasing role in the deepening mud.

At last, at the end of November, an assault on a modified scale was ready: the New Zealanders were to play their old deceptive role on the left while two other divisions made the main assault farther downstream. Once on the heights of the German Winter Line they were to fan out.

November 28th, by a miracle, was a fine day. Montgomery sent the troops in with this cry: "We will now hit the Germans a colossal crack". To the public at home this suggested that we were about to throw the Germans out of Italy. To the troops in the line it meant simply another bloody battle which would bring them another river and another mountain pass. Still, there was just the hope that the Germans *would* crack this time and allow us at least to reach Pescara.

The battle was one of those battles that went "as planned" —and nothing more. We already had a bridgehead across the river. Striking out from this springboard the soldiers carried the heights under concentrated artillery fire, and within thirty-six hours the German Winter Line was broken. A string of villages was overrun and a thousand prisoners were brought in within the first few hours. It was success with none of the rewards of success. This was no open desert. There could be no follow through. Having lost one winter line the enemy simply ran up another on the next range of mountains to the north. Ortona fell at Christmas and then the British momentum died away. On the left, Clarke, with the Fifth Army, was also in difficulties. The heartbreaking truth began to dawn on everyone—however many Sangros we crossed there was always another Sangro ahead. This was the dark and bitter part of the road, the period of unremitting danger and labour and no reward.

Even the men who were in those battles cannot tell you how they kept going through this winter. The Battle of the Sangro was followed by the tragic assault of Cassino; and after Cassino the long-drawn-out agony of the Anzio landing. These were affairs with which Montgomery had nothing to do, and lie outside this book. If one cannot admire the Allied planning of this winter struggle one must at least see and feel the nobility of the blind persistence of the Americans and the British. It was a period when the soldiers were greater than their commanders. People now forget how much they achieved. In the four months up to Christmas 1943 the Eighth Army traversed some four hundred miles from their starting-point and most of this in winter and in impossible campaigning country. Adversity drew the men together. There was one encouragement at least that never left them: no matter how hard the way they were always advancing.

And now, after a year's campaigning, after fighting across North Africa, Sicily and Italy, without a single failure, many had come to believe that with Montgomery there *could* be no failure, there *could* be no alternative but to advance. His name had become consonant with victory.

If one looks for good luck in Montgomery's career it probably lies most strongly here in this period. He was in Italy just so long as the Allies were making headway. He was recalled just at the point when things were starting to go seriously wrong. It is hard to conjecture what would have happened had he been ordered to remain with the Eighth Army. As a subordinate he could probably have made no radical alterations to the over-all plan. He might have argued and quarrelled with Eisenhower and Alexander; quite possibly he might have resigned. But luck—and the march of events—took him out of Italy just in time.

A few days after Christmas in 1943 Montgomery suddenly announced to the Eighth Army that he was going to leave them. He had been ordered, he said, to take a command in England. He was living at the time in a picturesque little

Adriatic town called Vasto, and several hundred staff officers and commanders gathered in the theatre there to hear him say goodbye. When Montgomery came on to the stage in his beret, his battledress with the ribbons, it was a curiously tense and emotional moment. There was no ceremony. He spoke very drily for about half an hour. Alamein. The desert. So many miles. So many different climates. So much that was planned and risked and done.

To an outsider the moment and the speech meant nothing—so much it was a compound of these people's lives. They had not yet grown old and garrulous about their exploits. The war was still on and everyone in that room still had the prospect of violently dying. There were no dramatics and no expressed emotion. This farewell of Montgomery to the Army which he had made—and which had made him—was a practical act, the last of many practical acts. Just once his voice caught on a phrase and he had nothing to say. Then he went on and finished his speech.

There was silence among the officers as he turned abruptly and began to walk off. Then a perfunctory, well-bred, parade-ground cheer broke out, and it had nothing much to do with the feelings of the speaker or the audience because what they felt could not be expressed by cheering or clapping. One does not applaud a surgeon after he has performed successfully an operation. And most of Montgomery's span of command had been an act of surgery.

To the soldiers he wrote: "What can I say to you as I go away? When the heart is full it is not easy to speak. But I would say this to you:

"You have made this Army what it is. You have made its name a household word all over the world. You must uphold its good name and its traditions.

"And I would ask you to give my successor the same loyal and devoted service that you have never failed to give me."

Among the soldiers there was no subtle reticence. They were still cheering, still waving to him and shouting from the roadside, "Jesus, there's Monty. Hi! Monty", when he drove down to his aircraft. This had happened to him every day across two thousand miles of campaigning. The Eighth Army. This was his family and these were his children. Could he not make his family a million men? Could he not embrace so many more like these? And could they not go anywhere together?

5

The aircraft did not make directly towards England. It turned south instead and flew to Marrakesh in Morocco for a rendezvous with Churchill, who was convalescing there from pneumonia.

The accession of Montgomery to this special command in England under Eisenhower had been by no means a cut-and-dried affair. Indeed Roosevelt and Churchill had taken the whole hierarchy of the High Command under review. At first Brooke had been chosen as the leader of the final great gamble of the western war—the invasion of France from England. Then, in view of the preponderance of the American forces, Marshall's name had been put up. Neither Brooke nor Marshall had wanted the job; both felt they were better placed as they were, exercising the real power in London and Washington. Finally Eisenhower had been elected, and he was formally asked by the British War Cabinet to name the man whom he would like as his British field commander. Eisenhower had answered that this was a matter best left for the British to decide for themselves. Churchill was in Tunis during these negotiations and he pressed Eisenhower to name his choice. Eisenhower repeated that he did not want to force the issue in any way but he was quite happy to continue with his existing field commander, General Alexander. From Tunis Churchill informed the Cabinet of this conversation, and added that it might be best to let Eisenhower have Alexander.

The position was one of the utmost power and importance; in some ways it was the most critical appointment of the war, since the British field commander would have control of the actual landing in France.

Cabinet was divided over the matter. Two names stood out clearly: Alexander or Montgomery? The steady and reasonable organizer or the man with the flair? Which? It was all too painfully obvious that Montgomery had been a disappointment as a co-operator either with his Allies or even with certain British service chiefs. There had already been some criticism in London and Algiers of Montgomery's work in the Sicilian and Italian campaigns. It was claimed that he was "too slow", too intent on getting the last ounce of supplies before he attacked. It was said that Patton in Sicily had "run rings round him". Other critics found him quarrelsome, negative, even defeatist.

To many in power in Whitehall the self-assurance had

appeared as nothing more than arrogance. The Eighth Army commander had been told bluntly in the War Office: You are making enemies fast and loose. You have kicked generals when they were down and you might have been generous. You have jeered and made cruel remarks about other officers and these remarks have got back to them. The Americans are reluctant to place themselves under your command. The whole of the First Army in Tunisia is bitter against you because they say you claimed the victory there. You have made no attempt to understand their difficulties—or anyone else's difficulties. You flatly contradict others in conference and sneer at their opinions. When officers come to your headquarters you will not see them. You have the reputation of high-handedly pushing people aside whenever it suits your purpose. All these men you have slighted are your enemies. You will have to ask yourself whether you can afford to go on like this.

Montgomery, hearing these charges, had been genuinely surprised. It was quite true that he had refused to be disturbed by visitors during the course of a battle, but he felt he had made particular concessions to allies and equals alike. Had he not mentioned them in his orders of the day? Had he not been at particular pains in Africa to explain to a group of American and British generals the art of making war? Had he not been obliged to submit to much inept planning? There had, of course, been incidents. The commander of the Canadian troops had flown out to the Mediterranean during the Sicilian campaign intending to see how his countrymen were getting on in their first action. Montgomery had forbidden him to land and the Canadian commander had flown back to England. But could not he have seen that he, Montgomery, was fighting a battle and did not want to be disturbed? And had not the Canadian general been issued with a cordial invitation to come once the battle was over? Victory was everything. Provided you got the victory what did these petty misunderstandings matter?

An old friend said to Montgomery in England: "It is true you have made a score of enemies. But you have made hundreds of thousands of friends as well."

Unfortunately the score of enemies were in high places. If Montgomery had no actual enemies in the Cabinet, there were at least key ministers who felt strongly that this new and vitally important post should go to a man who represented squarely the tradition and the character of the British Army, a man who had proved his ability to get along with his allies and his talent for combining armies in the field. These supported Alexander.

Brooke and Sir James Grigg, the Minister for War, though no opponents of Alexander, believed that this heady and dangerous experiment should be controlled by someone of Montgomery's tactical skill and power to galvanize the troops. In the end the vote had swung their way.

And now here was Montgomery entering Churchill's room at Marrakesh on New Year's Day 1944 to hear the terms of his new office. Churchill was in bed reading a bundle of papers. He tossed them across to Montgomery. "See what you think of it", he said. It was "Operation Overlord", the plan for invading Normandy in northern France, the "Second Front" for which the world had been waiting for the past two years.

Montgomery stayed up half the night reading it through. "Well?" Churchill asked in the morning.

"I can't give an opinion," Montgomery said. "I have not studied it. I have not consulted the Navy and the Air Force. And I am not, sir, your military adviser."

Churchill persisted. Surely the General had some opinion. Surely he could express a strictly private view. He could say what he liked without prejudice to any arrangements that might be made later on.

"Well, then," Montgomery said, "it will not do. It is not an operation of war. The organization of command is wrong. The frontage is too narrow. The whole plan will have to be drastically revised."

It was something of a bombshell. For many months General Morgan in England had been working on the plan with a secret staff known as "Cossac". To alter that plan now, so near the eve of this tremendous adventure, seemed foolhardy. How could Montgomery be certain that the plan was wrong? Why should he say with such flat conviction that "the frontage was too narrow", the landing forces not great enough? Surely this was a subject upon which everyone must have doubts. But Montgomery had no doubt. This was simply another technical operation with a right and a wrong way of doing it. You had only to manage things in the right way and the results were certain. He and his staff would be able to adjust the whole thing satisfactorily.

To Churchill and Beaverbrook (who was at Marrakesh) the General must have presented a slightly baffling picture. When all the world was desperately anxious about this thing, when the very best brains were balancing alternatives and doubtfully weighing the changing dangers of the prospect, here was one man who had no hesitations at all. Did he really know? Did he really have the remedy? Or was he merely a lucky adventurer? But then Alamein, Mareth, the Sicilian landing, all the other victories. As a builder of morale alone he was a potent instrument of war.

Churchill took Montgomery's book and in a somewhat scrawling hand (possibly because he was still ill in bed) wrote:

"The immortal march of the Eighth Army from the gates of Cairo along the African shore through Tunisia, through Sicily, has now carried its ever-victorious soldiers and their world-renowned commander far into Italy towards the gates of Rome. The scene changes and vastly expands. A great task accomplished gives place to a greater in which the same unfailing spirit will win for all true men a full and glorious reward."

With this blessing Montgomery set off on January 2nd for England. At the last moment they would not let him fly over that huge expanse of ocean in his own two-engined plane; a four-motored bomber was handed over instead. Right or wrong, genius or mere adventurer, Montgomery was too valuable to lose at this moment.

CHAPTER ELEVEN

THE TIDE TAKEN AT THE FLOOD

I

THESE were the rich days. High command. One more adventure—the biggest of all. Five months of freedom in England to take part in the planning and moulding of the expedition. Then back to France; not this time a young and bothered subaltern hurried away from his tennis, not a divisional commander compelled to fight on someone else's half-hearted ideas. This time Montgomery was going back at the head of a million men, and Europe would have a campaign, cold and clear and surgical, such as she had never seen before.

Promptly he moved back into his old school, St. Paul's, in Hammersmith, on the outskirts of London, and set up his headquarters there. Promptly de Guingand and the staff of planners arrived and moved into the schoolroom much as they would have made their encampments in the desert. Montgomery was fond of calling them his "first eleven". Sadly one of the outgoing non-Montgomery generals remarked: "The Gentlemen are out. The Players are coming in."

In a world of doubts no one at Hammersmith appeared to have any anxieties at all. It was, in many ways, a repetition of the scene in the desert before Alamein. Having made a first rapid inspection of the situation in England, Montgomery called his subordinates together, addressed them on his methods, on what he hoped to do and how he would do it: in fact, a short Montgomery course on "The Art of War". It was a gesture nicely calculated to raise the eyebrows of the outgoing Gentlemen. Was Montgomery the Supreme Commander? Was he going to take all the credit this time as well? Did he imagine that this was another one-man show? Had not "Cossac" already done the bulk of the work?

While the opposition gathered its ranks the staff at Hammersmith got down to the planning. Eisenhower's Chief of Staff, General Bedell Smith, was also in favour of a stronger assault. They applied for and got a wider front, a bigger initial landing, a much stronger rate of build-up. Three stages were envisaged: the "break-in", the entrenchment and the "break-out". The vital "break-in" period was to open with a heavy naval and aerial bombardment of the Normandy coastline followed by the landing of the British on the left and the Americans on the right.

Then the entrenchment of the bridgehead while the supplies flowed in, the British wheeling left to the capture of Caen while the Americans cut off the Cherbourg peninsula on the right and moved on to the capture of the supply port of Cherbourg itself. The final phase would resemble the tactics at Alamein and Mareth: the main enemy forces would be attracted to the British end of the line round Caen while the Americans launched their "break-out" on the right.

This would be the signal for all the armies to advance towards the Seine together and it was hoped that the river would be reached in ninety days. It was then expected that there would be a further battle on the Seine and, if it was successful, who could tell?—perhaps the war would be over by Christmas.

The over-all plan, of course, was not the product of Montgomery's brain; it was the result of many minds, British and American, working over many months and always within the limits allowed them by the Navy and the Air Force. But on his arrival in England, Montgomery was nominated commander-in-chief of all the Allied land forces in the field, and the actual working of the plan, its tempo, its tactical direction and application at the point of contact—all these matters fell to the staff of Montgomery's 21st Army Group, which was the initial striking force. In the broad strategic role, the politics and the administration, the Americans from now on played the leading part.

Montgomery was delighted to be out of Italy. And now that he was out on his own again, given his head in the biggest race of all, many good soldiers in England were darkly apprehensive that he was going to ride rough-shod over everyone and everything. Once again Montgomery had the rare good fortune to have a superior in Eisenhower who was willing to give him a free hand, and eagerly and gratefully he grasped the operational power.

"He will abuse it", the opposition cried. "He will take no advice. He will start a wave of capricious sackings. It has all happened before." But there was no wave of sackings. In the British Army, Ritchie (who had failed in the desert) was retained in his corps. Dick O'Connor, who had escaped from Italy, was also given a corps. So was Bucknall of the 5th Division. And Crocker of the First Army. None of these were Montgomery generals. Neither Horrocks, nor Leese, nor Harding was on the scene. Only Dempsey, a keen and logical craftsman, was brought back and put in command of the

British Second Army. Yet with Montgomery's "First Eleven" working at St. Paul's and with the return of the 50th, the 51st and the 7th (Armoured) Divisions, it remained an "Eighth Army", a strictly "Montgomery" command.

Outside this and running parallel to it, the Americans under General Bradley had in England their own Army Group, which managed its own domestic affairs. Bradley was simply obliged to accept general orders from Montgomery who, in turn, was answerable to Eisenhower. It was a situation which required a good deal of tact and forbearance, and at this stage, when everyone was under the cloud of the risks and dangers ahead, things worked smoothly. It was not until later on when the major risk was gone and the end in sight that loyalties became somewhat divided. For the moment Montgomery was accepted as the key man who was to lead the actual assault on Europe.

The truth was that he was mellowing and growing with his job. He had made a series of remarkable mental adjustments since he had gone out to Africa eighteen months before. He had grown much more tactful in his dealings with politicians and allies. He was more careful in what he said, more patient, and outwardly at least much more ready to listen to advice. The core of his character remained unrepentant, but an exterior façade of manners had grown up and he was much easier to approach. It was even a light-hearted and agreeable experience to have dinner with him. He began to take a mild interest in politics. And, what was much more important, he accepted his masters. Apart from Eisenhower, there were just three British leaders whom he admired and recognized as his superiors with the right to intervene. One was Churchill, another was Brooke and the third was Grigg. From these three he would accept orders and strictures. To them he would go for advice, though not perhaps in strictly tactical military matters. In Grigg at first Montgomery suspected an opponent, but they met and dined and had the matter out. "It will be no good if you start sending me 'stinkers'", Montgomery said. "If you criticize me we will only have a row. I know I am difficult. I know I'm a bit headstrong and apt to ride straight over opposition. But just caution me. Just tell me from time to time to take it steady." Upon this they became friends.

With Churchill, Montgomery was intrigued. The broad, sweeping gestures, the ardour, the warrior approach, the Elizabethan colour and enthusiasm—it was fascinating. Montgomery would go down to Chequers and promptly find himself invited to fight battles with rulers and inkstands and pens across the Prime Minister's desk. "If I did this, General," Churchill would say, moving the ashtray to the left, "what would you do?" Churchill was one of the few men whom Montgomery addressed as "Sir". But there were limits to the formalities. One night when Churchill telephoned and suggested a conference towards midnight, Montgomery protested mildly, "But, sir, I shall be in bed then. It's long after my bedtime." Wryly Churchill let the matter pass.

One might have expected a rich crop of anecdotes and incidents from these momentous days in England leading up to the invasion. It was the floodtide of Montgomery's life. He was working, thinking and acting on a huge canvas and he raced ahead with confidence and precision from one thing to another. But soldiers usually are the worst recorders of their own doings, and in any event, for England in general, this was a flat and forbidding time.

The dread of the coming battle lay like a leaden weight on everyone's mind. Could it be anything else than an appalling "blood bath"? There was something outrageous in this slow deliberate preparation for a massacre. The bombing of southern England went on. There were threats of rockets. Austerity followed one about like a lean and hungry dog. It sat by your table as you ate, followed you into the black streets at night and lay with you in the half-heated houses at night. The wreckage, the shabbiness and the overwhelming drabness of four years' garrison life stared one in the face all over England. When would it come? When? When?

Everywhere they went the leaders were met with the blank and fretful questioning. More and more people fixed their minds with a half-desperate faith on the little General in the black beret who kept bobbing about with his racy confidence, his curiously naive mixture of schoolboy slang and religious conviction: "We'll hit 'em for six. . . . The Lord mighty in battle."

Montgomery met the politicians with the same innocent and interested curiosity. One after another the Cabinet Ministers, Eden, Bevin and the others, went down to see him; and usually they came away impressed at least by the abounding assurance of the General. To Montgomery these visitors from the nebulous and intricate world of politics were even more strange phenomena than he was to them.

"What sort of a chap is he?" he would inquire when he was told that some dignitary was arriving. "Is he a good chap?" Gravely the prelates, the politicians and the great men filed by without quite knowing that they were being appraised on the level of whether or not they were "good chaps". Within these simple standards the General looked them over with considerable native shrewdness and he confided his opinions to his unpublished and unpublishable diary. Some third of Montgomery's waking day was given to the study and appointment of human beings.

An alarmingly high proportion of them were set down simply as "fools—quite useless". The people he particularly disliked were those with affectations and over-ornate manners, the smooth characters and many who were deeply immersed in money. In Montgomery's world there was no time to practise either the refinements of manner or the pursuit of material things: only the battle counted, the battle to be fought his way.

But for some time he had been interested in having his portrait painted. Several artists had attempted it without much success—possibly because they were nervous with the sitter. Augustus John was now commissioned for a fee of £500, and Montgomery began to drive down to John's studio in Tite Street, Chelsea, for the sittings. It was a strange performance. Montgomery would arrive with his A.D.C. in a Rolls-Royce, mount the stairs and enter an atmosphere which (despite the instruction of his wife) was as far away from him as voodoo worship. While the artist filled his canvas, the General sat there somewhat stiffly on the dais, in his beret, his ribbons and his battledress.

Bernard Shaw had long been wishing to meet Montgomery, and, intrigued by this scene, he dropped into the studio one day. There was no more painting at that sitting. Both had a very great deal to say. With unembarrassed gusto Shaw peeped across a lifetime of thinking and pacifism at the man of action and the man of war.

"General," he announced blandly, "I will tell you when the war is going to end."

Montgomery (from the dais): "Really?"

Shaw: "When money goes to five per cent. All wars end then."

The conversation touched lightly and fragrantly on politics. "Only five per cent. of the people are fit to rule," Shaw declared. "The difficulty is to find them and lift them up—and there are not enough men for the high jobs."

Montgomery: "Would you say that five per cent. of generals are efficient?"

Shaw: "No. Not that."

And amiably and understandingly they regarded one another across the studio.

An hour or two later Montgomery's chauffeur, waiting in the street outside, was surprised to see an old gentleman with a white beard step into the car with the announcement that he was to be driven home to the country: the General had loaned his car. They proceeded at a pace consonant with the age of the passenger, until the passenger himself protested and the speed was increased to sixty miles an hour. But again, to the chauffeur's astonishment, the white beard appeared at his elbow. Was this all that the car could do? Marvelling, the chauffeur put his foot down on the accelerator. So it was speed the old boy wanted. The speedometer shot up to ninety and riding thus, with the old boy leaning contentedly back in the cushions, they arrived at his home.

"Not bad", Shaw said as he stepped out and handed the soldier two half crowns. For to-day at least he was a man of action. Going inside, he sat down and wrote to Augustus John the liveliest comment on Montgomery yet to be set on paper.

"DEAR AUGUSTUS JOHN," he wrote. "This afternoon I had to talk all over the shop to amuse your sitter and keep his mind off the worries of the present actual fighting. And as I could see him with one eye and you with the other— two great men at a glance—I noted the extreme likeness between you. You, large, tall, blonde, were almost massive in contrast with that intensely compacted hank of steel wire, who looked as if you might have taken him out of your pocket.

"A great portrait painter always puts himself as well as his sitter into his work; and since he cannot see himself as he paints (as I saw you) there is some danger that he may substitute himself for his subject in the finished work. Sure enough, your portrait of B. L. M. immediately reminded me of your portrait of yourself in the Leicester Gallery. It fills the canvas, suggesting a large, tall man. It does not look at you, and Monty always does with intense effect. *He* concentrates all space into a small spot like a burning-glass; *it* has practically no space at all; you haven't left room for any. Now for it. Take that old petrol rag that wiped out so many portraits of me (all masterpieces) and rub out this one till the canvas is blank. Then paint a small figure looking at you straight from above, as he looked at me from the dais. Paint him at full length (some foreground in front of him) leaning forward with his knees bent back, gripping the edge of his camp stool, and his expression one of piercing scrutiny, the eyes unforgettable. The background: the vast totality of desert Africa. Result: a picture worth £100,000. The present sketch isn't honestly worth more than the price of your keep while you were painting it. You really weren't interested in the man.

"Don't bother to reply. Just take it or leave it as it strikes you.

"What a nose! And what eyes!

"Call the picture INFINITE HORIZONS AND ONE MAN.

"Fancy a soldier being intelligent enough to want to be painted by you and to talk to me! Always yours,

"G. B. S."

The following day, February 27th, 1944, Shaw wrote again:

"MY DEAR JOHN,—Having slept on it I perceive that part of my letter of yesterday must be dismissed as an ebullition of senile excitement; for as a matter of business the portrait, as it stands, will serve as the regulation one which its buyers bargained for and are entitled to have (plenty of paint and the sitter all over the canvas). And between ourselves it has a subtle and lovely Johannine colour plan which must not be thrown away.

"The moral would seem to be to finish the portrait for your customers and then paint the picture for yourself. Only, as he certainly won't have time to give you a second set of sittings, you must steal a drawing or two made from the chair in which I sat.

"The worst of being 87–88 is that I never can be quite sure whether I am talking sense or old man's drivel. I must leave the judgment to you. As ever, but doddering,

"G. BERNARD SHAW."

Doddering or not he was still the most charming letter-writer in the language.

Montgomery was inclined to agree with Shaw's estimate of the picture, which was now nearing completion (an A.D.C. sitting in Montgomery's jacket so that the rows of ribbons could be painted).

The "Johannine colour plan" appeared to Montgomery to be a rather nasty blue cloud and he was not happy about the likeness. Was he bound to take the picture since he had commissioned it? Certainly not, John said. It was hung in that year's Academy, a great centre of attraction for the crowds, and subsequently sold, it is believed, for £1000.

The matter cropped up once more when a London paper said that an Army officer had bought the portrait for £100.

John wrote to *The Times* correcting this. The £100 sale, he said, referred to a drawing of the same subject which he had shown at the Academy at the same time.

The General meanwhile went off in search of another artist more to his taste.

2

The invasion plan decided upon, Montgomery abandoned the details to de Guingand and the Americans and devoted himself entirely to the soldiers. He had a special train, and Addison Road, Hammersmith, was his private station. From here he set out each week with the intention of seeing and talking to every soldier and officer who was destined to go on the invasion, something like a million men.

There was almost a Wesleyan and revivalist fervour in this one-man expedition. The Army Intelligence reports had made it clear that the average young officer was expecting to die in the assault, and among the ranks there was that same heavy weight of apprehension and dismal foreboding. Very well. He would conquer this despondency. He would preach a new gospel of faith and hope. Let him get among the soldiers and they would understand. They would turn this invasion into a new crusade.

Up and down the country Montgomery went, talking sometimes to five or six meetings, addressing thirty thousand men in a single day. First he marched round the ranks peering into the soldiers' faces one by one. Then they came running in thousands towards him, to sit at his feet and listen to the thin religious voice: "Finish the thing off . . . you and I together . . . with God's help we will see the job through to the end". It was the same with each meeting, the same brand of faith and conviction, and he talked with the same assurance to Americans and Canadians, even to Norwegians and Poles.

To recapture the atmosphere one has to cast one's mind back to the time. It was a period when everything was a little larger than life—just as Montgomery himself was becoming larger than his own role in events. Conviction—any sort of conviction—shone out like a lighthouse in the dark sea of doubting about the immediate future. Most of the ordinary subtleties and niceties of life had vanished, and when Montgomery stood up and pounded out his simple faith he captured a rapt and believing audience at once.

And as upon a classical stage both audience and players are cast up into a new and cosmic world where all the issues are heroic, so now, preaching on the English football fields and the parade grounds, Montgomery made the soldiers feel that they were embarked upon something which made them larger and finer and more commanding human beings than they were before.

Presently reports began to flow back to London of the General's extraordinary crusade. He was here, there and everywhere. He was becoming a popular hero even in the remote villages. It was not just a matter of a general haranguing his soldiers before battle; it was growing very like an election campaign.

Nor did it stop with the Army. Montgomery began to address the railway workers, the miners, the stevedores. He held huge mass meetings in the factories. "Keep on working", he declared into the microphone. "Give us the tools and we will finish the job." They cheered him with a roar. Posters began to appear in the streets; pictures of that lean, intent face under the beret, a personal message underneath. In the towns the people shouted as he drove by: "Up there, Monty", "There goes Monty".

And just where, they wondered in Whitehall, was all this hullabaloo leading to? Was Montgomery a general or a candidate for the next Prime Ministership? In the House of Commons a cheer was raised at every mention of Alexander's name. At a reference to Montgomery the House fell silent. This became so marked that Grigg drew a few of the experienced members aside and reasoned with them; Montgomery had to be trusted, he was sincerely trying to raise morale—nothing more. But still the House watched suspiciously.

When the factory lectures started Montgomery was warned privately that he should call a halt. He would stand in better favour with the authorities, he was told, if he would just stick to his soldiering. He continued his campaign. A second warning arrived. Still he went on. The newspapers were now encouraged to "go slow" on Montgomery. Reports of his speeches were discreetly banned or cut by the censors. He was not asked to broadcast on the B.B.C. And finally a direct and official request to stop was passed on to Montgomery himself.

"I will not stop", he replied. "I have contracted to undertake a programme and I will go through with it because I am informed that it will be of value in heightening morale."

It was an awkward position. You could not suddenly muzzle the man whom you had chosen as the country's military leader at the moment of its major crisis. Thousands of people were now flocking to view his famous caravans which were sent on tour of the country to raise funds for the Red Cross. His

Eighth Army flag was publicly auctioned and was knocked down for two hundred and seventy-five guineas. People were naming babies after him, pleading with him to enter politics. Lady Oxford appealed to him in an impassioned letter to save the Liberal Party. Wherever he appeared the crowds came billowing round. But now the sands were running out. D-day was creeping closer and closer. Carefully opening and shutting the stops of publicity the authorities waited patiently until the invasion should sweep the over-popular General back to Europe and his proper affairs.

Not everyone in high places was alarmed by the General. Quite early in his morale campaign he had addressed a large gathering of the most eminent men in England at the Mansion House in London. It had been a great testing-point for Montgomery. Possibly there is no more urbane and long-headed assemblage in the world than that which gathers from time to time at the Mansion House ceremonies. With the Cabinet, the ambassadors, and the aldermen of England watching him in open curiosity, Montgomery rose and spoke as though he were addressing a platoon of soldiers on the heath. As always it was the way he spoke, his manner, his note of pronounced conviction—even his tense and ascetic appearance—which won the day and roused them to an exuberant and youthful cheering over the glasses of port. The words he used, in part, were these:

"It must forever redound to our shame that we sent out soldiers into this most modern war with weapons and equipment that were hopelessly inadequate; we have only ourselves to blame for the disasters that early overtook us in the field. Surely we must never let this happen again. Nor will we.

"But it is the man that counts and not the machine. If you have got men who are mentally alert, who are tough and hard, who are trained to fight and kill, who are enthusiastic, and who have that infectious optimism and offensive eagerness that comes from physical well-being—and you then give these men the proper weapons and the equipment—*there is nothing you cannot do*. Nothing. Nothing.

"Such men must have faith in God . . . and you must have mutual confidence between the commander and the troops; any steps you take to establish this confidence will pay a very good dividend.

"A study of the military disasters that have overtaken us in our history will reveal that they have been due, basically, to faulty command, or bad staff-work, or neglect of the human factor, and sometimes possibly all three.

"If you tell the soldier what you want, and you launch him

The Armorial Bearings of
FIELD MARSHAL the VISCOUNT MONTGOMERY
of ALAMEIN. G.C.B. .D.S.O.

The broken spear is the old Montgomery crest commemorating the ancestor who rode in a tourney against the King of France. The knight in chain armour recalls "Crusader", the code name used by the British Army in the desert. The other supporter is described: "on the sinister side a soldier in battle-dress all proper".

THE JOHN PORTRAIT

properly into battle, he will always do *his* part—he has never let the side down. Never. The British soldier is easy to lead; he is very willing to be led; and he responds at once to leadership.

"Only from an inspired nation can go forth an inspired army. It is absolutely vital that we realize that the 'tide in the affairs of men which, taken at the flood, leads on to fortune' will not be for this nation on Armistice Day or on Victory Day.

"*It will be when our men go forth to battle on this great endeavour.* The tide will flow *then* or not at all.

"That is the time when there must swell up in the nation every noble thought, every high ideal, every great purpose which has waited through the weary years. And then, as the sap rises, the men will feel themselves to be the instrument of a new-born national vigour. 'Let God arise and let His enemies be scattered.'

"All this is a necessity. The Promised Land is not now far off; if necessary we have got to hazard all, and give our lives that others may enjoy it. From a consecrated nation, such men will abundantly come. And the Lord Mighty in Battle will go forth with our armies and His special providence will assist our battle.

"Can you imagine this conversation in after years? 'What did you do in the World War?'

" 'I pulled hard to start with; but after a time I began to lose interest and let go the rope. I thought I wanted a rest; and I wanted more pay.'

" 'And did you win?'

" 'No. We lost. I let go the rope and we lost the match. God forgive me; we lost the match.'

"Is it possible that such a conversation could apply to us British? No. It is impossible. Thank God it is impossible.

"Then let us stand-to and get on the rope. How long will the pull last? No one can say for certain; it may last a year; it may take longer. But it will be a magnificent party. And we shall win."

The Church militant had found her champion. The Bishop himself could not have done better than his faithful son.

3

Across the Channel in France a piece of great good fortune had befallen the Allies. Hitler had decided to pit Rommel as his field-general for one last decisive throw against his old desert enemy, Montgomery.

7

It would be difficult to imagine anything more auspicious for the Allied cause. Rommel never was the match of Montgomery in a set-piece battle. Impulsive, erratic and restless by temperament he allowed his line to be flung off balance whenever a struggle dragged on.

Both Hitler and Rommel—and for that matter most of the British and American public as well—were gripped with a wholly erroneous idea of the nature of the coming battle. The collapse of the Maginot Line—and all the other defensive lines in the war—had taught them nothing. Nor had they gripped the fundamental difference between this war and the 1914–1918 war, the fact that this time, when so many wholly novel weapons were in use, the offence always prevailed at first against the defence.

Rundstedt and Montgomery and a few other professionals had grasped this fact; they read the lesson of Russia and the desert quite clearly—all defence must be fluid and mobile. You must meet and strike the advancing enemy in the open. No coastline was defensible. The French coast would crack as quickly as the Maginot Line. The massacre which the Allied public dreaded on the beaches would never happen because the real battle would never take place there; it would be fought inland.

Rommel, the impulsive, with Hitler impulsively at his back goading him on, was blind to all this. He did the very thing which Montgomery tried to prevent happening in similar circumstances in England in 1940. He rushed all his main defences up to the coast. Everything to Rommel depended on the Atlantic Wall. A complex about the Wall had grown up in the German Army. It *must* hold.

In vain for Rundstedt to protest that this was the same fatal mistake the French had made with their Maginot Line in 1940 (which Rommel himself had been instrumental in demolishing). In vain for him to argue that the Allies must be allowed to land, and later, when they had shown their hand, be met and defeated perhaps on the Seine or even farther back on the Rhine.

Hitler and Goebbels were determined to protect their flying-bomb and artillery bases in France. Given just a little more time they would demolish London. The invader must be flung back on the coast. And as Rommel stood on his Wall at Calais and looked across the narrow sea to Dover he was eager to begin the battle.

In England, Montgomery was ranged on the side of the planners who opposed an early landing in 1944. He refused to budge until all was ready, until all the railways were geared, all the stocks delivered to the ports, the pipe-lines and the Mulberry wharves completed and the latest tanks delivered from America.

Elaborate deception and double deception schemes were organized. In Kent fake encampments were erected and a full Army Group signalling station was kept transmitting coded messages to give the impression that the invasion was to be directed from there and the landing to fall on Calais. (Actually Montgomery's Tactical and Main Headquarters were outside Portsmouth, and Eisenhower also was miles away at Kingston.)

In Liverpool the British Intelligence Staff discovered an actor who bore a strong resemblance to Montgomery; a Lieutenant Clifton James who was serving in the Royal Army Pay Corps. He was brought down to London and he spent a week travelling around with Montgomery, observing all his gestures and mannerisms—hands behind his back as he walked, the pinching of the left cheek, the tense direct look, the rigid set of the head, the trick of throwing out a deprecatory hand as he punctuated his points in conversation. When the part was learned James was fitted out with the General's wardrobe, his beret with the badges, the beribboned battle-dress, the fur-lined flying-jacket. Then he was flown off to Gibraltar. He alighted on the airfield there, in full sight of the Fascist Intelligence agents who in those days perched like crows on the Spanish border a quarter of a mile away. A reception committee on the airfield underlined the occasion and James was driven through the narrow Gibraltar streets to Government House. There he was entertained by the Governor as though he were Montgomery. The following day James again appeared at the airfield and was flown to Algiers where he called at the headquarters of the Allied Commander-in-Chief, General Maitland Wilson. And then he disappeared.

The object of this charade was simple—to suggest to the Germans that a gigantic bluff had been played; that the real invasion was not aimed at northern Europe but was coming in through the Mediterranean from the south. Complicated shipping movements and other deceptions backed up the idea, and it was hoped that the trick would persuade the Germans to keep at least some forces in the south.

On his return to England it was suggested—perhaps with some justice—that James should be remunerated for his work at the rate of Montgomery's salary. Somewhat shocked by the suggestion the War Office eventually paid up—but only for those days when James was actually wearing Montgomery's uniform.

At home the last touches were being added to the expedition. Eisenhower and the commanders gathered at St. Paul's to hear addresses from the assault leaders on the final plans.

Admiral Sir Bertram Ramsay, speaking for the Navy, emphasized all the many dangers which might demolish the expedition in the Channel. Air-Marshal Sir Trafford Leigh Mallory, who, with Ramsay, was so soon to die, also spoke soberly of the capricious summer weather off the English coast.

But Montgomery as usual stood up brimming with assurance. Standing in front of a large floor-map on which he punctuated his points with his hand from time to time, he asserted that the plan was entirely sound. Stage by stage he traced the positions to which he hoped to lead his armies in the three months after D-day.

There followed a second talk to all ranks down to lieut.-colonel level. Arrangements were also made for the briefing of the soldiers throughout the entire force before they actually took off. All this was part of a deliberate scheme, not only to keep the organization running smoothly, but to reduce as far as possible the real enemy at this critical hour, the fear of the unknown in men's minds.

By now Montgomery had revived in England the idea of personal leadership in the military field, just as Churchill had done it some years previously in the political field: provided he had a success his position with the troops was secure. At his own level, among his equals and superiors, the arguments, the debatings and the doubts went on. In the last resort Montgomery's main difference from other leaders was that he never would blindly accept the advice of those above him. Perhaps, as many said, his besetting sin was vanity; certainly he appeared at times to be intransigent and stubborn to the point of bigotry, to oppose others simply for the love of opposing them. But these vices, if they existed in him, had also distilled a virtue which was regrettably lacking at times among the officers struggling up to a high command: he was nobody's sycophant, he could not be dined and wined into an amenable frame of mind, he could not be impressed by a show of authority nor were his wits clouded by ceremony. Nor was he unduly handicapped by the niceties of tact and diplomacy. He was wholly unbribable—even by the subtlest forms of bribery. And he never intrigued. This last was also a refreshing novelty. A very great part of Montgomery's success from

Alamein onwards was this habit of "talking back" to his superiors, of digging in his toes before a battle and demanding point-blank what he wanted in the way of men and supplies—otherwise he would not fight the battle. It is easy, as his enemies suggested, to win victories if you have the means. It is not so easy to extort and sometimes bludgeon those means out of governments and rulers. Nor is it easy to turn squarely against strong political pressure, to reject plans given you from very high authority and insist on the adoption of your own. This was the real basis of Montgomery's behaviour in High Command at this time and it was the least-known side of his character.

Obviously he was not always right; he himself said in 1944: "I have made many mistakes in the past and I shall doubtless make many more". It was impossible for the authorities, even had they wanted to, to give him *carte blanche* all the time. They had to oppose him sometimes. The eternal problem was to know just when you could give the rein to this headstrong and over-willing horse.

By the time the invasion was ready Churchill, most of the British Cabinet, and a great part of the Allied Command were ardent admirers of Montgomery's skill, his confidence and his toughness of moral character. But Churchill was a warm-blooded man. His was not the surgical approach to war. Once the conference was over and the planning was done he was a rip-roaring subaltern again, and his mind was riding once more in the charge of the 21st Lancers at Omdurman. Let us get at 'em. Let us take the monster by the throat. Let the cannon speak and this mighty host of free men would fall upon the skulking foe with fire and sword and all the ardour of a righteous cause. He announced his intention of landing with the troops on D-day.

From this he was restrained; but he chafed nevertheless at the endless preparations, the logistics, the mountainous tables of tonnage, the graphs, the figures, the loading priorities, the paraphernalia of workshops and bulldozers and spare parts, the radio wave-lengths, the ballistics and the statistics. Where was the bayonet in all this? Was the invasion an adding machine? Did the generals really need all those trucks and cranes and sacks of concrete on the landing-barges? Had not the organization become over-organized? Where was the charge up the beaches in all this? Had everyone forgotten that?

He queried the loading programme. Get the soldiers ashore. That was the thing. The paraphernalia could follow afterwards.

The answer from the generals was that all the equipment was, unfortunately, necessary. The men would be useless without it.

Churchill persisted. There were too many vehicles on the boats. Again Montgomery argued with him. It was reminiscent of the story of the king complaining to Mozart at the playing of one of the composer's symphonies: "Too many notes, my dear Mozart. Too many notes." Mozart had answered "No, sir, just enough". And Montgomery now repeated in the same way: "No, sir, we have just enough vehicles".

The Prime Minister remained restive. It so often happens in a crisis when one is exposed to a thousand anxieties the mind will fix on one and make it the sounding-board for all the rest. So Churchill fixed on this matter of the vehicles and the loading priorities. Barely a week before D-day he decided to go down to Montgomery's headquarters and address the General's staff upon the subject. Montgomery was waiting to receive him, but first led the way into a study. And there Montgomery put down his cards on the table.

It was unwise, he said, for the Prime Minister to speak to the staff at that moment. Even if he, Montgomery, was wrong it was too late now to alter things. The loaded trains were running to the ports. The boats were loading. The whole vast invasion machine was turning over and to alter things now would hopelessly dislocate the whole operation. He was absolutely confident that the loading programme was sound, that every single vehicle was necessary. If the Prime Minister could not accept his word on this—if he insisted on an alteration at this eleventh hour—then it was evident that the Prime Minister had lost confidence in his general.

Mr. Churchill protested at once that this was not so, but it was a highly charged moment. Churchill had had something more than a tolerable burden on his mind in the past few months; and now this was too much. Possibly he saw, and with a sense of overwhelming relief, that events had now reached the point where they were beyond the control of any one man, where inevitably this monstrous project was sweeping upward to its final crisis, that everyone was reacting in a certain way because he *had* to react that way and that there was no turning back or turning aside for anyone. And he gave way.

Possibly the Prime Minister was right in the matter but a difference of opinion between the two men at this moment was unthinkable and they both knew it. They remained a longer in the room while the tension slid away. Then

Montgomery reminded him that the staff was waiting outside.

Churchill got up and went out. The generals, the brigadiers and the colonels were drawn up in a line. One by one Montgomery introduced them. Everyone there sensed there had been a crisis. Most of them guessed what had taken place in the study.[1]

Churchill got to the head of the line and surveyed them for a moment without speaking. Then the old lion had his final roar. Some sly imp of genius made him say, and with dignity: "I'm not allowed to talk to you, gentlemen". Then he walked out. The scene was all his.

In Montgomery's book the Prime Minister had written:

"On the verge of the greatest adventure with which these pages have dealt, I record my confidence that all will be well, and that the organization and equipment of the Army will be worthy of the valour of the soldiers and the genius of their chief".

There followed the final conference on June 1st between Montgomery and the four Army generals under his command— Omar Bradley of the First American, George S. Patton of the Third American, Dempsey of the Second British and Crerar of the First Canadian. Then, a few days later, came that momentous meeting when Eisenhower decided to sail in the face of the rising wind rather than delay any longer.

To the troops Montgomery made his last appeal:

"The time has come to deal the enemy a terrific blow in Western Europe . . . in better days that lie ahead men will speak with pride of our doings. We have a great and righteous cause."

On the following day, June 6th, the blow was struck and Montgomery followed his shock troops over to Normandy. He set up his Tactical Headquarters in an old château at Creully half-way between the beaches and the firing-line.

---

[1] The authenticity of this incident has been questioned. Neither Churchill nor Montgomery made an official statement about it at the time and until their combined versions are heard the evidence cannot be regarded as complete.

CHAPTER TWELVE

GREAT ARGUMENT

I

WHEN Montgomery crossed to Normandy in June 1944 he believed that the Germans could have been thrown out of the war by the following Christmas and the Japanese defeated within six months thereafter. It was a belief he never forsook either during the campaign or afterwards. Even though the collapse of the Germans did not take place until May 1945— six months later than he anticipated—Montgomery stuck to his view that the war might have ended according to his time-table had he remained in control of the armies in the field.

There are, therefore, two versions of the campaign: the story of how it was actually fought, and the story (which we are concerned with here) of the campaign seen through Montgomery's eyes.

To the public the events flowed by in a coherent and connected pattern under the guiding hand of Eisenhower. One great milestone followed another: first the unbelievable success of the landing in June and the capture of Cherbourg. Then, through July and August, the long anxious battle of the bridgehead ending with the American break-out through St. Lô and the encirclement and destruction of the German Army in the Falaise Pocket. Then through the last days of the summer the kaleidoscopic and delirious pursuit, the fall of Paris, Brussels, Holland, the new American army sweeping up from southern France, and the Russian avalanche to the Oder. From day to day one talked of the ending of the war. Then the failure of Arnhem, the slow release of Antwerp, the abrupt halt all along the line ending with the ominous German counter-offensive at Christmas in the Ardennes. Then the dragging winter attacks up to the Rhine. And finally, in the spring, the breaking of the tidal wave which engulfed Germany from the east and the west.

Each event appeared to follow on logically and inevitably. But this was not so. The gravest divisions of opinion developed in the Allied High Command. Personal jealousies flared up. There were many moments of the most serious doubtings and hesitations. Vain and ridiculously emotional national rivalries clouded the issues. And often prejudices took fire through the lack of information and the unavoidable confusion of war.

Mainly because we had overwhelming strength and we were winning, and very largely through the patience and determined tact of General Eisenhower, these animosities never reached the point of open revolt. The Command was far more steady, far more complete and unified than it was in the previous war. One after another the simmering rivalries were composed and, in a sense, sublimated by the actual shock and movement of the fighting. And there were, as well, minor cross-currents that subdued the major waves. At Eisenhower's headquarters there were, for example, a group of British officers who by no means always supported Montgomery. And there were differences between the American commanders in addition to certain *malentendus* with the French and the goading silences of the Russians.

Montgomery wandered, a prickly and lonely prophet, through these political thickets. To his opponents he seemed to be forever growling vainly out of his lair: "Have done. Away with these arguments. There is only one way to settle the war and that is to let me finish it for you. Just relax and hand over the business to me." For thirty years he had fought the British Army, and now that he had achieved some success in that direction he found himself tilting against a whole group of armies. It must have seemed to him sometimes more than exasperating. When, from time to time, he was given his head he raced away with enormous gusto—only to find, after a brief moment of liberty, the reins dragging him back again. There were many other horses, mostly Americans, who also wanted to run in this final sprint. And since they had the preponderating weight of men and arms in the field they insisted on their rights.

But at first Montgomery was away on his own. From June until August, from the landing until the Falaise Pocket, he controlled the Allied armies in the field, and the general direction of the tactical battle was his own. Let us dip into his own account of the engagement:

"Once ashore and firmly established my plan was to threaten to break out on the eastern flank—that is, in the Caen sector; by this threat to draw the main enemy reserves into that sector, to fight them there and keep them there, using the British and Canadian armies for the purpose. Having got the main enemy reserves committed on the *eastern* flank, my plan was to make the break-out on the *western* flank, using for this purpose the American armies under General Bradley,

7*

and pivoting on Caen; this attack was to be delivered southwards down to the Loire and then to proceed eastwards in a
wide sweep up to the Seine about Paris.

"This would cut off all the enemy forces south of the Seine,
over which river the bridges were to be destroyed by air action.
This general plan was given out by me to the general officers

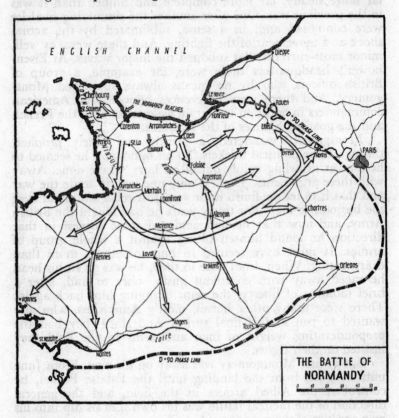

THE BATTLE OF
NORMANDY

of the field armies in London in March 1944—that is, three
months before D-day.

"The operations developed in June, July and August
exactly as I planned. I had given D plus 90 as a target date
for being lined up on the Seine; actually the first crossing of
the river was made on D plus 75."

About the details of the landing he says:

"My plan of assault, as approved by the Supreme Commander, provided for three simultaneous landings by eight

equivalent brigades—two British, two Canadian and two American. There were in addition on either flank British Commandos, U.S. Rangers and three airborne divisions, two of which were American. The British under Dempsey were to make straight for Caen and establish the pivot, while Bradley cut off the Cotentin (Cherbourg) peninsula and captured Cherbourg.

"I considered it essential for the success of the initial operations to have ashore, and ready for action by the end of D plus 3, seven divisions, together with the necessary proportion of armour, quite apart from the airborne troops. With these forces I was confident of being able to defeat the first German attempts to dislodge our forces and also of being able to retain the initiative."

The initiative was indeed maintained; but this was not apparent at the time. A "slogging match" developed, a bitter and excruciating series of battles which did not appear to be getting us anywhere. To the public who did not know the plan and the devious phases of its unfolding, and to the soldier who could not see the battle for the bullets, these hideous and changing conflicts of June and July seemed to be without pattern or direction, a chaos in which luck and courage governed all. Even some of those in command who knew the plan began to lose heart, so fierce and continuous was the struggle. And in the absence of detailed and consecutive news from hour to hour their minds began to fill with doubts.

And so a controversy developed over Montgomery, a controversy which continued with many permutations until long after the war. It was like some fungoid disease which, having been quenched at one place, lay dormant for a while and then broke out in a new form somewhere else. To those who were at Montgomery's headquarters and saw the orders go out day by day and watched the reports coming in, this controversy seemed childish and absurd. But whether or not this special view was right the fact remained that the argument was a very serious one: it touched the highest levels, it provoked the most emotional prejudices and here and there unseated the best reason.

It had been hoped in the planning that Caen would fall to the British in the assault. It did not fall; and immediately all those people who judge campaigns by the capture of towns and place-names began to imagine that we had failed. They forgot that it was not Caen we wanted but to attract the bulk of the German armour and artillery to this end of the bridge-head so that the Americans would be able to make an easier break-out at the other end. And this is precisely what happened. Although Caen did not fall in June, Rommel reacted entirely to Montgomery's plan by directing the bulk of his striking forces against the British on the outskirts of the city.

As these battles grew fiercer through June people at home began to suggest: "Montgomery has failed. He is getting nowhere. Why does not Caen fall?" At length Eisenhower was forced to take notice of them and his fears were confided to the Prime Minister. Did Monty really know what he was doing?

Mr. Churchill crossed to Montgomery's headquarters in France and found there the most surprising confidence. Set-backs? What set-backs? The battle was going excellently to plan. Having been beaten in the first assault Rommel was still hoping to wipe out the bridgehead and he was going about it in pre-cisely the wrong way. He was draining the rest of France of reserves in order to fight the decisive battle then and there in Normandy. Had he committed all these reserves together he might possibly have flung us back to the coast or at least con-tained us indefinitely in the bridgehead. But he had been bluffed by the Allied deception plans. He continued to fear a second Allied landing in the Pas de Calais area and so he was cautiously bringing down his reserves piecemeal into Nor-mandy. One by one they were being defeated, and in the end, if this went on, there would be no divisions left for a later stand on the Seine.

Montgomery reminded Churchill of the plan which had been agreed upon in March. Well, then, here was the plan in operation. Half a dozen panzer divisions were gathering round Caen in front of the British, while over on the left in front of the Americans the German line was tailing away. The shock of battle was enormous, the strain of fighting continuous. And the difficulties of manœuvring in close *bocage* country (a terrain intersected by thick hedges and small fields) were appalling. But still the plan was working out. Let the newspapers and critics hold their hands for a moment and they would see a victory.

Convinced, Churchill returned to England and passed on what had been said to Eisenhower. The Supreme Commander, if not exactly happy, was also inclined to put his trust in Montgomery, and from this moment until the closing of the gap at Falaise, Eisenhower loyally confirmed Montgomery's control.

The controversy might have ended here but for the appear-ance of several popular post-war books in America. Commander Harry Butcher, in his *My Three Years with Eisenhower*, reports that in June 1944 at S.H.A.E.F. there were constant complaints at the slowness of Montgomery, who "waited so long (at Caen) that two panzer divisions were drawn against him". This is set in contrast to Bradley's rapid progress on the right flank. Again, under the date of July 20th, Commander Butcher says, "Tedder says the British Chiefs of Staff would support any recommendation Ike might care to make with respect to Montgomery for not succeeding in going places with his big three-armoured division push (again near Caen)". It seems incredible (especially as Commander Butcher was Eisenhower's chief aide at the time) that the S.H.A.E.F. commanders could have had no notion of Montgomery's plan or that they could not have perceived that Montgomery was doing precisely what he had said he would do—attract the German armour to Caen so that Bradley could break out on the right flank.

Mr. Ralph Ingersoll, an American journalist who was attached to Bradley's staff, also wrote a book, *Top Secret*, which was published in 1946. He, too, makes the astonishing assertion that "Montgomery failed at Caen". He appears to believe (and the view was given wide currency in America) that the plan was for the British and Canadians to break out of Caen towards Paris, and that when this failed a dangerous stalemate developed. It is also suggested that at this point (in July) the strategy had to be changed: the feeble British were left behind at Caen while the Americans opened up an entirely new salient on the right.

In point of fact (as we now know from the officially published documents and the accounts of such leaders as Eisenhower and General Bedell Smith) the role of the British at this stage was never to break out and the strategy was never changed. The plan as laid down by Montgomery in March 1944 was followed to the letter and with overwhelming success. Very deliberately the British with their staying powers were set to attract and meet the great bulk of the German armour in a slogging match around Caen, while the Americans with their marvellous equipment, their mobility and their ardour for quick movement were given the fast-riding role in the west at St. Lô.

A study of Montgomery's directions to the Allied Army commanders throughout June, July and August 1944, brings out this point clearly. It also reveals that, at a time when all the world was puzzled and worried about the British and Canadian "slowness" at Caen, Montgomery was far more concerned about the delays in launching the American break-out at St. Lô.

Seen in the light of these documents, both British and American, Mr. Ingersoll's references to the British become so much sensational and irresponsible nonsense. The lamentable thing is not that he should be wrong, but that he should have been taken so seriously on both sides of the Atlantic; and that by 1946 Anglo-American relations should have drifted to the point where the book became the source of a misunderstanding between the two countries.

However, at the time, Montgomery's plan was going ahead. On July 25th the Americans started their break-out through St. Lô, the newly arrived American Third Army under Patton swinging right into Brittany and the remainder of the Americans racing round through Mayenne and Alençon to build up the southern wall of the pocket round the German Army.

Criticism for the time being expired. But there was one tense moment. The Germans made a desperate and bull-headed attempt to cut the American armies in two by breaking through their lines at the base of the pocket at Mortain.

"This was an exciting time", Montgomery says. "It was now to become apparent whether the enemy would stand and be defeated between the Seine and the Loire or whether he would endeavour to withdraw his forces behind the Seine. Between August 7th and the 11th it became clear that he had decided to fight the Battle of France on our side of the Seine. On the 7th a major counter-attack, employing up to six armoured divisions, was launched on Hitler's orders against the American forces in the area of Mortain. It was designed to cut off the forces operating south of Avranches by a drive to the sea. In the face of this counter-attack the Americans, assisted by the full weight of the Tactical Air Force, stood firm."

Then the denouement of this greatest battle of the western war: "I ordered the right flank of the Twelfth U.S. Army Group (the two American armies) to swing north to Argentan (the southern end of the mouth of the pocket) and intensified the British and Canadian thrusts southwards to the capture of Falaise (the northern end).

"It had become a race to trap the German forces deployed in the long salient (or pocket) between Falaise and Mortain. Meanwhile, the enemy received a tremendous hammering from the air. Falaise fell to the Canadian Army on August 16th; American forces reached Argentan, and fighting of tremendous intensity was in progress at the bottleneck with the German striving all he knew to force his way out."

With one last effort the Allies plugged the neck, the Air Force overran the enemy within the pocket, and the remainder of the Americans raced on to Paris, the Seine and eastern

France. It was the end. It was also probably the last of the classic land battles ever to be seen or endured in Europe.

The wreckage was fearful. There was a monstrous and horrifying debris of smashed horses, carts, vehicles and men choking up the country lanes. Twenty German corps and divisional commanders had been killed or captured, two others wounded. Forty-three divisions were knocked out. Half a million enemy soldiers had been eliminated. Fifteen hundred tanks and three thousand five hundred guns were either destroyed or captured. It was a victory on a cosmic scale.

There was even a personal triumph as complete as any leader of men could reasonably expect in this world. The long conflict of wills between Rommel and Montgomery was over. Having demolished his opponent's armies and utterly undone his generalship, Montgomery had the satisfaction of seeing the end of Rommel himself. The German Field-Marshal was struck down by the bullets of low-flying fighters in the village of Sainte Foy de Montgomery, in the midst of the battle area. The Montgomery clan had come to its birthplace for its revenge.

It is another revealing facet of Montgomery's mind that from this moment he lost all interest in Rommel. The picture was taken down from above his table in the caravan (the same caravan in which the photograph had first been posted at Alamein) and a photograph of Rundstedt, the new rival, set in its place. He no longer spoke of Rommel or thought of him. No sadistic (but perhaps understandable) pilgrimage was made to the spot where the arch-rival was hit. And when, months later, it was officially confirmed by the enemy that Rommel at last was dead,[1] Montgomery had no comment to make, no gesture of triumph. The truth was that he had long since ceased to rate Rommel as an equal.

But to those around Montgomery the passing out of Rommel added the last decorative touch to the victory. After so many doubts and so many months of waiting it was a transcendent moment. Montgomery had made good his word a hundred times over. The plan had been pure gold. He had fought his greatest battle, he had drawn hundreds of thousands of men to his will. He had manœuvred this vast and frightening host as though it were a platoon. And now he was entirely master of the battlefield and the road led on directly to the final *coup de grâce*.

[1] While Rommel was still convalescing it was discovered by the Gestapo that he was implicated in the bomb plot against Hitler. He was visited by Gestapo agents, and after the interview, he walked out alone into the woods. The following day his body was found: he had died of poisoning. Von Kluge, who replaced Rundstedt in the over-all command about this time, soon committed suicide also. Rundstedt was subsequently restored to his command.

It was at this point in August that Eisenhower sent word that Montgomery must step down. He must revert to the minor command of the two British armies while Eisenhower himself took up the operational direction in the field. To Montgomery the news could hardly be other than bitterly disappointing; a humiliating blow that took the edge off the whole victory.

It was a difficult moment for everybody. Eisenhower had done nothing which had not been pre-arranged. It had been accepted from the first that he was the Supreme Commander and that he must one day cross over to France and gather up the reins himself. There was no discourtesy and certainly no jealousy in the manner in which he took over the operational command; indeed he made it clear that Montgomery's future advice on the general conduct of the war would hold high priority.

To Eisenhower it seemed that he had no choice. There were now five American armies deployed as against two British. The American generals (let alone Congress and the American public) were wholly unwilling to continue under Montgomery's command—it was a slur on their own ability. Moreover, an Allied Headquarters had been created to meet this very situation, and Montgomery was not the man who had been nominated by Britain as the second in command. That position had been given to Air Marshal Tedder. If Montgomery continued to supplant Eisenhower and Tedder there would be an outcry in the United States Press and in Parliament.

To Montgomery these arguments were not conclusive. He had won a great victory. He had demonstrated a skill which had brought the Allies overwhelming success. Surely he was entitled to follow up that success. It was inefficient and dangerous to swop horses in mid-stream. As for the Supreme Allied Command there was nothing in the world to stop Eisenhower and Tedder from coming across to France and carrying on exactly as they had before. They could continue to control the rearward organization, to co-ordinate the flow of arms and men up to the front, to handle the *politics* of the battle, and the political resurrection of Europe.

As for the American Press, Montgomery argued, this point was of no account. *Victories were the only thing that mattered, not public opinion.* Victories moulded public opinion. Give the people victories and the public opinion would follow. There would be no criticism as long as we kept on winning. And the way to win the war quickly was to continue with the present command.

These two points of view were already irreconcilable enough, but something much more insoluble intervened. Supreme Headquarters and Montgomery were radically opposed on the actual tactics of the campaign as it should be fought from the Seine onwards.

Montgomery believed that the moment had come to throw Germany out of the war with one bold and decisive stroke. Given some forty divisions, or about a million men, and the cream of the Air Force, he was confident he could make one major thrust along the northern coast of Europe, enter the Ruhr and bring Germany to surrender. To do this he estimated that the Allies would have to halt on the right (in central France) and divert all priorities in petrol, vehicles and other equipment to the northern column. Indeed, with that plan in view he had already ordered Bradley to seize Paris, plug the gap between Paris and Orleans and then stop. Certainly, he argued, there were dangers in the scheme but the hour was propitious, the enemy was in a state of rout and once in the Ruhr we had only to maintain forces there for a maximum of three months—and that would be the end.

Supreme Headquarters strongly disagreed. One could not leave all France behind and expose a flank hundreds of miles in length. The thrust could never be maintained; a few soldiers might struggle into the Ruhr and then they would be cut off. It was absolutely necessary to capture first a large supply port on the North Sea. All the armies (there were now seven) must move up to the Rhine together.

Montgomery protested that this would mean that the war would drag on for months; that if we presented a long thin front to the enemy then Rundstedt would hold it off by simply maintaining a long thin line of his own, and we would be nowhere strong enough to break it. Now in August was the moment when he was unable to withstand one concentrated blow.

The arguments swayed back and forth through correspondence and subordinates, and were continued in a painful meeting between Eisenhower and Montgomery themselves in Montgomery's caravan. Montgomery would not and Eisenhower could not back down. And so it came to a matter of the senior man exerting his authority. Montgomery has summed up the issue himself:

"The speed of our advance through the Pas de Calais and Belgium convinced me that if the Allies could concentrate and maintain sufficient strength for the task, one powerful and full-blooded thrust deep into Germany would overwhelm the enemy and carry with it decisive results.

"The best axis along which such a thrust could have been developed was the route of the Ruhr leading to the plains of northern Germany. It was obvious that the enemy would concentrate strong forces to defend this vital axis, and the industrial area of the Ruhr.

"Speed was essential; the stroke could be effective only if carried out at once, taking advantage of the disorganized state of the enemy; moreover, weather conditions would inevitably deteriorate from mid-September onwards and handicap the use of our air power and airborne forces. But we would have to be strong enough on the selected axis to get decisive results quickly.

"Could sufficient troops be made available, and our maintenance sustain them on such a long line of communication? If so, the end of the war was in sight.

"The Supreme Commander came to the decision that we should not at this stage stick out our neck in one single thrust deep into enemy territory, owing to our lack of major deepwater ports. The lines of communication still stretched to the Normandy beaches and Cherbourg peninsula, and the autumn weather was close upon us. He therefore decided that the early opening up of deep-water ports and the improvement of our maintenance facilities were pre-requisites to the final assault on Germany proper. He directed that our immediate aim should be the establishment of bridges over the Rhine throughout its entire length, and that we should not go beyond this until Antwerp or Rotterdam could be opened."

Looking back on the event it is still difficult for the non-expert to decide who was right. That extra six months on the war in 1945 acutely intensified the ensuing famine in Europe, accelerated (through air bombing) the general downslide of civilization in the post-war years, killed many thousands of additional men and women, and probably lengthened the Japanese war as well. So Montgomery's thrust, if possible, was well worth trying. But even among the British he had opponents. The Russians at this time required 150 divisions to reach the Oder. Could the Western Allies have hoped to throw the Germans out of the war with just 30 divisions? Probably there was just one event which could have made Montgomery's scheme water-tight beyond all doubt. That was the success of the July bomb plot against Hitler. In the light of the evidence at the Nuremberg trials there can be no longer much doubt that had Hitler died then the collapse would have followed before the winter of 1944.

But the plot did not succeed, and Montgomery went off

obediently enough to clean up the deep-water port of Antwerp. No personal animosity remained between him and Eisenhower, any more than there had been with Alexander over the Sicilian and Italian campaigns. They had disagreed on a technical level, but each continued to respect the integrity and honesty of the other. Courtiers about the High Command whispered little stories and made the disagreement fester in secret, but Eisenhower and Montgomery reached across their heads and for the time being agreed to disagree. And it was at this moment that the British Cabinet made the somewhat obvious but acceptable gesture of creating Montgomery a field-marshal

Never perhaps had two such different personalities come together on a battlefield as Eisenhower and Montgomery. Their very appearance displayed their opposing and yet interlocking natures. On Eisenhower's broad and smiling face everything was boyishness, frankness and enthusiasm. Even in his loose-limbed easy walk and his warm full voice there was an air of friendliness and plain dealing. The heart warmed to him at once. Here was a man who was still the boy who once fished by the water-hole, an extrovert without any pretensions, a leader who knew and lived by all the weakness and failings and emotions of the ordinary human being; and finally a soldier of exceptional intelligence trying quite simply and devotedly to do his job as well as he could. Against this was set that "intensely compacted hank of steel wire" that made up the troubled and complicated nature of Montgomery. It was the difference between the fire and the burning-glass, the humanist and the individualist, the extrovert and the introvert, the determined amateur and the professional.

Eisenhower expressed truly the broad American attitude towards fighting: to get in there with the team and give it all you've got, to push on and exploit each success as it came along, to fight clean and fast. To the American public three thousand miles away the war never assumed the same aspect as it did to the people of Europe and Russia. It was never a desperate personal struggle for survival to-day or to-morrow in one's own home, but a fiercely dramatic game played at a distance. If an army were wiped out that did not mean that Kansas or Pittsburg was going to be blown to bits to-morrow. And yet, because the American soldier was offering his life in this distant arena, and his people at home could have no notion of what the fighting was like, the war possessed for the American public a thousand imagined terrors and triumphs; all its colours and even its viciousness were heightened, and the whole conception of the struggle was essentially dramatic and heroic. And just as we can become immensely moved in a theatre at a great tragedy, so the Americans were moved. But we react quite differently and far less dramatically when a real-life tragedy comes into our own lives. At the front the American soldier knew what this real-life tragedy was like. But at first, coming from the farm and the city office in the Middle West, he approached the war in the same dramatic way as the public at home, and later on the tragedy he came to know was for himself and not for his wife and children. Possibly because of this he had a double bravery: he fought not out of desperation but in the belief of a cause.

This was the altruism of Eisenhower's approach to war: he fought for an idea and perhaps a tradition. Montgomery fought for survival, with generations of struggling for survival behind him. With Montgomery there was no question of merely pitching in and giving it all you had: the thing to do was to kill with the utmost efficiency and on a long-term basis. You made a cold-blooded plan for killing and you stuck to it. You were never distracted by local successes, never carried away by enthusiasms or strokes of luck, never moved by public opinion; you stuck to the science of the matter. It is not suggested that Eisenhower and the Americans were amateurs, but their *emotions* were those of the amateur.

It followed, then, that there was a fundamental difference in the reactions of the Americans and the British leaders; those moments in the battle which seemed to the Americans to be the height of success sometimes appeared to be the very reverse to Montgomery, and he was urging "Pause and consolidate" when the Americans were crying "Push on". And sometimes when the Americans were advising caution Montgomery was all for advancing. Thus at Falaise, when the American plan was for taking all the armies steadily up to the Rhine together, Montgomery wanted to fling everything into the desperate gamble of an isolated spearhead march right into the centre of the Reich. And this, ironically, at a time when his critics were declaring he was "too slow, too cautious".

2

But now in August the bridgehead was done with. Eisenhower assumed the field command of the armies on September 1st and at once put his own plan into operation. He countermanded Montgomery's instructions that Bradley should halt at Paris and urged all the armies forward to the

Rhine together. Bradley was elevated to equal status with Montgomery as the commander of an army group.

Not one but two main thrusts were to be directed at Germany—one by General Patton aimed south of Paris towards the Saar, and the other by Montgomery in the north through Belgium and Holland to the lower Rhine. At the same time all other Allied forces were to be led up to the river with all possible speed and with more or less equal supplies.

It is interesting to follow the correspondence between Eisenhower and Montgomery from this point onwards.

On September 4th Montgomery wrote to Eisenhower stressing his opposition to the S.H.A.E.F. plan. He said in this letter that the plan meant a slow and deliberate campaign because the Allied armies would be spread on a very wide frontage, our administrative resources would be spread accordingly and would fall down. He reiterated that we would be nowhere strong enough to get decisive results quickly, the Germans would thus be given time to recover and we would become involved in a long winter campaign.

Again Montgomery asserted that there must be under Eisenhower a land force commander who would co-ordinate the armies and keep close up with the battle. The face of modern war was such, he argued, that a battle could very quickly get out of hand unless some one commander was able to give his sole and undivided attention to it. Eisenhower himself was already involved with too many problems: political, international, financial, governmental. Therefore let Eisenhower have an Army C.-in-C. just as he already had an Air and a Navy C.-in-C.

The letter can hardly have made agreeable reading to the soldiers at S.H.A.E.F. But Montgomery appended a startling suggestion. "If", he said, "I am not suitable for the appointment of C.-in-C. in the field, let Bradley have the job."

It was an offer which was kept secret at the time and has never been publicized since. Montgomery pressed it strongly. Not once, but a number of times, and in writing, he offered to serve under Bradley who was his junior both in rank and reputation. Since the Americans had so many more soldiers than the British, he wrote, it was only reasonable that the appointment should go to an American. At all events let *someone* be appointed.

Eisenhower's immediate reply to this was "No. British public opinion would never stand it." And, no doubt, he was right.

By now (September) the Supreme Commander had moved

his headquarters from England to Granville on the Atlantic side of the Cherbourg peninsula. Montgomery, holding the views he did, could hardly fail to note that Granville was some 500 miles from the front line, and the front line was getting farther away every day. However, on September 5th, Eisenhower issued the following order from Granville:

"12th Army Group (American) will capture the Saar and the Frankfurt area. 21st Army Group (British and Canadian) will capture the Ruhr and Antwerp."

Montgomery replied with repeated telegrams saying it was not possible to carry out these orders. 21st Army Group was not strong enough. S.H.A.E.F. was completely out of touch with the realities of the situation.

On September 15th Eisenhower followed up his orders with a letter to Montgomery, saying, "We shall soon have captured the Ruhr, and the Saar and the Frankfurt area, and I would like your views as to what we should do next".

Montgomery received this letter at a time when he was fighting increasing resistance on the Leopold Canal and other lines. He replied that he saw no chance of capturing the Ruhr *or* the Saar *or* the Frankfurt area unless the command and the strategy were reorganized in what he considered a more professional way.

However, an order was an order, and Montgomery proceeded with his attack towards the lower Rhine.

3

With the aid of three airborne divisions the British were asked first to seize bridgeheads at Grave, Nijmegen and Arnhem. The battle began on September 17th and reached a stalemate eight days later with the honours standing fairly even: we took two bridges and failed at the third—Arnhem. Arnhem was an incident magnified far beyond its strategic importance by the peculiar and exciting circumstances and the poignant tragedy of the stranded parachutists. Actually only a handful of divisions was involved, the over-all losses were small, and apart from the magnificent outburst of courage the battle had no more significance than half a dozen actions that were fought that same winter. "During the eight vital days of battle", Montgomery reported afterwards, "there were only two on which the weather permitted a reasonable scale of offensive air support and air transportation."

A longer and in some ways more gruelling engagement followed in October with the reduction of the approaches to

Antwerp, which was to become the main—the vital—port for
the Allies. In early November the port was clear. Meanwhile
things had not gone too well all along the line; somehow the
German rout at Falaise had turned into a bitter defence, and
all hope of finishing the war before Christmas had vanished.
Patton, having first outrun his supplies of fuel and ammunition,
was restocked, but still he was held up around Metz, and there
was no sign anywhere of the Allies achieving an early passage
of the river. The armies had come up to the Rhine together
and now they were blocked. In the thick of a particularly bitter
winter the battle had bogged down. And again there were
shortages in supply: even shells were rationed. It was impossible to deny that a great many of the dire things Montgomery
had predicted about the S.H.A.E.F. plan had actually come to
pass.

Restless, frustrated, and impatient, Montgomery wrote
again to the Supreme Commander. On December 13th the
letter was delivered to Eisenhower, who by then had taken up
his headquarters at Versailles, outside Paris. In it Montgomery
declared that the strategy since Falaise had not been successful.
Things indeed had gone wrong ever since Eisenhower himself
had taken over the direct command in his remote headquarters.
If the Supreme Commander would not appoint a deputy to
combine the battle at the front then Montgomery had another
suggestion. Let him organize the theatre into "fronts" with a
C.-in-C. in charge of each front. Resources should be allotted
to each front in accordance with its problems and tasks.

The northern front, Montgomery urged, should be given
to himself and it should extend southwards as far as the
Ardennes. This would mean placing the American Ninth Army
as well as the British and Canadians under Montgomery; and
thus they would proceed to the capture of the Ruhr.

General Bradley at once hotly opposed this plan. In
Washington also the idea of again placing American troops
under British command was strongly opposed—even resented.

In London the British Chiefs of Staff, reviewing the disappointing results of the autumn, on the whole, took Montgomery's side.

Here, then, was a disagreement running beyond personalities
into the sphere of governments, and Eisenhower needed a more
than human patience and tact to cope with it. The argument
was continuing in a desultory way when suddenly the Germans
struck in the Ardennes with the largest assembly of armour ever
seen in Europe; the object nothing less than the recapture of
Antwerp and the cutting of the Allied forces in half.

Some days of particularly bad weather had made air reconnaissance impossible, and thus the Germans came up to their start-line in secret, and delivered their opening blow with tremendous success. The American armies were split down the centre. Throughout December 16th and 17th the situation was out of control.

At Supreme Headquarters in Versailles there was a commotion as the appalling news came in.[1] Conference followed conference. It was useless now to discuss whether in fact the general strategy was wrong; the thing was to do something quickly before the situation developed into complete chaos. For the moment the chain of command had broken down. Over a large area generals were out of touch with the fighting, and the one imperative was to re-establish a command which would grip the situation together again. There were only a few hours in which to decide. Major-General Whiteley, a senior British officer attached to Eisenhower, suggested that Montgomery should be called in. At once, as though they had been waiting for this very day, the rivalries flared out. A strong faction at Supreme Headquarters (it was British as well as American) had never admitted Montgomery's skill in the Battle of Normandy; indeed it believed that he had mishandled it. They had urged his replacement while the battle was on and they could see no reason for calling him in now. They disliked his personality, they suspected he would be all too ready to crow over the matter and exacerbate feelings in every direction. Another group, while no lovers of the Montgomery manner, were willing to admit his skill and believed that at least he could be given some measure of control. As the argument raged back and forth at Versailles, still worse and worse news arrived. But at last, as always in a crisis, the issue devolved upon Eisenhower himself; he alone could settle the matter. He decided that Montgomery should have command of the First and Ninth American Armies then in the thick of the fighting in the north. Bradley meanwhile should continue in control of the remaining American forces on the southern flank of the battle.

Thus began the incident of the Ardennes, which was clouded by the crisis at the time and seems to have become more clouded by prejudices and emotional rivalries ever since.

What happened in the Ardennes? The facts as we read them in the intelligence reports and the war diaries seem clear enough. The Germans struck with two panzer armies and made

---

[1] In fairness it must be stated that General Bedell Smith denies there was any great concern at S.H.A.E.F.

a deep penetration at a point where the Americans were re-grouping; they demolished an untried American division and proceeded at speed towards Liége and the River Meuse, leaving isolated pockets of American resistance behind them. Mont-gomery, acting on his own initiative as the first reports came in, cancelled the mustering of his British armies for a battle in the extreme north and instead began to cover the approaches to Brussels and Antwerp. On December 20th he was given com-mand of the First and Ninth American Armies in the main battle area. Judging that the Germans intended to continue toward Liége he cancelled the American plans for counter-attack and instead formed a defensive line.

To continue in Montgomery's own words: "The Battle of the Ardennes was won primarily by the staunch fighting qualities of the American soldier, and the enemy's subsequent confusion was completed by the intense air action which became possible as weather conditions improved. Sixth S.S. Panzer Army broke itself against the northern shoulder of the salient, while Fifth Panzer Army spent its drive in the fierce battles which centred on Bastogne. Regrouping the First and Ninth U.S. Armies, assisted by British formations, made pos-sible the rapid formation of a reserve corps of four U.S. divisions under General Collins. The action of this corps, co-ordinated with the drive from the south by General Patton's Third Army, pinched the enemy forces out of the salient.

"The enemy had been prevented from crossing the Meuse in the nick of time. A detailed study of the battle would show how rapid re-grouping enabled the Allies to regain the initiative which the enemy had temporarily seized. Once we were sure of the Meuse crossings it became increasingly apparent that the opportunity had come to turn the enemy's position to our advantage. Hitler's projected counter-offensive ended in a tactical defeat, and the Germans received a tremendous battering." It was on New Year's Day, 1945, that the worst was over.

Those who were with Montgomery at this time were astonished at the snap and incisiveness of his orders. At times since he had lost the over-all command he had seemed lethargic, and as the long autumn battles in the mud had dragged on many people remembered a similar period under Montgomery's command in Italy during the previous year. Then, as now, he was living in a dreary village surrounded by mud, cold and rain, his convoys and soldiers straggling on the roads without the immediate prospect of getting anywhere. But now, under the stimulus of rapid action, all the old intensity and certainty came racing back. It might not be altogether wrong to say that he was enjoying himself.

He returned to Belgium after the fray full of enthusiasm. Dressed in a red beret and a camouflaged parachutist's jacket (he had recently been made Colonel-Commandant of the Parachute Regiment), he gathered the war correspondents to tell them his version of the story.

Curiously, Montgomery's Press conferences were never very successful. He tended to underrate the technical knowledge of his audience, and often he would speak with a monosyllabic simplicity that was impossible to pass on to a newspaper. "We are all one great team," he would say, "and we have all got to pull together." And he would return to the point again and again. Burning for real news the correspondents sat silently in rows on the wooden benches, wondering how on earth they could turn a homily on the team spirit into a news story. When they tried to pin Montgomery down to hard facts he frequently dodged the issue and escaped into generalities. More than anything else these conferences spread the already popular belief that the Field-Marshal, while a remarkable stimulator of men, was no ball of mental fire.

Moreover, Montgomery was not very good at dissembling. His thought processes *were* simple. They were also remarkably penetrating, but that did not appear at a Press conference. He rarely discussed the technicalities of which his head was full: this, he felt, would be "giving away his methods". While most commanders delighted in revealing their knowledge of tactics, with Montgomery it was the exact reverse. He cut all the preliminaries and, as it were, presented you with the finished solution of the problem. Because he conceived the Press more or less as a signalling set for the transmitting of atmosphere and news, and because he heard and read simple untechnical accounts of the battle on the radio and in the newspapers, he overlooked the fact that the correspondents themselves were not necessarily simple people, and that they, not he, were expert in rendering technicalities into newspaper simplicities. Further, he was by nature not always an impartial summer-up. He looked upon affairs from his own angle and it was foreign to him to analyse the thoughts and ideas of others. Often when he intended to be fair he simply neglected the other man's point of view. And when he was pleased and elated he could not disguise the fact.

He was elated on this morning after the Battle of the Ardennes. His red beret was in character with his brimming emotions. It was not an inaccurate summing-up as far as it went, but there was a slight flavour of patronage in his references to the part played by Bradley and the other American generals. At this special moment, when it seemed on the face of it that Bradley had been taken unawares in the Ardennes, and that the American commanders had allowed themselves to be out-manoeuvred, the report of this conference was bound to give offence. It was the signal for yet another public and a private flare-up over Montgomery and the position of the British vis-à-vis the Americans in the war.

For some time a section of the Press in England and America had been exchanging barely modulated abuse with one another. A good deal of it was childish and silly, but then quite a large number of people felt (unconsciously) childish and silly, and the argument was an expression of war-nerves which had been strained far too long. When it was suggested from Chicago and New York that the British were not pulling their weight, the British people looked at their drab cities and their drab and anxiety-ridden lives and remembered how long the United States had taken to enter the common war, how rich were the American soldiers billeted in England and how safe and well-fed were the American civilians. When London hinted that American generals were not very skilful and that New York business men seemed to think that the war was being run for their special benefit, people in the United States remembered that they were supplying the greatest number of troops and equipment in both Europe and the Pacific: that they were entitled to some gratitude for their help in a European cause which many in their hearts could not regard as their own. Why should they save the British Empire for the British?

This was the public quarrel. The private disturbance was just as acid. The Ardennes offensive inevitably had raised the suggestion that the American generals had been for a time out-witted by Rundstedt. Being human, they—and many of the staff—did not enjoy the spectacle of Montgomery appearing to come to the rescue. When Montgomery chose this moment to make his public statement on how he had fought the Battle of the Ardennes with American troops, and at the same time renewed his demands to be placed in permanent control of American forces—then feelings leaped into active dislike.

General Bradley complained that Montgomery's statements were making him (Bradley) ridiculous and lowering his authority in the eyes of his men. Discipline was suffering. When Bradley put out his own version of the Ardennes battle, a version which diminished the role Montgomery had played, the British Press flamed out angrily. And still Montgomery per-

sisted that, for the conquest of the Ruhr at least, he should be
given the full command in the north. To rival American
commanders it sounded as if he were saying: "There you are.
Look what happened in the Ardennes. You had to call on me
for assistance. I had to get you out of the mess." If Montgomery did not say quite this he did continue to indicate
strongly that he felt the general direction of the campaign was
at fault, and that the picking and thrusting at the Rhine was
advancing nobody. Things were getting very near an open
breach between Supreme Headquarters and 21st Army Group.
Staff officers who had the leisure to discuss these things were
becoming more and more acrimonious.

Looking back on the scene from a world at peace one might
marvel that the generals could brawl so cold-bloodedly with
one another at a time when so many thousands were exposing
themselves to death, and dying. But war—as one so easily
forgets—is a thing of emotion, of *amour propre*, of crude recourse
to violence. Each believed passionately in his own point of
view. It was a gunman's world. And now with the end in sight
many a man who had been missing in the crisis was hungering
for the honours. Many were desperate to prove themselves. All
believed they were acting for the best. It was a situation no one
quite knew how to tackle.

It was in the first week of January, immediately after the
Battle of the Ardennes, that Montgomery wrote to Eisenhower
yet again asking for a rearrangement of the command, on the
grounds that the strategical plan directed from Versailles was
continuing to fail. Eisenhower replied saying he could not alter
his position, and he added that the Field-Marshal by his
constant prediction of failure was doing harm to the Allied
cause. By now the argument was coursing strongly in America
and London, and Eisenhower was under some considerable
pressure from Washington. Again he reasoned: could not the
Field-Marshal see how impossible it was to fly against public
opinion in the United States? Doggedly Montgomery replied:
"Victories make public opinion. Give me the Ninth Army and
I will take the Ruhr."

This was a much more serious impasse than the earlier
contretemps in the autumn, and de Guingand was kept
shuttling between 21st Army Group in Belgium and Supreme
Headquarters in France. De Guingand was a master at smoothing out difficulties but this was getting beyond him.

At length Eisenhower declared, not without some feeling,
that the issue had gone too far. He had exhausted every
argument. He had gone to the limit of his powers in making

concessions to Montgomery. Both tact and reason seemed useless. In his earnestness he thumped upon the table. Very well. If Montgomery wanted a show-down he should have it. Let the matter go back to Washington and London. Let them decide. It was either he or Montgomery. One of them would have to go.

With this ultimatum in his pocket de Guingand posted back across France and Belgium to 21st Army Group, and arrived late at night. Montgomery heard the news silently. Since boyhood he had loved to sail up as close to the rocks as possible, and now he was very close to the rocks indeed. Well, he on his side had tried everything. He had pushed his beliefs to the climax, failed, and that was that. Here was a matter in which not even Churchill could intervene.

A telegram accepting Eisenhower's authority was written out and dispatched at once. Immediately a modest and charming reply was received from Eisenhower, assuring Montgomery of the widest powers Supreme Headquarters was able to give him. At the same time a friendly letter was sent by Montgomery to Bradley saying that it had been an honour to command American troops; and Bradley received a similar note from Churchill assuring him of the respect and support of the British Government.

It was at this point that Eisenhower did something which was both magnanimous and shrewd. Having established his authority he suddenly turned round and gave Montgomery what he wanted. The theatre was organized into fronts and the Ninth American Army was placed under Montgomery's command. Together the Allies crossed the Rhine in great force. The crisis was over. It was never to recur.

There was never anything more in the dispute than this, and subsequent attempts to magnify the disagreements were simply mischievous and untrue. When the campaign was over Montgomery himself summed up the matter very clearly. "When Allies work together", he wrote, "there are bound to be different points of view, and when these occur it is essential that they are thrashed out fully and frankly; but once a final decision is given, it is the duty of all members of the team to carry out that decision loyally. The Allied team worked in this spirit, and by its team work achieved overwhelming victory.

"In June 1945, when the German war was over and Supreme Headquarters was being dissolved, I wrote to General Eisenhower and thanked him for all that he had done for the British armies, and for myself. I said that I wanted him to know that I, a British general, had been proud to serve under

American command. Ike, as I like to call him, wrote me this very charming letter:

" 'DEAR MONTY,—Your note to me written on the 7th is one of the finest things I have ever received. I am intensely gratified that you feel as you do. In the aftermath of this Allied effort enduring friendships and feelings of mutual respect among higher commanders will have a most beneficial effect. The team must continue to exist in spirit.

" 'Your own high place among leaders of your country is firmly fixed, and it has never been easy for me to disagree with what I knew to be your real convictions. But it will always be a great privilege to bear evidence to the fact that whenever decision was made, regardless of your personal opinion, your loyalty and efficiency in execution were to be counted upon with certainty.

" 'I hope you realize how deeply appreciative I am of your letter and the spirit that prompted you to write it, as well as of the tremendous help and assistance that you have been to me and to this whole Allied Force since it was first formed. In whatever years are left to both of us, possibly we may occasionally meet, not only to reminisce, but to exemplify the spirit of comradeship that I trust will exist between our two countries for all time.

" 'With warm personal regards,

" 'As ever,

" 'IKE.' "

Montgomery's book, *Normandy to the Baltic*, which deals with these affairs, is an astonishing piece of documentation, full of terse authoritative writing. It will probably remain as a standard work for students of the north-west European campaign. In it one obtains an entirely new picture of Montgomery, his extraordinarily detached view of the battle as a whole, his incisive grip on the development of the struggle day by day, his honesty and his unaffected admiration of the Americans. Not one hint of personal animosity emerges. American and British, generals and privates, are regarded impartially and unemotionally as counters in an elaborate and highly technical game. One reads here of the fantastically intricate planning by which he laid not one but two encircling layers round the German armies west of the Seine, of the complicated approach to the Ruhr; and there is an entirely unprejudiced account of his dealings with S.H.A.E.F.

However, this is all material for the professional student and lies outside the personal business of biography. What we are concerned with here is that in January, having brought their differences to a crisis, Eisenhower and Montgomery offered one another the fullest co-operation.

Why had Montgomery persisted so implacably in his demands? His enemies said—personal vanity. Yet when we look into his own mind and remember all his background of experiences from childhood onwards we find the matter much more complicated. With some truth he could say: "Whenever I was given a free hand to fight the war as I thought right, success was complete and decisive: and the end of the war was brought nearer, *e.g.* Alamein, Sicily, Normandy, the Ardennes, the crossing of the Rhine. Whenever my advice was not followed we got into grave difficulties."

And when the casualties came to be counted one had to acknowledge this point as well: "I always stood not only for the need to win victories, but to win them with the minimum loss of life. For this reason I refused always to start till I was ready— and the soldiers knew this. Hence their regard for me."

Finally, it was impossible for Montgomery not to believe that he had agitated all through the dark autumn days of 1944 for a new organization of command; and that it took the crisis of the Ardennes and a really first-class row to get what he wanted. Then all went well.

Whether or not all this builds up into a combination of vanity and luck and persistence, the fact remains that it is a logical case, a case for the serious attention of history.

And now the spring was breaking. With first the King, and then Churchill, staying at his side in his headquarters, Montgomery planned and made his crossing of the Rhine. Then the avalanche burst over Germany to Berlin.

Visiting Normandy six days after the landing, Churchill had written in Montgomery's autograph book:

"As it was in the beginning so may it continue to the end".

On November 6th he had added:

"The conquest of Germany remains". On March 4th, 1945, he wrote again: "The British Army has reached the Rhine on a broad front and with its Allies from America and its Canadian brothers will presently pass this obstacle as it has so many others. Such are the rewards which fall to the brave when led with unwearying energy and unequalled skill."

In March 1945 as he watched the British stream across the river the Prime Minister made another entry: "The Rhine with all its fortress lines lies behind the 21st Group of Armies. Once again they have been a hinge upon which massive gates revolved. Once again they have proved that physical barriers are vain without the means and spirit to hold them.

" A beaten army, not long ago Master of Europe, retreats before its pursuers. The goal is not to be denied to those who have come so far and fought so well under proved and faithful leadership.

"Forward all on wings of flame to final Victory."

Soberly Montgomery notes that the Germans had, in his opinion, made three major mistakes: "The first was the decision to fight the Battle of France south of the Seine. By failing to surrender the territory between the Seine and the Loire and to take advantage of the Seine obstacle they suffered tremendous losses . . . and widespread political repercussions.

"Then came the second mistake. They launched a counter-offensive in the Ardennes, designed to hit the Allies so hard that the German striking force could subsequently be switched to the east. But they failed to win the air battle first; they had not the air resources nor adequate supplies of fuel for a major counter-stroke, and were wrong to attempt it. While some progress was made in the short period of bad weather, the enterprise was doomed to failure. A counter-attack, Yes; a counter-offensive, No.

"The third big mistake was the decision to stand and fight west of the Rhine in the hope of masking the Ruhr."

4

Two scenes on Lüneburg Heath in northern Germany, the scenes with which Montgomery ended the war.

A funeral cortège comes winding through the trees in the bright spring sunshine. A gun carriage, the coffin with the Union Jack draped round it, Montgomery walking a little ahead. A group of senior officers waiting on the road falls in behind and follows the coffin across the grass to an open grave beside a bank of trees. It is an afternoon of unusual and beautiful fresh-ness, so still that the voice of the chaplain sounds clearly across the field and, at the firing of the rifles in the air, the birds rise screaming and a dog barks in the farmyard in the valley.

Montgomery is the first to go up to the grave and salute the body of his friend John Poston, of the 11th Hussars. Some thirty months have gone by since they first met quite for-tuitously in the Egyptian desert on Montgomery's arrival there. Since then the boy of twenty-five and the man in his fifties have been everywhere together in ten countries along the Army's line of march, Montgomery directing, Poston riding

THE LUNEBURG SURRENDER

MONTGOMERY, EISENHOWER AND BRADLEY

out each day in his jeep to the front line to gather the news and bring it home in the evening. "Home" was Tactical Headquarters, a group of caravans and vehicles, the two puppies "Rommel and Hitler", and this was very much a piece of England in whatever country it was though it never stayed more than a few days in the same place. The grave lies in Tactical Headquarters, now. Poston would never take care. He was always discovering short-cuts back along roads which had not been reconnoitred. He was taking a short-cut when a little group of fanatical German boys, firing some of the last shots of the war, ambushed him. He drove the jeep straight at them as they fired, he was wounded, shot it out from a ditch and died; and Montgomery sent out a party to bring the body in. And now, saluting shortly, he walked back to his caravan and wrote this letter to *The Times* in London:

"There can be few young officers who have seen this war from the inside as did John Poston.

"He knew everything that was going on and was in possession of much information that is secret and must remain secret for all time. We trod the path together from Alamein to the Elbe.

"I gave him my complete trust and confidence and he would come to me with his own personal troubles. He had been through this war from the beginning and he saw the end approaching. The Promised Land was not so very far away and he gave his life that others might enjoy it.

"I was completely devoted to him and I feel very sad."

From the funeral Montgomery went up to the hill-top outside Lüneburg to receive the German commanders coming in to surrender. It was a grey evening: grey heather, grey heavy clouds, grey coats on the Germans and grey in their faces.

"Tell me," said Montgomery in his caravan to Admiral Friedeburg, the leader of the enemy delegation, "is this a good likeness of Field-Marshal Rundstedt? I always like to study my opponents."

Friedeburg looked at the photograph and dully agreed that it was excellent. Rundstedt, the man who had said "Montgomery is the ablest of the British generals"; the German Field-Marshal who was now making his private surrender somewhere in the south.

Never had anyone seen Montgomery so jocular as he was on this occasion. He kept the Germans waiting. Motioned them to stand here and here. Read them the terms of surrender as though they were a classroom of schoolboys taking dictation. Ordered them to sign one by one.

8

And now in this first week in May the story was almost complete. Hitler was dead. Goebbels was dead. Himmler was in hiding. Goering a prisoner. And the Russians were in Berlin. The British Army had crossed to the Baltic to join hands with them. The German Army was a bewildered and panic-stricken herd streaming into the Anglo-American lines in front of the Russians. And by a curious stroke of fortune the German High Command had come first to Montgomery to offer their unconditional surrender. He looked at them quietly over the rims of his glasses; Germans, the enemy, the beaten enemy, the unskilful and foolish enemy, and therefore nothing. They were of no interest any longer. They might as well be dead.

Montgomery made his last address to the troops:

"What I have to say is very simple and quite short. I would ask you all to remember those of our comrades who fell in the struggle. They gave their lives that others might have freedom, and no man can do more than that. I believe that He would say to each of them: 'Well done, thou good and faithful servant'.

"And we who remain have seen the thing through to the end; we all have a feeling of great joy and thankfulness that we have been preserved to see this day. . . . 'This is the Lord's doing, and it is marvellous in our eyes.'

"Few commanders can have had such loyal service as you have given me. I thank each one of you from the bottom of my heart. We have won the German war. Let us now win the peace."

And Churchill wrote the final chapter in the autograph book:

"At last the goal is reached.

"The terrible enemy has unconditionally surrendered.

"This record of military glories, predicted or celebrated, now in its tenth chapter, reaches its conclusion. The fame of the Army Group, like that of the Eighth Army, will long shine in history, and other generations besides our own will honour their deeds and above all the character, profound strategy and untiring zeal of their Commander who marched from Egypt through Tripoli, Sicily and southern Italy, and through France, Belgium, Holland and Germany to the Baltic and the Elbe without losing a battle or even a serious action."

CHAPTER THIRTEEN

1946 IN LONDON

I

A FULL seven rows of medals decorated the Field-Marshal's chest. In addition to his G.C.B. conferred at the end of the war, he had been created a chief commander of the United States Legion of Merit and had received that country's Distinguished Service Medal. From the Russians he had the Order of Suvorov and the Order of Victory. From the French the Grand Cross of the Legion of Honour and another Croix de Guerre to add to his old one from the earlier war. From the Belgians he had the Grand Cordon of the Order of Leopold and still another Croix de Guerre. He had the Grand Cross of the Order of the Lion of the Netherlands, and the Danes made him a first-class member of the Order of the Elephant. At Prague he was given the Order of the White Lion, the Star of Victory and a fourth Croix de Guerre. From the Poles he had the Order of Virtuti Militari, from the Greeks the Order of King George of the Hellenes, from Morocco the Order of the Sultan and from Tunisia the Order of the Bey. They shone together, some thirty ribbons in all, in a solid plate of colour on his battledress.

He was the controller of the British Zone of Occupation with twenty million German subjects, and he was the British member of the Allied Control Commission in Berlin.

At home in Britain and in the Empire there was scarcely a region that had not hastened to do him honour. In addition to his official receptions in Antwerp, Brussels and Falaise he had been made a freeman of Londonderry, Belfast, Canterbury, Portsmouth, London, Huddersfield, Newport, Edinburgh, Manchester, Lambeth, Brentford and Chiswick, Warwick, Maidenhead, Dover and Hastings.

He was an honorary Doctor of Civil Laws of Oxford, a Doctor of Laws of Cambridge, Belfast, St. Andrews, the McGill University in Canada and the Louvain University in Belgium. He was a freeman of the Mercers' Company in London and a Governor of the King's School in Canterbury. His patronage and his presidencies extended over hospitals and football clubs, boys' and Bible societies, Army regiments and benevolent funds.

In Berlin he toasted Marshal Zhukov in champagne (a special occasion), in Paris he was the guest of President de Gaulle, and in England he dined with his Prime Minister in Downing Street and his King in Buckingham Palace.

From America came offers of half a million dollars for his autobiography (refused), and City business men were thinking of appointing him to the Boards of their companies. As a Field-Marshal of the first grade he had a salary of £9 a day with allowances (and a pension of some £1600 a year later on). It was the highest rate of pay in the Army with the exception of that of the Chief of the Imperial General Staff (who received £10 a day). All in all, it was a formidable edifice which the penniless young subaltern from Tasmania had erected around himself.

As he flew around Europe, from Prague to Berlin and Copenhagen, from London to Ireland and Scotland, receiving ovations, making speeches, accepting the applause of these first rich days of peace, there was a sudden double jolt in the triumphal progress, and death twice brushed by the Field-Marshal very quickly.

Except for occasional bombings and bombardments Montgomery's life had not been seriously threatened through the war. Once in the early days in Normandy he had been shelled out of his château at Creully, and again at the end of the war in the German township of Soltau even the cooks and clerks in his headquarters had to turn out to ward off marauding German patrols at night. But there had been no deliberate attempt on his life until he went to Copenhagen a week or two after the victory.

His visit had been announced in advance and a young Danish terrorist of Nazi sympathies rented a flat on the route of the procession. He equipped himself with hand-grenades and stood poised at the window when suddenly he lost his nerve. Danish police grabbed the man before he could change his mind again. Montgomery heard nothing of the matter until afterwards.

But then a little later something more serious happened. Montgomery was flying in a light single-engined plane to inspect Canadian units near Oldenburg. The engine cut out as the machine was about to land. The pilot banked, tried to land on a road, and finally they dropped vertically on to some high bushes where the plane was reduced to a total wreck. Montgomery crawled out apparently unharmed. He took a cup of tea and went on with his tour of inspection.

That night he flew back to his headquarters and there he

was X-rayed. It was discovered that a small chip of bone had been detached from one of the vertebræ and he was for a short time in bed.

Possibly as a result of the accident, possibly because the strain of the war was beginning to tell, he was not well in the summer of 1945 and again in the early autumn. His old war wound had made him susceptible to colds and other minor ailments which he combated by simply intensifying the simplicity of his habits. But he continued steadily with his rounds of receptions and soon he was back in his old tireless groove of health again.

2

The business of governing Germany was going surprisingly well in the British sector. Montgomery treated the whole affair as if it were simply another operation of war. When the peace was not a day old he astonished his staff by suddenly announcing that he had made certain plans for the civil government of north-west Germany. No one had even guessed he had put his mind to the matter, and there was intense curiosity mixed with misgiving about the outcome. The uneasiness about the appointment of Montgomery as Controller in Germany was strongest in London, and was about equally divided between the Left and the Right.

Those who regarded the Field-Marshal as a martinet with totalitarian ideas despaired of his ever handling the trades unions, the political parties and the re-education of German youth in the right way. Humanitarians who saw him simply as a soldier deplored that he had never shown the slightest interest in the feeding and rehabilitation of starving people. The jingoes feared that he would succumb to the nonsense about "putting the Germans on their feet again" under a sort of professional soldier's agreement with the German generals. To the economist he was too inexpert, to the diplomat too naive, to the leftist too churchy, to the conservative too popular. The one thing on which most people had agreed was that he had no training for the complexities of the job.

However, the appointment raised no great interest at the time; everyone was sick and tired of Germany and only thankful that the Germans were not able to menace England any more. Montgomery was able to go ahead with his administration under a not too bright light of publicity.

Actually Montgomery's opponents had overlooked two things. In the first place the problem of Germany *was* a military problem—or at least it was a crisis that required direct action, and the politics for the moment were of second-rate importance. Starvation, cold and general misery governed every issue and the Germans had not the strength—the mere physical strength—to consider politics even had they wanted to.

The second thing (which the opponents had no means of knowing about) was Montgomery's method of always accepting the advice of experts.

At the point of victory Montgomery took one look at Germany and saw what anyone else with two eyes in his head could have seen, that he was in charge of a disordered rout, that millions of people were running wild without a police force or a government, and that presently they would starve and start looting and wrecking unless something were done quickly. It was not a long-range strategical and political problem, but a short-range tactical and economic problem.

He was quite unmoved by a sense of revenge or non-revenge. Abstract emotions — mass emotions — had never touched him in the least.

He had never talked or thought about Loyalty or Courage or Generosity in the abstract but only as applied to particular things. The Job was all. *Why* the job should be done was quite another matter and outside his province. The job here was to stop a rout from becoming a riot, to diminish the possibility of disease sweeping Europe.

And so on this first day of peace he emerged from his caravan and announced:

A. That the German military command, as the only existing authority able to cope with these millions, would continue to operate (under his orders) for the time being.

B. That the people must be fed in an orderly fashion, and the only way to do this was to get German farm labourers out of the army and on to the land as quickly as possible.

C. To assist in distributing the food, repairing and heating the houses, all technicians in railways, bridge building and so on should be put to work in the same way.

D. All remaining vestiges of control—the police, the local Kreis administrations, the hospitals—were "frozen" for the time being and would continue to operate in the crisis until they could be replaced by something better.

He then called in the experts to make the project work. One of the first experts was Field-Marshal Busch, who was the German in military command of a good deal of Montgomery's territory; and Busch started by criticizing Montgomery's methods fairly freely. Montgomery sent for him; bit his head off; told him he would be sacked on the spot if he did not obey orders and sent him away.

Then came a meeting with the team of civil administrators who were being sent out from England. Montgomery explained that they would operate exactly as if they were at war. They would handle all details themselves or take them to the Chief of Staff. When they wanted to see Montgomery himself they would have to state their business inside ten minutes. For the present they would occupy themselves entirely with getting through the crisis.

There followed Operation Barleycorn (to get the soldiers on to the land), Operation Coal Scuttle (to gather fuel for the winter) and all the other schemes.

During this transitional period, the period of moulding the German chaos into some workable form, inevitably two things happened which disturbed and angered people at home: too few Nazis were removed from their jobs and too many British soldiers due for demobilization were kept in Germany. Montgomery was criticized on both counts. Moreover, it was all too clear that the black market was raging in Germany. Despite his protestations that public opinion did not count in war, he was not insensitive to it in peace. Again the experts were called in, and as the long, hideously painful winter of 1945–1946 dragged on it began to seem possible that Montgomery would hand over to his successor a situation which at least was susceptible to treatment.

If his administration had not been flawless he had established law and order. Neutral observers were almost unanimous in agreeing that of the four zones in Germany the British was by far the best organized. In both the Russian and French sectors a certain ruthlessness prevailed, an instinctive desire for revenge *per se* and immense official looting. The Americans at this early stage were suffering from a lack of trained administrators and a wave of nostalgia which swept the soldiers with an intense desire to get out of the mess of Europe. In all four sectors perhaps the Russians were the only ones who had a really coherent long-term political policy. They alone appeared to be quite coldly and clearly preparing to convert their area of Germany into a satellite of their own Government.

At heart Montgomery was not really interested in the Germans. He traversed his district, attended the Control Commission meetings, made speeches full of facts about railroads and coal tonnage, and performed his job punctiliously enough. But his heart was in the Army. The real business of governing Germany fell more and more upon his subordinates;

his "team of experts". More and more the C.-in-C. was to be found touring the British soldiers' camps. He was constantly awarding medals, opening workshops and universities for them, presiding at sports meetings and discussing their training.

It was something more than a successful general's affection for his men; it was a genuine and permanent interest in professional technique—an interest which had already survived the anti-soldiering period following the 1914–1918 war.

During the German campaign he had begun (and it was distinctly unorthodox) a policy of issuing personal "merits" signed by himself to soldiers who performed some unusual feat of devotion or courage. These merits were really an additional decoration designed to enthuse the soldier and attach him more closely to their general. Many a good democrat in England, scenting dictatorship, raised his eyebrows at this practice. And now in place of these merits Montgomery issued a personal card to every soldier leaving his command: "I feel I cannot let you leave 21st Army Group on your return to civil life without a message of thanks and farewell. Together we have carried through one of the most successful campaigns in history, and it has been our good fortune to be members of this great team. God bless you and God speed—B. L. MONTGOMERY."

Was he really planning to go into politics? Was he preparing the electorate in advance? Again the old questions came up. There was much to provoke them. He seemed, through these post-war months, to be forever popping over to England in his aircraft to receive a new "freedom" at some city or other. Always the crowds, the cries of "Monty" . . . "Monty". His chauffeur had an instruction to slow down whenever children stood beside the road, so that the Field-Marshal could bestow a special wave of the hand and a smile.

To many it was evident that Montgomery had broadened again with his experience as a civil governor of Germany. He had done well with the Russians; they liked his forthrightness, the "soldierly" attitude. At a meeting of the Control Commission in Berlin, Zhukov's chief of staff pointed to Montgomery (who was in the chair) and whispered to one of the British staff—"I could be chief of staff to that man". Clearly Montgomery was learning, if not diplomacy, a certain *patience* in a post-war world that was approaching his own standards of bluntness. And he obviously enjoyed authority, obviously wanted to keep it.

However, of late Montgomery had been steadily falling

out of the news as generals do once a war is over. The British
elections of the summer had come and gone without his making
a move. The successful Labour Party was by no means sym-
pathetic to him. More and more people were engrossed in the
frantic struggle to take up civilian careers again—and somehow
keep body and soul together through the arid poverty of the
times. But the atom bomb now brooded over the world, and
with it a seemingly senseless brawling among the spokesmen
of the major Powers. Apparently there was still a use for
generals in the world—even though they were becoming a
little out of date, the tools of the scientists.

3

All through this period—the autumn and the winter of
1945—Montgomery was reverting strongly to type. The
teacher was coming up in him again. And with this the desire
to make a record of all he had experienced and learned through
the war. Throughout the time of his government of Germany
this undercurrent of thought was continuing strongly; it was
probably far more real to him than his outward life. It went
beyond the normal human craving for immortality; it was the
old passion for teaching others, a determination to "tidy-up"
the whole incident of the war by getting the story down in
print, by getting everything explained and illustrated for the
history books.

When nearly everyone else in the world was talking about
the atom bomb and beset with the problems of the civilian
future, Montgomery was quietly writing about the precise
tactics by which he had won his battles in the desert, and
tabulating lists of shipping tonnages. Let everyone else say
that the methods of the last war were out of date, he was not
convinced of it; the same principles would prevail in the future,
atoms or no atoms.

A stream of pamphlets and printed lectures flowed from
Montgomery's headquarters; booklet after booklet covering
every department of the Army, every turn of the campaigns.
These were printed solely for distribution among officers, but
public lectures were given as well. Maps were reproduced,
photographs printed. His orders of the day were collected
and handsomely bound for private circulation. So was his
autograph book. Only the diary remained secret. For the rest,
Montgomery went on patiently with the help of his staff until
he had got every important particle of his story down on paper.
At one lecture in London he continued for two solid hours

8*

with only a short break in between; this was his account of the
Battle of North-west Europe. Like the ancient mariner he
was determined that he should be heard, because he believed
that what he had to say would make his hearers better and
wiser men.

To the layman the pamphlets make dull reading. For the
most part they consist of flat statements of opinion or fact.
There is a Delphic ring about them, and each truism follows
hard upon the heels of the last. There is no argument, no
concession to possible alternatives. The reader can either
take it or leave it—and if he leaves it he is wrong: not only
wrong but damnably wrong.

The pamphlet, *Principles of War*, opens: "A war is won by
victories in battles". Then: "You must first win the air battle
before you embark on the land, or sea battle.

"The enemy must be made to dance to your tune and react
to your thrusts.

"Morale is the most important single factor in war. The
surest way to obtain high morale is by success in battle."

One after another the maxims and the sayings pile up until
you have a kind of soldier's Koran. The more salient points
like "Morale is the first factor in war" are repeated again and
again as though the author were trying to drive it into his
audience's brains by the sheer weight of repetition. Even in
the minutest things there is this same bland presumption of
prophetic and indisputable rightness. And as you read on, the
points do fix themselves in your mind with a mesmerizing
persistence. The overwhelming simplicity which at first repels
the mind in the end attracts it.

This was especially so while the war was being fought.
One of Montgomery's commanders used to say that in the
thick of an action, when all reason seemed on the point of
vanishing in the chaos of explosion and killing, he would
remember that thin insistent voice pronouncing its simple
lucid advice—and it had the effect of an anchor.

In point of fact there was a great deal of ordinary common-
sense in all Montgomery's sayings and, added together, they
did contain the learning of an extraordinarily wide experience
in commanding men. Had these pamphlets been available
at the beginning of the war, and had they been acted upon,
there can be no doubt that many unsuccessful actions could
have been avoided. But Montgomery himself, like everyone
else, had to learn. And the interesting thing is that so much of
his teaching is a list of necessary abstract virtues, and fairly
obvious ones at that. Thus he says "be successful, be healthy,

be simple, be inspiring, be quick, be surprising, be reflective, be courageous". Each point is put down with the positivism of the Beatitudes in the Bible. "Follow this rule", he cries, "and you will be saved." As with most prophets the thing he cannot altogether impart is his own spirit and determination. He cannot pass on the secret of *how* one manages to acquire all these excellent virtues.

He tried in these pamphlets and in many addresses to define the quality of leadership, to issue an easy guide for future commanders. There are many useful hints, but somehow this part of the teaching never quite comes off, probably for the very good reason that leadership is an individual spark susceptible to analysis but beyond mimicry. Wrestling with the problem—"Why did I succeed", he really ends by explaining himself to himself. He writes:

"One of the first responsibilities of a C.-in-C. in the field is to create what I would call atmosphere, and in that atmosphere his staff, his subordinate commanders and his troops will live and work and fight.

"Above all, commanders must have a moral courage, that resolution and that determination which will enable them to stand when the issue hangs in the balance.

"The battle is, in effect, a contest between two wills, his own and that of the enemy commander.

"It is absolutely vital that a C.-in-C. should keep himself from becoming immersed in details. He must spend a great deal of time in quiet thought and reflection. He will refuse to sit up late at night conducting the affairs of his army; he will be well advised to withdraw to his tent or caravan after dinner at night.

"He must trust his subordinates. The only orders issued from a commander's Tactical Headquarters are those given verbally to army commanders by the C.-in-C.; these are never confirmed in writing.

"Every single soldier must know, before he goes into battle, how the little battle he is fighting fits into the larger picture. The troops must be brought to a state of wild enthusiasm. They must enter the fight with the light of battle in their eyes and definitely wanting to kill the enemy.

"When the issue hangs in the balance radiate confidence in the plan and in the operations even if inwardly you do not feel too certain of the outcome."

And finally:

"Never worry".

There is also much technical advice along these lines :

"In all offensive operations endeavour to hit hard on a

narrow front and keep on hitting, penetrate deeply and then turn outwards, *i.e.* the *schwerpunkt* and the *aufrellen*. The momentum of the attack must be kept at all costs.

"All divisions are different; some are outstandingly good at the break-through attack, but not so good at the deliberate set-piece affair; some divisions are best at night; some by day. For a solid killing match certain types of men are better than others—and so on."

The words often sound strangely archaic, as though they are dealing with events in another world, a bygone age. In 1945 and early 1946, when these pamphlets were written, not only was the world intensely antipathetic to war, not only were most people bored with its technicalities, but the discovery of the atomic bomb made the whole subject appear to be hopelessly out of date.

How were the movements of tanks and infantry and battle-ships going to affect the issue now? The next war—and it was unthinkable—would be a matter purely of atomic rockets and other incalculable horrors. To speak now of guns and machine-guns was like harking back to the bows and arrows and the sword play of the Roman wars. H. G. Wells was writing in England too, about this time, but from the opposite pole of thought to Montgomery. "This is the end", he declared. "Progress has stopped. The world is now rushing to its ruin." It expressed the way many people were thinking.

But was it the end? In 1918 people had also said it was the end, that another war was impossible. In 1938 at Munich and in 1939 they had said that air bombing would destroy civilization. But it is not the end, Montgomery argued. An antidote to the atomic bomb would be discovered. Meanwhile it was necessary to marshal intelligently the forces that we did possess. "Reason alone", he insisted, "will never prevent war." You must be strong. A strong British Empire was his first essential for keeping peace in the world.

Yet there was something else in his teaching. Apart from the tactics and the weapons, apart even from war itself, it contained a simple philosophy of life, a thesis that was a compound of boy scoutery, of Victorian discipline and Bishop Montgomery's absolute faith. In 1946 Montgomery was still a Victorian figure, an empire builder of the world of Rhodes and Kipling and Gordon. It was not necessarily out of date; it was certainly much nearer the feeling of the people than a hopeless defeatism or the iconoclasm and absolute lack of faith of the intellectuals. For Montgomery the old Spartan virtues remained, and to practise them revealed the happy life—or if not the happy life, the just and correct life. It remained an exactly prescribed world: on this side the practical issues which man must tackle with his courage and his common-sense; on that side the divinity that watched over the universe. Like a good operational plan every issue was covered by some department in the supreme order of things. There were no mysteries; but simply human weaknesses which, unless checked, led to a state of untidiness.

Like most rebels Montgomery was in a constant state of war against "untidiness"; he was aiming continually towards orthodoxy, a composed and efficiently managed world. At heart Montgomery was not an explorer or an experimenter but a revivalist. He accepted the world as it was and religion as he found it. His self-appointed task was to reorganize existing things on a more tidy pattern.

If there was any key to Montgomery's character, now, in his late fifties, it was very possibly his "detachment", his horror of scandal, his life-long aversion to "becoming involved". All his life Montgomery has kept slightly apart. He has found his closest friends among the very young or the very old—rarely among his contemporaries. One might say that Montgomery has never found a way of dealing with his equals: either above or below he feels at ease, never on the same plane. To such a nature the ordinary ties of family and relations could not make a strong appeal. Immediately Montgomery felt himself becoming involved in some emotional attachment or drawn into some position where claims could be made upon him, his immediate instinct was to break away. The great exceptions to this were his father, his wife and his son. All the rest was a series of friendships and relationships conducted carefully and logically on his own terms. It is interesting to note that when he had to find a home for his son he turned not to his immediate family but to acquaintances. And in the same way most of Montgomery's private life has been organized so that he will not "become involved". To this severe and sometimes lonely man anything resembling an emotional debt is intolerable.

Someone who knew him well wrote this cool appraisal at this time: "His initial mental gifts, though good, were not outstanding. But he saw that more brilliant men could be caught and surpassed if he went his own logical way. He saw that many men failed to do themselves justice because they allowed themselves emotions and 'untidiness' in their private lives. He is a shrewd and detached observer, and when he repeats, as he likes to do, "I am a student of human nature", he is speaking the truth.

"Whereas the lives of most men resemble a river, Montgomery's was planned as a canal. And never has the life of a great man been lived with less frictional loss of energy from the sides of the watercourse."

Whom, then, did he resemble? In the end he was not a martinet like Cromwell, nor an eccentric like Gordon; not a soldier of the Church like Stonewall Jackson, nor a fire-eater like Garibaldi; and he did not mount to the subtle realism and magnetism of the Napoleons and the Hitlers. Most strangely, of all the people in the world, the man he probably resembled was not a man of war at all, but of peace. At first sight the comparison with Mahatma Gandhi seems ridiculous. But between the prophet in Asia and the general in Europe there was a marked physical likeness: the pointed face, the arresting eyes, the wiry body. Their voices were even very similar and they shared the same dry sense of humour. Both were wholly indifferent to worldly pleasures and both enjoyed the genial conviction that what they said and did was absolutely right, a conviction which they managed to impart to a good many other people. Both were excellent choosers of men, especially intellectuals, both were shrewd domestic politicians and each of them gathered his group of devoted disciples. Equally they adored argument and opposition, equally they went to the crowd and the common man and found their strength there. Theirs was a parallel world of essential simplicities, a world without mystery but full of practical errors which needed correction. Each of them could be kind and generous to his friends, and they were entirely devoid of snobbery. Both of them, too, could be intransigent and they were not altogether lost to the pleasures of making mischief, of "sailing as close as possible up to the rocks". An unbridgeable gulf of philosophy and background might separate the two men, but their methods and their basic mental reactions were much the same. For the man of peace it was the same as with the man of war, one crying "Be weak", the other "Be strong".

Both believed in a world governed by love and the loyalty of love; both sought to surround themselves with love—Gandhi and his starving millions, Montgomery with his dedicated soldiers. The loin-cloth was just as much a symbol as the black beret.

4

In November 1945 Montgomery went up to St. Andrews University in Scotland to receive the honorary degree of Doctor of Laws. At the ceremony he made a speech which was unusually interesting if only for the fact that he revealed that the three military commanders of the past whom he most admired were Moses, Cromwell and Napoleon. He also settled the question of whether or not he was going into politics.

"Moses", he said, "was already old when he was called to lead the Children of Israel out of the land of Egypt. His task was an immense one. Israel had been living for about four hundred years as slaves . . . they lived in the Nile Delta, a bad and enervating climate.

"I believe that Moses intentionally kept Israel for forty years in the desert—for two generations—in order to breed and train a fighting race capable of undertaking the task of conquest which lay ahead. . . . He is most careful never to risk failures in action . . . he had an unbroken record of military successes."

But in the end Moses failed; he sinned by his presumption against the Lord.

Cromwell, too, Montgomery found, was an inspiring trainer of men. With "fire in his belly" he set about reorganizing his soldiers after the action of Edgehill, and in fifteen months he was a lieut.-general. And this was done in his middle age.

"Cromwell was not a very likeable man. He was quick-tempered; he believed in a rigid discipline and constant exercises, and he drove his men hard. But he believed with a blinding certainty in the righteousness of his cause, he enthused his soldiers with its righteousness and he was convinced of his own ability to achieve success in battle. And he did achieve success; he had no failures."

But Cromwell sinned too; he sinned by his presumption against the people. He entered politics where he was "uncertain and perplexed" and he became a dictator.

Napoleon, unlike the others, was a professional soldier but he also was a dominator of men. His great power, according to Montgomery, was his power of simplifying problems. His sin was a little more commonplace. He sinned against common-sense: "From the time he became First Consul, political rather than military factors influenced his decisions, and his failure to reconcile his political aspirations with what was militarily possible finally led to the disasters of Moscow and the Peninsula, from which no recovery was possible".

"What", Montgomery asked, "did Moses, Cromwell and Napoleon have in common without which they would not have achieved success?" Two things, he replies—supreme confidence in themselves and the ability to pass on this confidence.

Finally he reaches this conclusion:

"The three leaders whom I have considered succeeded so long as they kept in mind their clear military purpose and were not deflected from it by other considerations. But many battles have been fought for political and not for military reasons, and these have been the graveyard of many a soldier's reputation. The soldier is the servant of the politician and is therefore bound to be subject to political pressure. He must be strong enough to resist such pressure whenever it conflicts with his clear military purpose.

"In history the military leader has frequently been tempted, and frequently succumbed to the temptation, to aspire to political leadership. The whole training and experience of the soldier is to take direct action down certain well-defined lines, and he has in his hand a military machine which responds immediately and with precision to his touch. The politician is trained in subtlety in debate, in weighing up the conflicting interests of his supporters, and finally in compromise; and the government machine is much less precise or exact than the military, and is much more liable to deviation unless in highly skilled political hands.

"Now in war, if a commander compromises on essentials he fails. Furthermore, the time factor forces the commander in the field to adopt the best expedient in the time available, which is usually short. The politician, on the other hand, is seldom forced to give an immediate decision; rather he delays in order to find the right and accurate answer and avoids any temporary expedient. One seizes time by the forelock and adopts the best expedient; the other procrastinates in order to ensure that what he does is exactly right.

"Therefore a leader, who is primarily a soldier, when he meddles with politics loses his clear, simple military purpose; he no longer sees the essentials; he is at sea in a political world. There have been few soldiers who have made good politicians and few politicians who have made great soldiers."

Privately, Montgomery went even further than this. He had been approached unofficially by both the Conservatives and the Liberals, and no doubt the Labour Party might have been glad to have had him as well. All offers were refused, and he declared that he would never enter politics. The question then remained—what was he going to do? Alexander had already been appointed Governor-General of Canada. For Montgomery, the soldier, there were not very many worlds left to conquer.

5

The course of the war was pretty nearly done. Japan was finished. The Nazi leaders were being led to their cells at Nuremberg. Years of slow convalescence lay ahead, but at least the actual surgery of the fighting was finished. One after another the generals and the soldiers were drifting back to civilian clothes, in business, in the City and the factories. Montgomery remained in his battledress. The season for wars was over, but he was a permanent resident on the past and future battlefields. Wars were simply major incidents in an Army career, a time of examination, as it were, and, having passed, one went on with the course again.

Little by little events were falling into a perspective and the hurried and enforced relationships of the war were sorting themselves out. Churchill and Grigg, Montgomery's two acknowledged leaders in the Cabinet, had been turned out of office by the election. De Guingand, his health affected by the overstrain of the war, left the Army. From Eisenhower, to whom Montgomery had sent a copy of his lecture on the North-west Europe campaign, came a letter which sealed a friendship that was stronger than their differences during the battle:

"DEAR MONTY,—Thank you very much for sending me a copy of your lecture. I have read some of it with great enjoyment, and will finish it as soon as I get an opportunity.

"My blood-pressure went up very considerably the other day to read in an American magazine that I 'disliked' you. My first reaction was to write to the editor and tell him what a skunk and a liar he is, but on second thought it seemed to me that to take notice of such a silly falsehood would be simply playing into the hands of some newspaper gossip.

"I shall probably see you in Berlin to-morrow.—As ever, your devoted friend, "IKE."

From London, Churchill wrote:

"MY DEAR MONTY,—. . . Certainly the relations which I had with you, with Alexander and with the High Command of the three Services generally, were of a most intimate character in spite of the great stresses through which we went. How different from the rows of the 'Frocks' and 'Brass Hats' which characterized the last war."

At the anniversary of Alamein some hundreds of the old soldiers gathered at Claridge's Hotel in London under Montgomery's chairmanship. Churchill, the guest of honour, rolled out one more period: "Up to Alamein we survived; after Alamein we conquered". Montgomery, he said, "is one of the greatest living masters of the art of war". And he went on to relate one of those after-dinner after-war stories that multiply and magnify as the years go on. This was the story:

When Montgomery was first appointed to the command of the Eighth Army he was driven to the airport by General Ismay. Montgomery had philosophized on the "tragical life of the soldier"—at one moment he is up and at another down; he wins a battle and gains promotion; he wins again and his name becomes a household word; he wins a campaign and he develops into a national hero. Then suddenly a defeat. He is in disgrace. He is forgotten.

Ismay (according to Churchill) had sought to cheer Montgomery. "Why", he asked, "should that happen to you?"

"To me?" Montgomery said in astonishment. "Certainly not. I am referring to Rommel."

At the dinner table Montgomery threw back his head and joined with Churchill in the long shout of laughter that went round the room. In defeat unthinkable: in victory insufferable: the phrase was dying at last.

There followed the granting of the honorary degrees to the Allied war leaders at Oxford on St. Crispin's Day. Of Montgomery the Public Orator said:

"On this day of St. Crispin what could be happier than the presence among those guests whom our laurels crown, of one who has twice matched the knightly prowess of our ancestors at this very season of the year? It was close on St. Crispin's day that he earned, in his youth, the award for Distinguished Service in the field; and close on this day when, later in life, he faced his old adversaries on Egyptian soil, in a contest with our Empire as the stake. How I wish I could now display to you, as a tale not told before, the full grandeur of that campaign, showing you in every detail:

'How each man stood; how hot the noonday glowed;
How clean a pair of heels the Axis showed'.

"Past all praise is that high-hearted, knightly valour which led soldiers of our Empire through uninhabitable wastes, through fire and flood, by way of cliff and forest, from Egypt to Berlin.

"I present the paragon and flower of Britain's chivalry,

Bernard Law Montgomery *Africanus*, G.C.B., for admission to the honorary degree of D.C.L."

In Germany the flower of Britain's chivalry had now, at last, obtained a portrait of himself to his liking. While he stood for seven consecutive hours in a room at his headquarters, Mr. Frank O. Salisbury executed a painting which delighted the Field-Marshal. It is a vigorous and concise piece of work showing Montgomery in his beret, his battledress and his woolly flying-jacket, pointing to Normandy on the map of Europe, with the heraldic emblems of Montgomery's command on the top left-hand corner.

At home the Field-Marshal had composed many of his affairs. His son David was at Winchester and developing a strong inclination to become, not a soldier, but an engineer. On his long week-ends from Germany, Montgomery himself retreated quite alone to his son's former school in Surrey, where for some years now a room had been kept for him; apart from the wandering Tactical Headquarters it had been his only home in the world since his house had been blitzed in Portsmouth. It contained a truckle bed, a direct telephone to Germany and a wooden plaque over the door which announced that here Montgomery had made his personal headquarters during the German war. Downstairs, before the reverent eyes of the schoolboys, various paintings and photographs of the Field-Marshal hung on the wall, a Nazi flag captured from Rommel, a cartoon or two. In the corner were kept the Field-Marshal's baton in gold and velvet and some of the many clocks, silver salvers and trophies presented by the cities of England and Europe.

Montgomery loved being with the boys. He sat with them for his meals, set them puzzles and made jokes across the roaring hubbub of the dining-room.

Sitting afterwards on the lawn under the oak-trees he had leisure to think about his future. There were many offers. He had been asked to become Chief Scout. The British Legion and a dozen other organizations wanted him as president. There was mention of a governor-generalship. Well, there was still time. He was only in his sixtieth year. Until the spring of 1946 at least he must continue in Germany.

Looking back over the sixty years he concluded that he would have changed nothing in his life. He believed that he would always have chosen this career and that he had been destined to become a general since his heart was set upon it. "I have always been supremely confident that I can do anything that I attempt—due to hard study", he said.

Perhaps in his old age he would devote himself to youth movements. From the nation he wanted nothing very much. A house in the west country perhaps—not another Blenheim— but a small place with a garden and two or three spare bedrooms. Outside a car and a few clothes and presents he had no possessions whatever. His career had brought him no wealth. He had his salary (less income tax), a few hundreds of private income, nothing more. But then he had never wanted to spend money and he wanted none now.

The Field-Marshal was far from frail, but he seemed to his old friends to have shrunk a little in stature. He weighed ten stone four pounds in his uniform, and stood five feet eight inches in height. If anything his life was simpler than ever: he ate little, drank a cupful of a warm milk drink each morning and night, and when his work was done read the usual run of novels and latest books. He seldom played cards but he liked to make moderate bets occasionally to back up his opinion in an argument. His face had grown a little thinner but it was still the face of the subaltern who had sailed for India in 1908 and the face of his father before him. The chin was sharper, the grey moustache clipped back almost to nothing.

That extraordinary detachment that enabled him to sleep at will, to withdraw by himself for hours at a time every day, and to throw all minor troubles aside, now enabled him to cross the bridge from war to peace, from excitement to routine, much more easily than most men. He could never quite understand the lack of detachment in other men—even in the men on whom he loaded the details of his work day after day. Speaking of the political and military leaders in Whitehall he used to exclaim: "How can they ever think clearly? They go to conference after conference. They rush from their desks to official lunches and dinners and then back again to their desks where the work piles up. They stay up until midnight. They never have time to think. They must be perpetually tired."

In 1946 Montgomery carried on in his own handwriting an exceptionally large correspondence with all sorts of people— former batmen and servants, foreign generals and politicians, soldiers' wives and the secretaries of innumerable societies. Every pamphlet he wrote, every bound copy of his speeches, went off to a large circle of particular friends all over the world, These friends, who had supported him through the struggling years, he treated with an avuncular interest which almost went beyond loyalty. He assisted their sons in the Army, he subscribed to memorials, he drove miles to take a cup of tea with families who had been kind to him in the past. No letter ever went unanswered. Football clubs, schools, hospitals and city councils could usually count on him to accept their invitations if some charity was involved.

Some people still looked on this patronage with suspicion. Their theme was "Vanity of vanities: all is vanity".

"It is his besetting sin", said one of his generals (not an antagonist). "Montgomery has genius, but it is a restricted genius marred by just this one thing—his vanity."

This to Montgomery was absurd. To a host of admirers it was envious heresy. They argued that here was a man who was really disinterested, seeking no luxury, no property, no political power. His pleasure in the crowd must therefore surely be innocent. At all events, most people agreed that Montgomery, if ruthless, was never an intriguer. At least you knew exactly where he stood on every issue.

The Field-Marshal's views had crystallized a good deal. He was fond of saying: "You must be strong. We had a second world war because we never destroyed the German Army the first time: we were not strong."

The past to Montgomery was full of avoidable errors, mainly due to our weakness, our failure to "grip the problem tightly". He even liked to recall that several times he was very nearly ejected from the Army for misbehaviour, which was true enough.

His mother, an indomitable old lady who took her first aeroplane flight at the age of seventy-eight, was still living at New Park in Northern Ireland, but Montgomery seldom saw her or the rest of his brothers and sisters scattered around the world. His life was in his son. Of late, however, his attitude towards women had softened, although he had some misgiving about women in power. "Imagine a woman Secretary for War", he said. "She might be having a baby while a campaign was being fought."

Religion was still the backbone of his thoughts, but it was not the sort of revivalist ardour generally attributed to him. He rarely introduced religion in a conversation. He did not attend Communion nor would one have described him as an excessively devout and penitent Christian. He used Christianity instead as part of his practical everyday life, and the Church was incorporated in the Army in a way that sometimes left more sensitive minds a little aghast.

Thus before Alamein Montgomery dismissed a padre for preaching an eve-of-battle sermon which he considered too woebegone and lacking in inspiration. Later on he found a senior padre more to his liking, and it became the practice of

Canon Hughes to preach a personal sermon to the Commander in his Tactical Headquarters every Sunday morning.

Montgomery personally supervised the appointments of all priests in his command, for he regarded them as "vital for morale", as "essential to winning victories". At the conquest of Germany he even worked out a plan with Canon Hughes for the Christian education of the Germans in the British occupied zone; and Hughes was put into an aircraft for London to obtain the Archbishop of Canterbury's immediate approval. Dr. Temple signed the document—it was one of his last acts before he died.

In private Montgomery returned often to his favourite passages in the Bible; the parable of the Good Samaritan and Solomon's prayer for a wise and understanding heart. This last passage[1] has perhaps a particular reference to Montgomery's life as he has wanted to live it:

> "Give therefore thy servant an understanding heart to judge thy people, that I may discern between good and bad. . . . And God said unto him . . . Behold I have done according to thy words: lo, I have given thee a wise and an understanding heart. . . . And I have also given thee that which thou hast not asked, both riches and honour: so that there shall not be any among the kings like unto thee all thy days. And if thou wilt walk in my ways, to keep my statutes and my commandments, as thy father David did walk, then I will lengthen thy days."

All this for Montgomery has had a special meaning. He has tried hard to emulate his father.

Those who saw him at this time, sitting peacefully in the English garden in his old grey sweater, the boys playing around him, might well have thought that the rocket had spent itself at last, that the career might be ending gracefully here. A title, a dignified old age, an appearance or two at school speech-days and Empire reunions—this surely was the inevitable course of things.

In actual fact, another blistering row was brewing over Montgomery and very shortly he was going to be in the thick of it himself.

Alan Brooke was retiring. A new man was wanted as Chief of the Imperial General Staff, the highest post in the British Army. Montgomery, as the most successful commander in the war, was an obvious choice on merit. But—Montgomery. The diehards leapt to their guns. He would turn the whole War Office into a circus. How could you have a C.I.G.S. strutting about in a comic hat? He would fire everyone whom he did not know and appoint his own people instead. He would

[1] 1 Kings, chapter iii.

quarrel with the other Services and other countries. He would
never grasp the intricacies of the job. How on earth could you
expect him to deal with such a problem as the atomic bomb?
The whole Army would be used for the self-glorification of
Montgomery.

Random shots came in from all sides. The opposition was not
yet quite dead; but now there was more sound than fury in
the attack—indeed, it was more like a rearguard action.

Had the appointment been a purely political one the
opposition no doubt would have been a good deal stronger; the
Government had already decided to make no money grants
to the generals, and the names of Montgomery and his fellow-
commanders had been pointedly omitted from the official vote
of thanks on the Victory in the House.

But the war had created a solid body of men at the top who
knew Montgomery, not as the public hero and the cheer leader
on the battlefield, but as the planner at the conference table.
They were aware that Montgomery had spent forty years of
his life studying the Army, and that most of his theories had
proved correct. They also knew that as C.I.G.S. he would call
in the experts and take their advice, and that the matter of the
atomic bomb would be handled in this way. And finally, they
had seen Montgomery develop with his job in the past few
years; he had mellowed, he had broadened, he was learning
patience at last. Those who met him now for the first time were
astonished at his good humour and a certain gentleness and
kindliness.

"He is a man", Sir James Grigg noted, "who not only
became a greater man as his responsibilities grew . . . but a
much more agreeable one as well." And Sir James added: "I
am positive he is not a self advertiser. Everything he says and
does publicly is considered with a view to its effects on the
troops under his command: they arrogate to themselves a part
of the glamour that attaches to him".

Yes, the glamour was there. It would always be there.

In the 1946 New Year's Honours List Montgomery was
raised to the peerage, taking the title of Viscount Montgomery
of Alamein, of Hindhead in the county of Surrey, and a few
weeks later it was announced that he would succeed Brooke at
the War Office. The rocket was gathering itself for the final
flight. The struggle to the target was over.

For those who had watched him through the years one
thing was apparent above everything else: the rebel was a rebel
no longer. And it was not Montgomery but the opposition
which had given in. One after another the things which had

been withheld and forbidden were now under his command. At last his ideas and the Army had locked together. The hands were off the reins again. The days of defiance, from Bishop's Court in Tasmania to the Battle of the Rhine, were over. When Montgomery marched to the War Office in June 1946 there was still perched firmly on his head the symbol of it all—the black beret.